# 500
## RECIPES
# COOKING FOR TWO

# 500
## RECIPES
# COOKING FOR TWO

### Edited by
# Wendy James

TREASURE PRESS

# *Notes*

All measurements in this book are given in metric, imperial and American. Follow one set only because they are not interchangeable.

Standard spoon measurements are used in all recipes

1 tablespoon = one 15 ml spoon
1 teaspoon = one 5 ml spoon
All spoon measurements are level.

Ovens and grills (broiler) should be preheated to the specified temperature or heat setting.

First published in Great Britain
in 1984 by Octopus Books Limited

This edition published in 1989 by
Treasure Press
Michelin House
81 Fulham Road
London SW3 6RB

Reprinted 1990, 1991

ISBN 1 85051 476 3

Printed in Czechoslovakia

50539/04

# Contents

# Chicken and Lemon Soup

METRIC/IMPERIAL
1 x 295 g/10¼ oz can chicken
   consommé
2 tablespoons rice
2 egg yolks
3 tablespoons lemon juice
salt and white pepper
chopped chives to garnish

AMERICAN
1 x 10 oz can chicken consommé
2 tablespoons rice
2 egg yolks
3 tablespoons lemon juice
salt and white pepper
chopped chives for garnish

Make the consommé up to 750 ml/1¼ pints (3 cups) with water, pour in a pan and bring to the boil. Add the rice and reduce the heat to a simmer.

Beat the egg yolks in a small bowl and gradually whisk in the lemon juice. Stir in 3 or 4 tablespoons of the hot soup, a spoonful at a time, then slowly pour the mixture back into the hot soup, stirring all the time.

Heat, stirring, until the rice is cooked and the soup is glossy and slightly thickened – do not allow the soup to boil or it will curdle. Season with salt and pepper to taste and garnish with chives. Serve with wholewheat buttered toast.

VARIATION:
**Fish and Lemon Soup** – substitute fish stock for the chicken consommé. Fish stock can be made by boiling fish trimmings (bones, heads, etc.) with an onion, carrot, celery stalk, parsley and lemon thyme sprigs, 1 bay leaf and 8 black peppercorns in 750 ml/1¼ pints (3 cups) water and 2 tablespoons white wine vinegar. Bring to the boil slowly, simmer for 45 minutes, then strain. Reduce slightly by rapid boiling, then use in the soup as above.

# Asparagus Soup

METRIC/IMPERIAL
*15 g/½ oz butter*
*15 g/½ oz plain flour*
*300 ml/½ pint milk*
*150 ml/¼ pint stock (see Note)*
*1 x 340 g/12 oz can asparagus*
  *pieces, drained*
*salt and freshly ground pepper*

AMERICAN
*1 tablespoon butter*
*2 tablespoons all-purpose flour*
*1¼ cups milk*
*⅔ cup stock (see Note)*
*1 x 12 oz can asparagus pieces,*
  *drained*
*salt and freshly ground pepper*

Melt the butter in a pan, stir in the flour and cook for 1 minute. Remove from the heat and gradually blend in the milk and stock. Cook, stirring, until the soup thickens a little. Add the asparagus, reserving two tips for garnish, and simmer for 5 minutes.

Rub the mixture through a sieve, or purée in a blender or food processor. Add salt and pepper to taste.

Reheat the soup and pour into two warmed bowls. Garnish with the reserved asparagus and serve with Croûtons (see page 147).
**Note:** use some of the liquid from the canned asparagus if it is not too salty.

# Chinese Beef and Tomato Soup

METRIC/IMPERIAL
*1 tablespoon dry sherry*
*1 tablespoon soy sauce*
*freshly ground pepper*
*2 teaspoons cornflour*
*100 g/4 oz lean beef, thinly sliced*
  *and cut into bite-size pieces*
*1 tablespoon oil*
*1 litre/1¾ pints chicken stock*
*2 teaspoons salt*
*2 tomatoes, skinned and roughly*
  *chopped*
*2 eggs, beaten*
*1 tablespoon chopped spring onion*

AMERICAN
*1 tablespoon pale dry sherry*
*1 tablespoon soy sauce*
*freshly ground pepper*
*2 teaspoons cornstarch*
*¼ lb flank steak, thinly sliced and*
  *cut into bite-size pieces*
*1 tablespoon oil*
*4¼ cups chicken stock*
*2 teaspoons salt*
*2 tomatoes, peeled and roughly*
  *chopped*
*2 eggs, beaten*
*1 tablespoon chopped scallion*

Mix together the sherry, soy sauce, pepper and cornflour (cornstarch) in a bowl. Add the beef and turn until well coated.

Heat the oil in a pan. Add the beef and stir-fry until it becomes brown. Add the stock and salt and bring to the boil. Add the tomato pieces. Cook for 5 minutes, reduce the heat and slowly pour in the beaten eggs, without stirring so that they resemble clouds floating on top of the soup. Garnish with the chopped spring onion (scallion) and serve immediately.

# Fresh Mushroom Soup

METRIC/IMPERIAL
1 litre/1¾ pints chicken stock
1 clove garlic, crushed
225 g/8 oz large flat mushrooms
50 g/2 oz butter
salt and freshly ground pepper
1 egg yolk
4 tablespoons single cream
2 button mushrooms, thinly sliced

AMERICAN
4¼ cups chicken stock or broth
1 clove garlic, crushed
½ lb large flat mushrooms
¼ cup butter
salt and freshly ground pepper
1 egg yolk
¼ cup light cream
2 button mushrooms, thinly sliced

Heat the stock with the garlic in a large heavy pan. Roughly chop the large mushrooms and put about one-third of them into a blender or food processor. Add one-third of the butter and one-third of the stock and process until smooth. Pour into a pan for reheating. Repeat twice with the remaining butter, chopped mushrooms and stock. Heat the mushroom mixture gently until very hot, then season with salt and pepper to taste.

Beat the egg yolk with the cream until well blended. Stir in a little of the hot soup, then pour the mixture back into the pan and stir until the soup becomes glossy and thickens slightly, but do not allow to boil.

Serve the soup immediately, garnished with mushroom slices and with croûtons (see page 147).

# Italian Marriage Soup

METRIC/IMPERIAL
900 ml/1½ pints beef or chicken
    stock
25 g/1 oz fine egg noodles, broken
    into pieces
25 g/1 oz unsalted butter
25 g/1 oz Parmesan cheese,
    freshly grated
1 egg yolk
4 tablespoons single cream
freshly grated nutmeg

AMERICAN
3¾ cups beef or chicken stock
¼ cup fine egg noodles, broken
    into pieces
2 tablespoons unsalted butter
¼ cup freshly grated Parmesan
    cheese
1 egg yolk
4 tablespoons light cream
freshly grated nutmeg

Bring the stock to boiling point in a pan. Add the noodles and cook for 3 to 4 minutes, or until tender.

Blend the butter with the cheese and egg yolk, and gradually add the cream. Stir a little hot soup into the egg mixture, then pour back into the soup and stir until the mixture is thickened and creamy. Add nutmeg to taste and serve at once.

# Curry Soup with Rice

METRIC/IMPERIAL
50 g/2 oz ghee, clarified butter or
   2 tablespoons oil
2 onions, thinly sliced
1 clove garlic, crushed
1 teaspoon ground turmeric
2 teaspoons curry powder
¼ teaspoon ground ginger
1 litre/1¾ pints chicken or beef
   stock
50 g/2 oz cooked rice
salt and freshly ground pepper
1 tablespoon lemon juice

AMERICAN
¼ cup ghee, clarified butter or
   2 tablespoons oil
2 onions, thinly sliced
1 clove garlic, crushed
1 teaspoon ground turmeric
2 teaspoons curry powder
¼ teaspoon ground ginger
4¼ cups chicken or beef stock or
   broth
⅓ cup cooked rice
salt and freshly ground pepper
1 tablespoon lemon juice

Heat the fat or oil in a heavy pan and gently fry the onions and garlic until soft and golden, stirring to prevent sticking. Add the turmeric, curry powder and ginger to the pan and continue frying for 1 minute. Pour in the stock, bring to the boil and simmer for 10 minutes.

    Add the rice and cook for another minute or two until the rice is heated through. Add salt and pepper to taste, and the lemon juice. Serve with hot buttered toast.

# Zuppa alla Pavese

METRIC/IMPERIAL
600 ml/1 pint well-flavoured
   chicken stock
salt and freshly ground pepper
50 g/2 oz butter
2 thick slices crusty bread
25 g/1 oz Parmesan cheese, grated
2 eggs at room temperature

AMERICAN
2½ cups well-flavored chicken
   stock or broth
salt and freshly ground pepper
¼ cup butter
2 thick slices crusty bread
¼ cup grated Parmesan cheese
2 eggs at room temperature

Gently heat the stock in a saucepan and season to taste with salt and pepper.

    Heat the butter in a large frying pan and sauté the bread on both sides until golden. Place a slice of bread in each warmed soup bowl. Sprinkle with a little salt and grated cheese.

    Break an egg into each bowl. Bring the stock to a rolling boil and carefully ladle over the eggs. (Keep the stock on the heat while working, so that it remains hot enough to poach the eggs.) Serve at once.

# French Onion Soup Gratinée

METRIC/IMPERIAL
25 g/1 oz butter
1 tablespoon olive oil
4 large onions, thinly sliced
1 teaspoon sugar
25 g/1 oz plain flour
900 ml/1½ pints beef stock
4 tablespoons dry white wine
salt and freshly ground pepper
2 tablespoons brandy
TOPPING:
4 thick slices French bread
1 clove garlic, cut in half
25 g/1 oz butter
50 g/2 oz Gruyère cheese, grated

AMERICAN
2 tablespoons butter
1 tablespoon olive oil
4 large onions, thinly sliced
1 teaspoon sugar
¼ cup all-purpose flour
3¾ cups beef stock
¼ cup dry white wine
salt and freshly ground pepper
2 tablespoons brandy
TOPPING:
4 thick slices French bread
1 clove garlic, cut in half
2 tablespoons butter
½ cup grated Gruyère cheese

Heat the butter and oil in a large heavy pan, add the onions, stir well and cover. Cook gently for 15 minutes, then remove the lid and sprinkle in the sugar. Continue to cook, stirring often, until the onions are deep golden brown.

Sprinkle in the flour, stir for 2 minutes, then gradually blend in the stock and wine. Season with salt and pepper to taste. Cover and simmer for 20 minutes.

Meanwhile rub the bread with the garlic. Butter the bread, sprinkle with grated cheese and grill (broil) until melted. Place the bread in heated bowls. Stir the brandy into the soup and pour into the bowls. Serve at once.

# Spinach and Bean Curd Soup

METRIC/IMPERIAL
750 ml/1¼ pints well-flavoured
   chicken or beef stock
225 g/8 oz spinach, torn into small
   pieces
2 cakes bean curd, cut into 2.5 cm/
   1 inch cubes
1 spring onion, chopped
salt
freshly ground black pepper

AMERICAN
3 cups chicken or beef stock
½ lb spinach, torn into small pieces
2 cakes bean curd, cut into 1 inch
   cubes
1 scallion, chopped
salt
freshly ground black pepper

Bring the stock to the boil in a pan. Add the spinach and bean curd. Bring back to the boil, then add the spring onion (scallion) and salt and pepper to taste. Simmer the soup for about 10 minutes – do not overcook or the spinach will lose its green colour and the bean curd will become tough. Serve immediately.

# Tomato Soup with Basil Paste

METRIC/IMPERIAL
1 teaspoon olive oil
1 medium carrot, sliced
1 small leek, sliced (white part
  only), or 8 spring onions,
  chopped
1 clove garlic, crushed
1 x 396 g/14 oz can tomatoes
1 tablespoon tomato purée
300 ml/½ pint chicken stock
1 sprig fresh or small pinch dried
  thyme
½ bay leaf
salt and freshly ground pepper
BASIL PASTE:
2 handfuls basil leaves (see Note)
2 teaspoons olive oil

AMERICAN
1 teaspoon olive oil
1 medium carrot, sliced
1 small leek, sliced (white part
  only), or 8 scallions, chopped
1 clove garlic, crushed
1 x 16 oz can tomatoes
1 tablespoon tomato paste
1¼ cups chicken stock or broth
1 sprig fresh or small pinch dried
  thyme
½ bay leaf
salt and freshly ground pepper
BASIL PASTE:
2 handfuls basil leaves (see Note)
2 teaspoons olive oil

Heat the olive oil in a large heavy pan, add the carrot, leek or spring onions (scallions) and garlic. Cover and cook gently for 5 minutes.

Place tomatoes and their juice in a blender with the tomato purée (paste) and stock and blend till smooth. Add to the pan with the herbs. Heat the soup until simmering, add salt and pepper to taste and simmer, half covered, for 20 minutes.

Meanwhile put the basil leaves and olive oil in a blender or food processor fitted with the steel blade and blend to a paste.

Rub the soup through a sieve and return to the saucepan (or purée in a blender or food processor and strain back into the pan). Reheat and serve the soup, swirling a small spoonful of the basil paste into each serving.

**Note:** if fresh basil is unavailable, use the basil sauce called "pesto" from good delicatessens.

# Tomato and Onion Soup

METRIC/IMPERIAL
1 tablespoon dripping or butter
225 g/8 oz chopped onion
1 clove garlic, peeled and crushed
500 g/1 lb ripe tomatoes, quartered
900 ml/1½ pints chicken or
   vegetable stock
1 teaspoon sugar
salt
freshly ground pepper
2 tablespoons broken vermicelli
croûtons, to serve

AMERICAN
1 tablespoon drippings or butter
½ lb chopped onion
1 clove garlic, peeled and crushed
1 lb ripe tomatoes, quartered
3¾ cups chicken or vegetable
   stock
1 teaspoon sugar
salt
freshly ground pepper
2 tablespoons broken vermicelli
croûtons, to serve

Heat the fat in a heavy-based pan, add the onion and garlic and fry gently until golden – about 15 minutes. Add the tomatoes, stock, sugar and salt and pepper. Bring to the boil, stirring occasionally, then lower the heat and simmer, uncovered, for 20 minutes.

Purée in an electric blender and then sieve (strain), or press mixture through a sieve (strainer). Return the soup to the rinsed-out pan and bring to the boil again. Add the vermicelli and cook for 6 to 10 minutes until pasta is tender yet firm to the bite. Taste and adjust seasoning. Serve immediately with freshly made croûtons.

# Buttermilk Pepper Soup

METRIC/IMPERIAL
1 small onion, finely chopped
15 g/½ oz butter
½ red or green pepper, finely
   chopped
1 chicken stock cube, dissolved in
   120 ml/4 fl oz hot water
400 ml/⅔ pint buttermilk
salt and white pepper
GARNISH:
whipped cream
chopped chives

AMERICAN
1 small onion, finely chopped
1 tablespoon butter
½ red or green pepper, finely
   chopped
1 chicken bouillon cube, dissolved
   in ½ cup hot water
2 cups buttermilk
salt and white pepper
GARNISH:
whipped cream
chopped chives

Fry the onion gently in the butter for about 5 minutes until soft but not brown. Add the pepper, cover the pan and cook over a low heat for another 5 minutes. Add the stock, cover and simmer gently for 15 minutes.

Add the buttermilk and salt and pepper to taste and heat through. Purée the soup in a blender.

Serve hot or chilled, garnished with a swirl of whipped cream and the chives.

# Chilled Tomato Soup

METRIC/IMPERIAL
2 tablespoons olive oil
1 large onion, peeled and chopped
2 cloves garlic, peeled and crushed
750 g/1½ lb ripe tomatoes, skinned
    and quartered
1 bay leaf
1 thyme sprig
1 teaspoon sugar
salt
freshly ground pepper
soured cream and snipped chives,
    to serve

AMERICAN
2 tablespoons olive oil
1 large onion, peeled and chopped
2 cloves garlic, peeled and crushed
1½ lb ripe tomatoes, peeled and
    quartered
1 bay leaf
1 thyme sprig
1 teaspoon sugar
salt
freshly ground pepper
sour cream and snipped chives, to
    serve

Heat the oil in a heavy-based pan and fry the onion and garlic gently until tender but not browned. Add the tomatoes, bay leaf, thyme, sugar, and salt and pepper and cook over a moderate heat, covered, for 20 minutes. Press the tomatoes occasionally to break them up.

Discard the bay leaf and thyme. Press through a vegetable mill or purée in an electric blender, then sieve (strain). Leave until cool, then chill in the refrigerator for at least 3 hours. Taste and adjust seasoning. Serve topped with a swirl of sour cream and a sprinkling of chives.

# Carrot Cheese Soup

METRIC/IMPERIAL
3 large carrots, diced
750 ml/1¼ pints chicken or beef
    stock
175 ml/6 fl oz milk, scalded
freshly grated nutmeg
salt and white pepper
25 g/1 oz Gruyère cheese, grated
2 tablespoons grated Parmesan
    cheese

AMERICAN
3 large carrots, diced
3 cups chicken or beef stock
¾ cup milk, scalded
freshly grated nutmeg
salt and white pepper
¼ cup grated Swiss cheese
2 tablespoons grated Parmesan
    cheese

Cook the carrots in the stock until tender. Rub through a sieve (or potato ricer) or purée in a blender and return the mixture to the pan.

Add the milk, nutmeg and salt and pepper to taste and bring to the boil. Pour into two flameproof bowls and sprinkle with the cheeses. Place under a preheated grill (boiler) for 2 minutes, or until the cheese melts. Serve with warm Herb Bread (see page 147).

# Piquant Iced Avocado Soup

METRIC/IMPERIAL
½ chicken stock cube
4 tablespoons boiling water
1 avocado, peeled and stoned
2 tablespoons lemon juice
150 ml/¼ pint plain yogurt
3 drops Tabasco sauce
salt and freshly ground pepper
2 crisp lettuce leaves, shredded, for
　garnish

AMERICAN
1 chicken bouillon cube
¼ cup boiling water
1 avocado, peeled and seeded
2 tablespoons lemon juice
⅔ cup plain yogurt
3 drops hot pepper sauce
salt and freshly ground pepper
2 crisp lettuce leaves, shredded, for
　garnish

Dissolve the stock (bouillon) cube in the water and leave to cool. Purée the avocado, lemon juice and stock in a blender or food processor. Add nearly all the yogurt and the Tabasco (hot pepper) sauce. Mix well and add salt and pepper to taste.

　Pour the soup into serving bowls and chill. Serve topped with shredded lettuce and a swirl of the remaining yogurt.

VARIATION:

**Peppered Avocado Soup** – instead of the Tabasco (hot pepper) sauce, use 1 tablespoon canned green peppercorns. Drain, then place them in the blender with the avocado.

# Creamy Cucumber Soup

METRIC/IMPERIAL
½ small cucumber, diced
450 ml/¾ pint chicken stock
1 small onion, peeled and chopped
15 g/½ oz butter or margarine
15 g/½ oz plain flour
1 teaspoon lemon juice
salt and pepper
3-4 tablespoons single cream
coarsely grated cucumber for
　garnish

AMERICAN
½ small cucumber, diced
2 cups chicken stock
1 small onion, peeled and minced
1 tablespoon butter or margarine
2 tablespoons all-purpose flour
1 teaspoon lemon juice
salt and pepper
3-4 tablespoons light cream
coarsely grated cucumber for
　garnish

Put the diced cucumber, stock and onion into a pan. Bring to the boil, cover and simmer for 20 minutes or until tender. Cool slightly, then liquidize or sieve until smooth. Melt the butter or margarine in another saucepan. Stir in the flour and cook for 1 minute. Gradually stir in the cucumber purée and bring to the boil. Add the lemon juice then season well with salt and pepper and simmer for 4 to 5 minutes. Allow to cool completely then chill. Just before serving, stir in the cream and sprinkle with grated cucumber.

# Iced Apple-Curry Soup

METRIC/IMPERIAL
25 g/1 oz butter
1 small onion, chopped
1 tablespoon curry powder, mixed
  with 1 tablespoon sherry
1 large dessert apple, peeled,
  cored and diced
300 ml/½ pint chicken stock
120 ml/4 fl oz apple juice
120 ml/4 fl oz single cream
1 tablespoon lemon juice
salt and freshly ground white
  pepper
chopped spring onions to garnish

AMERICAN
2 tablespoons butter
1 small onion, chopped
1 tablespoon curry powder, mixed
  with 1 tablespoon sherry
1 large apple, peeled, cored and
  diced
1¼ cups chicken stock
½ cup apple juice
½ cup light cream
1 tablespoon lemon juice
salt and freshly ground white
  pepper
chopped scallions for garnish

Heat the butter in a pan, add the chopped onion, curry mixture and apple and cook, stirring occasionally, for 5 minutes. Stir in the stock and bring to the boil, then simmer for 5 minutes. Leave to cool, then place in blender and blend until smooth.

Stir in apple juice, cream, lemon juice and salt and pepper to taste. Chill well. Serve in chilled bowls, garnished with spring onions (scallions).

# Chilled Herb Soup

METRIC/IMPERIAL
400 ml/⅔ pint plain yogurt
250 ml/8 fl oz tomato juice
6 parsley sprigs
6 mint sprigs
2 tablespoons chopped chives
sea-salt and freshly ground pepper
½ large cucumber

AMERICAN
2 cups plain yogurt
1 cup tomato juice
6 parsley sprigs
6 mint sprigs
2 tablespoons chopped chives
sea-salt and freshly ground pepper
½ large cucumber

Place the yogurt, tomato juice, parsley, mint and half the chives and salt and pepper to taste in a blender or food processor fitted with the steel blade. Blend until well combined, then chill.

Peel the cucumber and scoop out the seeds. Chop finely and chill. To serve, divide the cucumber between soup bowls and ladle the chilled soup over. Garnish with the remaining chives and serve with fresh crusty bread and butter.

DISHES

# Fish Dishes

FOR TWO

## *Avocado Fish Surprise*

METRIC/IMPERIAL
*350 g/12 oz whiting fillets, cut into*
*  strips*
*2 tablespoons plain flour*
*2 tablespoons arrowroot*
*2 egg whites*
*1 large ripe avocado*
*2 tablespoons lime or lemon juice*
*oil for shallow frying*
*salt*
*freshly ground black pepper*

AMERICAN
*¾ lb whiting fillets, cut into strips*
*2 tablespoons all-purpose flour*
*2 tablespoons arrowroot flour*
*2 egg whites*
*1 large ripe avocado*
*2 tablespoons lime or lemon juice*
*oil for shallow frying*
*salt*
*freshly ground black pepper*

Discard any skin from fish. Place plain (all-purpose) flour in a bowl. Put arrowroot in another bowl with egg whites and whisk together with a fork until light and fluffy. Peel avocado, remove stone (pit) and cut each half into 5 slices lengthways. Place in another bowl and sprinkle with lime or lemon juice. Heat about 1 cm/½ inch oil in large frying pan (skillet).

Season fish strips with salt and pepper, then coat in flour. Shake off excess, dip strips into egg white mixture. Add to hot oil a few at a time and cook for 2 to 3 minutes each side until golden and tender when pierced with a skewer. Drain on absorbent paper towels, then pile on to a warmed serving plate.

Pour lime or lemon juice from avocados over the fish. Dip slices in flour, then egg white and fry in hot oil until golden (1 to 2 minutes each side – do not overcook). Arrange around fish and serve with plain boiled rice, lemon wedges and Tartare Sauce (see page 148).

# Crispy Herrings in Oatmeal

METRIC/IMPERIAL
2 x 300 g/10 oz herrings, scaled
  and cleaned
milk
medium oatmeal for coating
100 g/4 oz butter
GARNISH:
lemon wedges
parsley sprigs

AMERICAN
2 x 10 oz herrings, scaled and
  cleaned
milk
medium oatmeal for coating
½ cup butter
GARNISH:
lemon wedges
parsley sprigs

Cut off the heads, fins and tails of the herrings. Open out flat and place, skin side up, on a board. Press down with knuckles all along the backbone to loosen it. Turn fish over and, with the point of a knife, ease out the backbone in one piece, starting at the tail end. Pull out as many of the small bones as possible. Wipe the fish.

Place the milk on one plate, oatmeal on another. Dip the fish first in the milk, then in the oatmeal. Melt the butter in a pan and fry the fish, skinless side first, until crisp, then turn and fry other side. (If the herring has roe, fry it separately and place it down the centre of each fish.)

Serve very hot garnished with lemon wedges and parsley.

# Fried Fish with Sweet and Sour Sauce

METRIC/IMPERIAL
1 egg white
½ teaspoon salt
2 teaspoons dry sherry
2½ tablespoons cornflour
oil for frying
350 g/12 oz sole, plaice or whiting
  fillets, cut into pieces
150 ml/¼ pint water
1 tablespoon sugar
1 tablespoon wine vinegar
½ teaspoon grated root ginger

AMERICAN
1 egg white
½ teaspoon salt
2 teaspoons pale dry sherry
2½ tablespoons cornstarch
oil for frying
¾ lb sole fillets, cut into pieces
⅔ cup water
1 tablespoon sugar
1 tablespoon wine vinegar
½ teaspoon minced ginger root

Beat the egg white lightly, then beat in the salt, sherry and 2 tablespoons of the cornflour (cornstarch) to make a smooth batter.

Heat enough oil in a heavy-based frying pan to come 1 cm/½ inch up the sides. Fry the fish pieces in the oil until crisp and golden; drain.

Bring the water to the boil in a pan. Add the sugar, vinegar and ginger. Blend the remaining cornflour (cornstarch) with a little water and add to the pan. Simmer the sauce, stirring, until it thickens. Add the fish and reheat. Serve hot with boiled rice.

# Spanish Fish

METRIC/IMPERIAL
500 g/1 lb white fish fillets
25 g/1 oz plain flour, seasoned with
    salt and freshly ground black
    pepper
3 tablespoons olive oil
1 x 227 g/8 oz can tomatoes
1 fresh chilli, seeded and chopped
1 green pepper, cored, seeded and
    chopped
2 cloves garlic, crushed
1 tablespoon tomato purée

AMERICAN
1 lb white fish fillets
¼ cup all-purpose flour, seasoned
    with salt and freshly ground black
    pepper
3 tablespoons olive oil
1 x 8 oz can tomatoes
1 fresh chili, seeded and chopped
1 green pepper, seeded and
    chopped
2 cloves garlic, crushed
1 tablespoon tomato paste

Cut the fish into largish chunks and coat in seasoned flour. Heat the oil in a heavy-based casserole, add the fish and cook for a few minutes until golden all over. Remove fish and reserve.

Chop tomatoes and add to the casserole with the juice from the can, the chilli, green pepper, garlic and salt and pepper to taste. Cook, uncovered, until near boiling, then add fish chunks, cover and cook gently for 20 minutes. Stir in tomato purée (paste) and cook for a further 5 minutes. Serve with chunks of crusty fresh bread.

# Whiting with Wine and Mustard Sauce

METRIC/IMPERIAL
50 g/2 oz butter
2 shallots, peeled and finely
    chopped
2 tablespoons chopped parsley
salt
freshly ground pepper
500 g/1 lb whiting fillets
2 teaspoons prepared hot mustard
4 tablespoons dry white wine
2 tablespoons single cream
2 tablespoons lemon juice

AMERICAN
¼ cup butter
2 shallots, peeled and finely
    chopped
2 tablespoons chopped parsley
salt
freshly ground pepper
1 lb whiting fillets
2 teaspoons prepared hot mustard
4 tablespoons dry white wine
2 tablespoons light cream
2 tablespoons lemon juice

Melt 25 g/1 oz (2 tablespoons) butter in a flameproof casserole and add the shallots, parsley and salt and pepper to taste. Place the whiting on top and sprinkle with more salt and pepper. Mix the mustard and wine together, pour over the whiting. Cover and cook in preheated moderately hot oven (200°C/400°F, Gas Mark 6) for 10 minutes until the fish is tender.

Carefully transfer fish to warmed plates and keep hot. Boil the cooking juices on top of the stove for 2 to 3 minutes, then stir in the remaining butter, the cream and lemon juice. Taste and adjust seasoning, then pour over the fish and serve immediately with croquette potatoes.

# Poached Trout with Cucumber

METRIC/IMPERIAL
*2 x 350 g/12 oz trout*
*250 ml/8 fl oz water*
*4 tablespoons white wine*
*½ bay leaf*
*2 spring onions, chopped*
*½ cucumber*
*25 g/1 oz butter*
*2 sprigs of chopped fresh dill weed*
*or 1 teaspoon dried dill*
*salt and white pepper*
*lemon wedges to serve*

AMERICAN
*2 x ¾ lb trout*
*1 cup water*
*¼ cup white wine*
*½ bay leaf*
*2 scallions, chopped*
*½ cucumber*
*2 tablespoons butter*
*3 sprigs of chopped fresh dill weed*
*or 1 teaspoon dried dill*
*salt and white pepper*
*lemon wedges to serve*

Wash the trout well and dry with kitchen paper towels. Trim the fins and tail. Put the water and wine into a flameproof dish and add the bay leaf and spring onions (scallions). Add the trout, and cover with buttered paper with a tiny hole in the centre. Bring just to simmering point, reduce the heat, cover with foil and poach for about 5 minutes.

Peel the cucumber and cut into small, even cubes, discarding the seeds. Heat the butter in a pan and stir in the cucumber, then cover and cook slowly for 5 to 6 minutes. Remove from the heat and add the dill weed or dried dill. Season with salt and pepper to taste.

Place the fish on a warm serving plate. Remove part of the skin of the trout to reveal the flesh but leave the heads and tails intact. Arrange the fish on a warmed serving dish, serve with the cucumber and lemon wedges.

VARIATION:
**Trout with Mustard Sauce** – make a mustard sauce to accompany the trout. Boil the poaching liquid until reduced by one-third, then whisk in small amounts of beurre manié (1 tablespoon each of butter and flour and 2 teaspoons dry mustard) until the sauce thickens. Add salt and pepper to taste and strain the sauce into a sauce boat to serve.

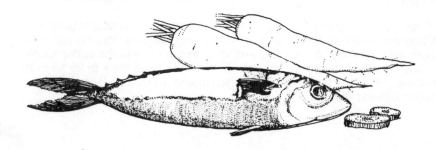

# Fish Fillets with Mushrooms

| METRIC/IMPERIAL | AMERICAN |
|---|---|
| 4 skinless sole fillets | 4 skinless sole fillets |
| butter | butter |
| 3 spring onions, chopped | 3 scallions, chopped |
| 8 small mushrooms, sliced | 8 small mushrooms, sliced |
| salt and white pepper | salt and white pepper |
| 250 ml/8 fl oz water | 1 cup water |
| 4 tablespoons white wine | ¼ cup white wine |
| 15 g/½ oz butter | 1 tablespoon butter |
| 1 tablespoon plain flour | 1 tablespoon all-purpose flour |

Wipe the fish fillets with kitchen paper towels. Lightly butter a flameproof dish, sprinkle in the chopped spring onions (scallions) and half the sliced mushrooms and arrange the fish on top. Cover with the remaining mushrooms and season with salt and pepper to taste. Pour over the water and wine. Cover with a sheet of buttered paper with a small hole in the centre. Bring the liquid to simmering point, cover and reduce the heat. Poach the fish for 8 to 10 minutes.

Using a broad spatula, remove the fish and vegetables to a warmed serving plate and keep warm while making the sauce. Reduce the liquid in the pan to about 250 ml/8 fl oz (1 cup). Cream the butter and flour to a smooth paste and whisk into the liquid in small pieces.

Add salt and pepper to taste and spoon the sauce over the fish. Serve with plain boiled potatoes.

# Italian-Style Fish

| METRIC/IMPERIAL | AMERICAN |
|---|---|
| 2 large fish fillets or steaks | 2 large fish fillets or steaks |
| salt and freshly ground pepper | salt and freshly ground pepper |
| 1 x 227 g/8 oz can tomatoes | 1 x 8 oz can tomatoes |
| 25 g/1 oz grated Parmesan cheese | ¼ cup grated Parmesan cheese |
| ½ teaspoon dried oregano | ½ teaspoon dried oregano |
| 25 g/1 oz butter, melted | 2 tablespoons melted butter |

Place the fish in a shallow baking dish and season with salt and pepper. Chop the tomatoes and pour over the fish with the juice from the can. Sprinkle over the cheese and oregano, then drizzle over the butter. Cook in a preheated moderately hot oven (200°/400°F, Gas Mark 6) for 15 to 20 minutes until the fish flakes easily when tested with a fork. Serve with jacket baked potatoes.

# Baked Sole with Oysters

METRIC/IMPERIAL
50 g/2 oz butter
1 stick celery, finely chopped
1 tablespoon chopped parsley
1 tablespoon chopped onion
6 fresh, bottled or canned oysters
25 g/1 oz fresh white breadcrumbs
4 small sole or plaice fillets
salt and freshly ground pepper
4 tablespoons dry white wine
4 tablespoons oyster liquor or water
chopped parsley to garnish
CREAM SAUCE:
15 g/1 oz butter
1 tablespoon plain flour
4 tablespoons single cream

AMERICAN
1/4 cup butter
1 stalk celery, finely chopped
1 tablespoon chopped parsley
1 tablespoon chopped onion
6 fresh, bottled or canned oysters
1/2 cup soft white bread crumbs
4 small sole or flounder fillets
salt and freshly ground pepper
1/4 cup dry white wine
1/4 cup oyster liquor or water
chopped parsley for garnish
CREAM SAUCE:
1 tablespoon butter
1 tablespoon all-purpose flour
1/4 cup light cream

Melt the butter in a pan and sauté the celery, parsley and onion until soft. If using bottled oysters, drain them and reserve 4 tablespoons liquor. Chop the oysters. Add the oysters and breadcrumbs to the pan and stir over a moderate heat for 30 seconds, then remove.

Sprinkle the fish fillets lightly with salt and divide the stuffing equally between them. Roll up and secure the ends with wooden cocktail sticks (toothpicks). Arrange the rolls in a greased shallow baking dish and pour the wine and reserved liquor or water over them. Cover and bake in a preheated moderate oven (180°C/350°F, Gas Mark 4) for 20 minutes, or until the fish flakes easily. Sprinkle lightly with pepper and remove to a warmed serving dish. Reserve the cooking liquid to make the sauce.

Melt the butter in a pan, add the flour and cook for 1 minute. Stir in the reserved cooking liquid from the fish and the cream, and cook over a gentle heat for a minute until the sauce thickens. Check for seasoning and spoon over the rolls. Serve at once, sprinkled with parsley, with boiled potatoes and broccoli.

VARIATIONS:
**Special Baked Sole** – make this dish extra special by adding 50 g/2 oz peeled prawns (shelled shrimps) to the cream sauce.
**Baked Sole with Mussels** – use canned mussels instead of oysters, but not those bottled in vinegar as the flavour would be too strong.

# Fish with Vegetables

METRIC/IMPERIAL

25 g/1 oz butter or margarine
2 carrots, thinly sliced
1 small onion, thinly sliced
1 large stick celery, finely chopped
350 g/12 oz white fish fillets
2 tomatoes, skinned and chopped
1 tablespoon water or white wine
1 bay leaf
2 teaspoons chopped fresh herbs
    (thyme, parsley, fennel, dill,
    chervil, tarragon, chives)
salt and freshly ground pepper
2 tablespoons single cream

AMERICAN

2 tablespoons butter or margarine
2 carrots, thinly sliced
1 small onion, thinly sliced
1 large stalk celery, finely chopped
¾ lb white fish fillets
2 tomatoes, peeled and chopped
1 tablespoon water or white wine
1 bay leaf
2 teaspoons chopped fresh herbs
    (thyme, parsley, fennel, dill,
    chervil, tarragon, chives)
salt and freshly ground pepper
2 tablespoons light cream

Melt the butter or margarine in a frying pan. Add the carrots, onion and celery. Stir, then cover and cook gently for 5 to 7 minutes until soft but not browned. Cut the fish into serving pieces.

Push the vegetables to one side, place the fish in the pan and cook for 1 minute on each side. Add the tomatoes, water or wine, bay leaf and herbs, then spoon the vegetables over the top. Add salt and pepper to taste. Cover and cook gently for 7 to 10 minutes or until the fish flakes easily when tested with a fork.

With a slotted spoon, remove the fish and vegetables to a hot serving dish. Stir the cream into juices left in the pan, then spoon over the fish. Serve with plain boiled rice or noodles.

VARIATION:

**Baked Fish with Vegetables** – place 4 frozen fish fillets in a greased ovenproof dish and add the contents of a 290 g/10 oz can of vegetable soup. Sprinkle with 2 tablespoons fresh herbs of your choice and add salt and pepper to taste. Cook in a preheated moderate oven (180°C/350°F, Gas Mark 4) for 30 minutes. Serve with creamed potatoes.

# French Fish Bake

METRIC/IMPERIAL
25 g/1 oz butter
1 clove garlic, crushed
225 g/8 oz courgettes, sliced
1 onion, sliced into rings
½ red pepper, cored, seeded and
 sliced
½ green pepper, cored, seeded
 and sliced
100 g/4 oz mushrooms, sliced
2 x 225 g/8 oz red mullet or
 snappers
salt and freshly ground pepper

AMERICAN
2 tablespoons butter
1 clove garlic, crushed
½ lb zucchini, sliced
1 onion, sliced into rings
½ red pepper, seeded and sliced
½ green pepper, seeded and sliced
1 cup sliced mushrooms
2 x ½ lb snappers
salt and freshly ground pepper

Melt the butter in a pan and sauté the garlic, courgettes (zucchini), onion, peppers and mushrooms for 15 minutes.

Using a sharp knife, slit the fish along the belly and remove the guts. Snip off the fins and wash the fish well. Place each fish on a piece of foil and season with salt and pepper.

Arrange the vegetables around each fish, fold over the foil to make two parcels and seal tightly. Place the fish parcels on a baking sheet and cook in a preheated moderately hot oven (190°C/375°F, Gas Mark 5) for 30 minutes. Before serving, remove the fish eyes. Arrange the fish on warmed serving plates with the vegetables and serve with boiled new potatoes.

# Smoked Fish Hash

METRIC/IMPERIAL
350 g/12 oz smoked haddock or
 cod, cooked and flaked
2 medium potatoes, cooked and
 diced
1 small onion, finely chopped
1 tablespoon chopped parsley
1 teaspoon grated lemon rind
50 g/2 oz butter
salt and freshly ground pepper
2 tablespoons soured cream
chopped chives to garnish

AMERICAN
¾ lb smoked haddock or cod,
 cooked and flaked
2 medium potatoes, cooked and
 diced
1 small onion, finely chopped
1 tablespoon chopped parsley
1 teaspoon grated lemon rind
¼ cup butter
salt and freshly ground pepper
2 tablespoons sour cream
chopped chives for garnish

Mix together the fish, potatoes, onion, parsley and lemon rind.

Heat the butter in a heavy-based frying pan, then add the fish mixture, pressing it down well to form a cake. When the base starts to brown, turn the mixture, add salt and pepper to taste and pour over the soured cream. Cook until very hot. Garnish with chives and serve.

# Gingered Fish

METRIC/IMPERIAL
500 g/1 lb white fish fillets
grated rind and juice of 1 lemon
50 g/2 oz butter
1 small onion, finely chopped
2.5 cm/1 inch piece fresh root
ginger, grated
2 cloves
1 teaspoon brown sugar
1 tablespoon dry white wine
salt and freshly ground pepper
2 spring onions, shredded, to
garnish

AMERICAN
1 lb white fish fillets
grated rind and juice of 1 lemon
¼ cup butter
1 small onion, finely chopped
1 inch piece fresh ginger root,
grated
2 cloves
1 teaspoon brown sugar
1 tablespoon dry white wine
salt and freshly ground pepper
2 scallions, shredded, for garnish

Cut the fish into serving pieces. Place the fish on a plate and sprinkle with the lemon rind and juice. Leave for 15 minutes.

Melt the butter in a large frying pan, add the onion and ginger and cook gently until golden but not browned. Add the cloves, brown sugar and wine, then push mixture to one side and add the fish and marinating juices. Add salt and pepper and spoon the onion mixture over the fish. Cover tightly and cook on a low heat for 8 to 10 minutes until the fish flakes easily.

Garnish with spring onions (scallions) and serve immediately with plain boiled rice and a cucumber salad.

# Curried Fish

METRIC/IMPERIAL
2 large fish fillets
3 tablespoons lemon juice
1 teaspoon ground turmeric
2 teaspoons curry powder
25 g/1 oz plain flour
1 teaspoon paprika
oil for shallow frying
chopped chives to garnish

AMERICAN
2 large fish fillets
3 tablespoons lemon juice
1 teaspoon ground turmeric
2 teaspoons curry powder
¼ cup all-purpose flour
1 teaspoon paprika
oil for shallow frying
chopped chives for garnish

Marinate the fish in the lemon juice for 10 minutes. Combine the turmeric, curry powder, flour and paprika on a plate. Dip the fish fillets into the mixture to coat both sides. Heat the oil in a pan, add the fish and fry for 4 to 5 minutes each side.

Sprinkle the fish with chives and serve with plain boiled rice, finely sliced cucumber in plain yogurt, and a tomato and onion salad.

VARIATION:

**Grilled (Broiled) Curried Fish** – place the coated fish fillets on a foil-lined grill (broiler) pan and cook for about 4 minutes on each side.

24

# Chinese Braised Fish

METRIC/IMPERIAL
2 x 500 g/1 lb whole white fish
   (sole, plaice, snapper, cod, etc.),
   cleaned
oil for shallow frying
1 clove garlic, crushed
1 tablespoon chopped root ginger
2 tablespoons chopped spring
   onion
1½ tablespoons hot soy bean
   paste
2 tablespoons dry sherry
3 tablespoons soy sauce
½ teaspoon salt
1 teaspoon sugar
1 tablespoon red wine vinegar
2 teaspoons cornflour, blended with
   4 tablespoons water
shredded spring onion to garnish

AMERICAN
2 x 1 lb whole white fish (sole, sea
   bass, cod, etc.), cleaned
oil for shallow frying
1 clove garlic, crushed
1 tablespoon chopped ginger root
2 tablespoons chopped scallion
1½ tablespoons hot bean sauce
2 tablespoons pale dry sherry
3 tablespoons soy sauce
½ teaspoon salt
1 teaspoon sugar
1 tablespoon red wine vinegar
2 teaspoons cornstarch, blended
   with ¼ cup water
shredded scallion for garnish

Slash the fish on both sides with diagonal cuts, 1 cm/½ inch deep and
1.5 cm/¾ inches apart. Heat just enough oil in a pan to make a thin film.
Place the fish in the pan and fry until light brown on both sides. Transfer
to a warmed plate.

Add 4 tablespoons oil to the pan and heat. Add the garlic, ginger and
spring onion (scallion) and stir-fry over high heat for a few seconds. Put
the fish on top and add the soy bean paste (bean sauce), sherry, soy
sauce, salt, sugar and vinegar. Bring to the boil and simmer for
10 minutes, covered. Remove fish to serving plates.

Add the cornflour (cornstarch) mixture to the pan and simmer, stirring,
until the sauce has thickened. Pour over the fish, garnish with the
shredded spring onion (scallion) and serve with vegetables of choice.

# Fish Pies

METRIC/IMPERIAL
*350 g/12 oz cod*
*1 small onion, sliced*
*300 ml/½ pint milk*
*blade of mace*
*25 g/1 oz butter*
*½ teaspoon dry mustard*
*25 g/1 oz plain flour*
*50 g/2 oz Cheddar cheese, grated*
*500 g/1 lb potatoes, mashed*

AMERICAN
*¾ lb cod*
*1 small onion, sliced*
*1¼ cups milk*
*blade of mace*
*2 tablespoons butter*
*½ teaspoon dry mustard*
*¼ cup all-purpose flour*
*½ cup grated Cheddar cheese*
*2 cups mashed potatoes*

Place the cod, onion, milk and mace in a pan and heat gently until nearly boiling. Remove from the heat, cover and leave for 15 minutes.

Lift out the fish, flake it and divide evenly between 2 shallow flameproof dishes. Strain the milk and reserve.

Melt the butter in a small pan, add the mustard and flour and cook for 1 minute. Gradually stir in the reserved milk and cook, stirring, until the sauce thickens. Add the cheese and season. Pour over the fish.

Place the mashed potato in a piping (pastry) bag fitted with a large fluted nozzle and pipe the potato over the fish and sauce in the dishes. Place under a preheated moderate grill (broiler) until golden brown. Serve immediately with a salad made with whole green beans, flaked (sliced) almonds and French (vinaigrette) dressing.

# Oriental Fish

METRIC/IMPERIAL
*2 thick fillets white fish*
*1 tablespoon soy sauce*
*2 slices fresh root ginger, chopped*
*½ teaspoon 5-spice powder*
*1 tablespoon oil*
*½ teaspoon sugar*
*freshly ground black pepper*
*1 tablespoon sweet sherry*
*coriander sprigs to garnish*

AMERICAN
*2 thick fillets white fish*
*1 tablespoon soy sauce*
*2 slices fresh ginger root, chopped*
*½ teaspoon 5-spice powder*
*1 tablespoon oil*
*½ teaspoon sugar*
*freshly ground black pepper*
*1 tablespoon sweet sherry*
*Chinese parsley sprigs for garnish*

Place the fish in a small shallow dish. Mix together the soy sauce, ginger, spice, oil, sugar, pepper to taste and sherry and pour over the fish. Turn to coat, then leave for 1 hour to marinate.

Line the grill (broiler) pan with foil, heat well and place the fish on it, skin side up. Pour over half the marinade and grill (broil) at high heat for 4 minutes. Turn the fish, pour over remaining marinade and cook for a further 5 to 6 minutes until the fish flakes easily. Transfer to a warmed serving dish and pour over any marinade in the pan.

Garnish with coriander (Chinese parsley) sprigs and serve with rice.

# Celebration Seafood Pie

| METRIC/IMPERIAL | AMERICAN |
|---|---|
| PASTRY: | DOUGH: |
| 100 g/4 oz plain flour | 1 cup all-purpose flour |
| pinch of salt | pinch of salt |
| 65 g/2½ oz soft margarine | 5 tablespoons margarine |
| 2 tablespoons water | 2 tablespoons water |
| beaten egg to glaze | beaten egg for glaze |
| FILLING: | FILLING: |
| 150 ml/¼ pint milk | ⅔ cup milk |
| 175 g/6 oz cod, cubed | 1¼ cups cubed cod |
| 15 g/½ oz butter | 1 tablespoon butter |
| 15 g/½ oz plain flour | 2 tablespoons all-purpose flour |
| 150 ml/¼ pint dry white wine | ⅔ cup dry white wine |
| 75 g/3 oz peeled prawns | ½ cup shelled shrimp |
| 1 x 99 g/3½ oz can pink salmon, drained and flaked | 1 x 3½ oz can pink salmon, drained and flaked |
| 1 tablespoon chopped parsley | 1 tablespoon chopped parsley |
| salt and freshly ground pepper | salt and freshly ground pepper |

To make the pastry (dough) put half the flour, salt, margarine and water in a bowl and mix with a fork until well blended. Stir in the remaining flour and mix to a stiff dough, adding just a little more water if necessary. Knead on a board until smooth, then chill.

To make the filling: place the milk and fish in a pan and poach for 10 minutes. Remove the fish with a slotted spoon, strain and reserve the liquor.

Melt the butter in a pan, stir in the flour and cook for 1 minute. Gradually blend in the fish liquor and wine. Cook the sauce, stirring, until it thickens. Continue to cook for 1 minute, then stir in the cod, prawns (shrimp), salmon and parsley. Add salt and pepper to taste. Place in a 600 ml/1 pint (2½ cup) pie dish (pan) and leave to cool.

Roll out the pastry to an oval larger than the dish. Cut a strip 1 cm/½ inch wide from the edge and place around the moistened rim of the pie dish. Moisten the strip and place the pastry over the top to make a lid. Trim, seal and crimp the edges. Roll out any trimmings and cut into fish shapes. Moisten these and place on top of the pie. Brush with beaten egg.

Cook in a preheated moderately hot oven (200°C/400°F, Gas Mark 6) for 40 minutes until the top is cooked and golden. Serve hot with creamed potatoes, peas and baked tomatoes.

# Salmon Pizzas

METRIC/IMPERIAL
BASE:
*100 g/4 oz self-raising flour*
*pinch of salt*
*25 g/1 oz hard margarine*
*3 tablespoons milk*
TOPPING:
*1 x 397 g/14 oz can tomatoes,*
*drained and chopped*
*50 g/2 oz mushrooms, sliced*
*½ green pepper, cored, seeded*
*and sliced*
*2 tablespoons chopped spring*
*onions*
*1 x 213 g/7½ oz can pink salmon,*
*drained*
*50 g/2 oz Cheddar cheese, grated*
*salt and freshly ground pepper*

AMERICAN
BASE:
*1 cup self-rising flour*
*pinch of salt*
*2 tablespoons hard margarine*
*3 tablespoons milk*
TOPPING:
*1 x 16 oz can tomatoes, drained*
*and chopped*
*½ cup sliced mushrooms*
*½ green pepper, seeded and sliced*
*2 tablespoons chopped scallions*
*1 x 7½ oz can pink salmon, drained*
*½ cup grated Cheddar cheese*
*salt and freshly ground pepper*

Sift the flour and salt into a bowl and rub (cut) in the margarine until the mixture resembles fine breadcrumbs. Stir in enough milk to make a firm dough. Turn on to a floured surface and knead until smooth.

Divide the dough in half and roll out each piece to a 15 cm/6 inch round. Place on a large greased baking sheet and pull the edges up to make a rim on each. Arrange the tomatoes, mushrooms and green pepper on each pizza. Sprinkle over the spring onions (scallions). Remove any skin and bones from the salmon and arrange chunks on the pizzas. Sprinkle over the grated cheese and salt and pepper to taste.

Cook in a preheated moderately hot oven (200°C/400°F, Gas Mark 6) for 20 to 25 minutes until the dough is cooked and the cheese bubbling and golden. Serve immediately with a crisp salad.

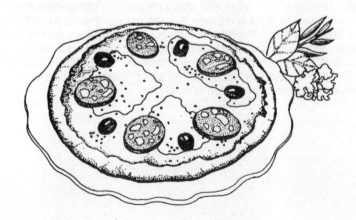

# Devilled Fish

METRIC/IMPERIAL
2 large or 4 small white fish fillets
25 g/1 oz butter
2 small onions, finely chopped
2 teaspoons curry powder
2 tomatoes, skinned and chopped
1 tablespoon lemon juice or cider
  vinegar
salt
a few drops Tabasco sauce
chopped parsley to garnish

AMERICAN
2 large or 4 small white fish fillets
2 tablespoons butter
2 small onions, finely chopped
2 teaspoons curry powder
2 tomatoes, peeled and chopped
1 tablespoon lemon juice or cider
  vinegar
salt
a few drops hot pepper sauce
chopped parsley for garnish

Cut the fish into pieces, discarding any skin and bones.

Melt the butter in a pan and fry the onions and curry powder gently until golden. Add the tomatoes to the pan. Place the fish on top and cook, covered, over a low heat, without stirring, until the fish juices begin to run.

Raise the heat and cook, stirring lightly and flaking the fish with a fork, so that the juice thickens slightly. Stir in the lemon juice or vinegar and add salt and Tabasco sauce to taste. Sprinkle with parsley and serve with toast.

# Fish Kebabs with Lemon Rice

METRIC/IMPERIAL
350 g/12 oz haddock
2 tablespoons vegetable oil
salt and freshly ground black
  pepper
1 tablespoon lemon juice
6 bay leaves
1 lemon, sliced
6 stuffed olives
150 g/5 oz long-grain rice
grated rind and juice of ½ lemon
15 g/½ oz butter
½ teaspoon freshly grated nutmeg

AMERICAN
¾ lb haddock
2 tablespoons vegetable oil
salt and freshly ground black
  pepper
1 tablespoon lemon juice
6 bay leaves
1 lemon, sliced
6 stuffed olives
¾ cup long-grain rice
grated rind and juice of ½ lemon
1 tablespoon butter
½ teaspoon freshly grated nutmeg

Remove any skin and bones from the haddock and cut the fish into cubes. In a bowl, blend together the oil, salt and pepper and lemon juice. Add the fish and leave to marinate for about 30 minutes.

Arrange the fish, bay leaves, lemon slices and olives on two skewers. Brush with the marinade and place under a preheated moderate grill (broiler) for 10 minutes turning several times.

Meanwhile cook the rice in boiling salted water for 15 minutes or until tender. Drain and rinse. Stir in the lemon rind and juice, butter and nutmeg. Spoon the rice on to a hot serving dish and arrange the skewers on top.

# Crispy Tuna Supper

METRIC/IMPERIAL
1 x 99 g/3½ oz can tuna
½ onion, finely chopped
25 g/1 oz butter
25 g/1 oz plain flour
300 ml/½ pint milk
100 g/4 oz Cheddar cheese, grated
salt and freshly ground pepper
2 tomatoes, sliced
25 g/1 oz fresh breadcrumbs

AMERICAN
1 x 3½ oz can tuna
½ onion, finely chopped
2 tablespoons butter
¼ cup all-purpose flour
1¼ cups milk
1 cup grated Cheddar cheese
salt and freshly ground pepper
2 tomatoes, sliced
½ cup soft bread crumbs

Drain the oil from the tuna into a small frying pan and sauté the onion until soft. Flake the tuna and place in a greased 600 ml/1 pint (2½ cup) flameproof dish. Arrange the onion over the top.

Place the butter, flour and milk in a pan. Cook the sauce, whisking continually, until it thickens. Continue to cook for 1 minute, then stir in 75 g/3 oz (¾ cup) of the cheese; and salt and pepper to taste.

Arrange the tomatoes over the tuna and onion, then pour over the sauce. Mix the breadcrumbs with the remaining cheese and sprinkle over the top. Cook under a preheated moderate grill (broiler) until golden.

# Fish Steaks Casalinga

METRIC/IMPERIAL
50 g/2 oz butter
1 small onion, chopped
120 ml/4 fl oz dry white wine
1 tablespoon chopped parsley
2 thick white fish steaks
5 anchovy fillets, rinsed
1½ tablespoons beurre manié (mix
  1 tablespoon flour with 15 g/½ oz
  butter)
salt and freshly ground pepper
1 tablespoon lemon juice

AMERICAN
¼ cup butter
1 small onion, chopped
½ cup dry white wine
1 tablespoon chopped parsley
2 thick white fish steaks
5 anchovy fillets, rinsed
1½ tablespoons beurre manié
  (mix 1 tablespoon flour with
  1 tablespoon butter)
salt and freshly ground pepper
1 tablespoon lemon juice

Melt the butter in a heavy-based frying pan, add the onion and cook gently until golden but not browned. Add the wine and parsley, bring to the boil, then place fish in pan. Cook for ½ minute on one side, then turn the fish. Tightly cover the pan and simmer for about 8 minutes or until the fish is tender and the flesh can be pushed away from the bone slightly with a fork.

Meanwhile pound the anchovies to a paste. When the fish is cooked, remove and keep warm. Add the anchovies to the pan and bring to the boil. Add small pieces of the beurre manié, stirring until the sauce is the required thickness. Cook over medium heat for 5 minutes, stir in the lemon juice. Spoon some over the fish and serve the rest separately.

# Poached Turbot with Hollandaise Sauce

METRIC/IMPERIAL
2 serving-size turbot steaks
2 slices lemon
250 ml/8 fl oz milk
salt
2 eggs yolks
1 tablespoon water
115 g/4½ oz butter, melted
1 tablespoon lemon juice or white
  wine vinegar
freshly ground white pepper
parsley sprigs and lemon halves, to
  garnish

AMERICAN
2 serving-size turbot steaks
2 slices lemon
1 cup milk
salt
2 egg yolks
1 tablespoon water
9 tablespoons melted butter
1 tablespoon lemon juice or white
  wine vinegar
freshly ground white pepper
parsley sprigs and lemon halves,
  for garnish

Place the turbot in a pan with lemon slices and milk. Add salt to taste and enough water just to cover fish. Bring to the boil, then reduce heat, cover and poach gently for about 15 minutes until flesh is tender.

Meanwhile, make the sauce. Put the egg yolks and water in a bowl over a pan of simmering water (the bottom of the bowl must not touch the water). Whisk over low heat until mixture begins to thicken, then gradually add 100 g/4 oz (8 tablespoons) butter, whisking constantly. Make sure each addition is well incorporated before adding more butter. Stir in lemon juice then taste and adjust seasoning. Remove from heat and allow to cool to warm (the serving temperature).

Drain the turbot and place on warmed plates. Brush with remaining melted butter and garnish. Serve with the sauce and plain boiled potatoes.

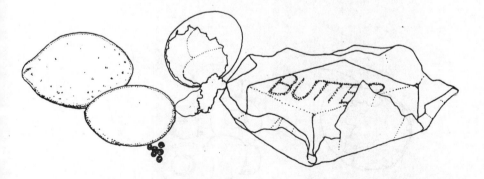

# Fish with Mushroom Sauce

METRIC/IMPERIAL
1 bay leaf
1 onion, sliced
6 peppercorns
1 teaspoon salt
300 ml/½ pint water
2 large or 4 small fish fillets
50 g/2 oz mushrooms, finely sliced
1 spring onion, chopped
15 g/½ oz butter
1 tablespoon chopped parsley
1 egg yolk
5 tablespoons single cream
salt and freshly ground pepper

AMERICAN
1 bay leaf
1 onion, sliced
6 peppercorns
1 teaspoon salt
1¼ cups water
2 large or 4 small fish fillets
½ cup sliced mushrooms
1 scallion, chopped
1 tablespoon butter
1 tablespoon chopped parsley
1 egg yolk
⅓ cup light cream
salt and freshly ground pepper

Place the bay leaf, onion, peppercorns, salt and water in a large frying pan and bring to the boil. Simmer for 5 minutes, then add the fish fillets, cover and remove from the heat. Leave to poach for 6 to 8 minutes, then lift out with a slotted spoon and place on a warmed serving dish. Keep hot.

Sauté the mushrooms and spring onion (scallion) in the butter for 3 to 4 minutes, remove from the heat and stir in the parsley. Mix the egg yolk with the cream and add to the mushrooms. Return to a low heat and stir until the sauce thickens. Add salt and pepper to taste, then spoon over fish and serve with sauté potatoes and green beans.

VARIATIONS:
**Fish with Wine Sauce** – replace half the water with white wine. After poaching the fish, strain the cooking liquid, then boil to reduce it a little. Proceed as in recipe above.
**Fish with Piquant Sauce** – use soured cream instead of single (light) cream, or add 1 tablespoon cider vinegar to the poaching liquid.

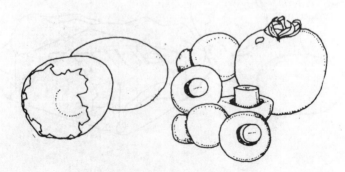

# Haddock with Orange Sauce

METRIC/IMPERIAL
2 x 225 g/8 oz haddock steaks
salt and freshly ground black
  pepper
150 ml/¼ pint milk
15 g/½ oz butter or margarine
1 tablespoon plain flour
1 orange
parsley sprigs to garnish

AMERICAN
2 x 8 oz haddock steaks
salt and freshly ground [
  pepper
⅔ cup milk
1 tablespoon butter or margarine
1 tablespoon all-purpose flour
1 orange
parsley sprigs for garnish

Place the fish steaks in a shallow pan, season with salt and pepper and add the milk. Bring gently to near boiling, then turn off the heat, cover and leave for 15 minutes. Remove fish with a slotted spoon and arrange on a serving dish. Keep hot.

Strain the cooking liquid and reserve. Melt the butter or margarine in a pan, add the flour and cook for 1 minute, then gradually blend in the reserved milk. Cook the sauce, stirring, until thick. Grate rind of orange and stir into sauce with salt and pepper to taste. Pour the sauce over the fish.

Cut away all the remaining skin and pith from the orange and slice the orange. Arrange the orange slices and parsley sprigs on the fish and serve immediately.

VARIATION:
**Haddock with Lime Sauce** – instead of the orange, use 1 lime for a much sharper flavour.

# Baked Haddock with Tomatoes

METRIC/IMPERIAL
350 g/12 oz haddock fillet, skinned
salt and pepper
1 tablespoon chopped onion
2 tomatoes, skinned and chopped
1 tablespoon tomato purée
1 garlic clove, crushed
2 teaspoons lemon juice
3-4 tablespoons white wine or cider
40 g/1½ oz fresh breadcrumbs

AMERICAN
¾ lb haddock fillets, skinned
salt and pepper
1 tablespoon minced onion
2 tomatoes, skinned and minced
1 tablespoon tomato paste
1 garlic clove, crushed
2 teaspoons lemon juice
3-4 tablespoons white wine or
  apple cider
3 tablespoons soft bread crumbs

Lay the haddock in a buttered ovenproof dish and season well with salt and pepper. Combine the onion, tomatoes, tomato purée (paste), garlic, lemon juice and wine or cider and spoon over the fish. Sprinkle with the breadcrumbs and cook in a preheated moderately hot oven (200°C/400°F or Gas Mark 6) until cooked through and browned.

# ᴌackerel with Cider

METRIC/IMPERIAL
2 x 500 g/1 lb whole fresh mackerel
salt and freshly ground black
   pepper
4 bay leaves
sprig of fresh thyme
sprig of fresh rosemary
½ lemon
1 onion, sliced into rings
300 ml/½ pint dry cider
150 ml/¼ pint water
2 teaspoons arrowroot

AMERICAN
2 x 1 lb whole fresh mackerel
salt and freshly ground black
   pepper
4 bay leaves
sprig of fresh thyme
sprig of fresh rosemary
½ lemon
1 onion, sliced into rings
1¼ cups hard cider
⅔ cup water
2 teaspoons arrowroot

To prepare the mackerel: slit along the belly and remove the guts. Cut off the head and fins and wash well. Season the fish inside with salt and pepper, then place a bay leaf in each.

Place the herbs and remaining bay leaves in a shallow ovenproof dish and lay the fish on top. Pare the rind from the lemon and sprinkle over the mackerel with the onion rings. Pour in the cider and most of the water. Cover the dish with foil and cook in a preheated moderate oven (180°C/350°F, Gas Mark 4) for 30 minutes.

Strain off 300 ml/½ pint (1¼ cups) of the cooking liquid into a pan. Blend the arrowroot with the remaining water and stir into the fish liquid. Cook the sauce, stirring, until it thickens and clears.

Arrange the fish and onions on a warmed serving dish, pour over the sauce and serve immediately with mashed potatoes and peas.

VARIATION:
**Greek-Style Mackerel** – cut the lemon into fine slices and use white wine instead of cider. After 20 minutes' cooking, add 12 green olives to the dish. Continue as recipe above but garnish fish with onions, lemons and olives.

# Fried Prawns with Broad Beans

METRIC/IMPERIAL
150 g/5 oz baby broad beans,
 shelled
1 tablespoon dry sherry
2½ teaspoons salt
freshly ground pepper
1 small egg white
2 teaspoons cornflour
500 g/1 lb uncooked prawns,
 shelled and deveined
½ teaspoon sugar
1 tablespoon water
2 tablespoons oil
1 spring onion, chopped

AMERICAN
1 cup podded lima beans
1 tablespoon pale dry sherry
2½ teaspoons salt
freshly ground pepper
1 small egg white
2 teaspoons cornstarch
1 lb raw shrimp, shelled and
 deveined
½ teaspoon sugar
1 tablespoon water
2 tablespoons oil
1 small scallion, chopped

Cook the beans in boiling salted water for 5 to 7 minutes until just tender. Drain well. Mix together 1 tablespoon of the sherry, 1 teaspoon of the salt, pepper, egg white and 1 teaspoon of the cornflour (cornstarch) in a bowl. Add the prawns (shrimp) and leave to marinate for 30 minutes.

Mix together the remaining sherry, salt and cornflour (cornstarch) with the sugar and water. Heat the oil in a pan. Add the prawns (shrimp) and stir-fry for about 1½ minutes or until pink. Transfer to a serving dish.

Add the beans to the pan and stir-fry for a few seconds. Add the spring onion (scallion). Stir-fry for 30 seconds, then add the sugar mixture. Simmer, stirring, until thickened. Add to the prawns (shrimp) and serve at once with noodles.


# Fish Parcels

METRIC/IMPERIAL
4 fish fillets
50 g/2 oz butter
4 spring onions, chopped
2 teaspoons chopped dill weed
2 tablespoons lemon juice
4 tablespoons double cream
salt and freshly ground pepper

AMERICAN
4 fish fillets
¼ cup butter
4 scallions, chopped
2 teaspoons chopped dill weed
2 tablespoons lemon juice
¼ cup heavy cream
salt and freshly ground pepper

Cut 2 squares of doubled foil large enough to wrap around the fish. Grease one side of each piece of foil, then arrange 2 fish fillets in the middle of each and top with equal amounts of the remaining ingredients, adding salt and pepper to taste.

Bring the edges of the foil to the middle and join together to seal tightly. Place the fish parcels under a hot grill (broiler) for about 10 minutes. Turn off the heat and leave for 5 minutes before serving.

# Prawns (Shrimp) with Tomato Sauce

METRIC/IMPERIAL
1 teaspoon salt
1 egg white
4 teaspoons cornflour
500 g/1 lb prawns, shelled and
    deveined
6 tablespoons oil
3 spring onions, finely chopped
2 slices root ginger, finely chopped
2 tablespoons tomato ketchup
1 teaspoon sugar
1 teaspoon red wine vinegar or
    lemon juice
3 tablespoons water

AMERICAN
1 teaspoon salt
1 egg white
4 teaspoons cornstarch
1 lb shrimp, shelled and deveined
6 tablespoons oil
3 scallions, finely chopped
2 slices ginger root, finely chopped
2 tablespoons tomato ketchup
1 teaspoon sugar
1 teaspoon red wine vinegar or
    lemon juice
3 tablespoons water

Mix together the salt, egg white and 1 tablespoon of the cornflour (cornstarch) with a fork until frothy. Add the prawns (shrimp) and turn until coated with the batter.

Heat the oil in a pan. When very hot, add two-thirds of the spring onions (scallions), the ginger and tomato ketchup and stir-fry for 30 seconds. Add the prawns (shrimp), sugar, a pinch of salt, and the wine vinegar or lemon juice. Stir well.

Blend the remaining cornflour (cornstarch) in the water and add to the pan. Simmer the mixture, stirring, until thickened. Serve hot, garnished with the remaining spring onion (scallion), with plain boiled rice.

# Flemish Carbonnade of Beef

METRIC/IMPERIAL
500 g/1 lb beef topside, cut into thin
slices
2 tablespoons oil
2 onions, sliced
100 g/4 oz mushrooms, sliced
1 tablespoon plain flour
1 teaspoon brown sugar
250 ml/8 fl oz beer
about 120 ml/4 fl oz beef stock
salt and pepper
1 bouquet garni (3 sprigs parsley,
1 bay leaf and 1 sprig thyme, tied
together)
Dijon mustard
6 thick slices buttered French bread

AMERICAN
1 lb beef (eye of round or top
round), cut into thin slices
2 tablespoons oil
2 onions, sliced
1 cup sliced mushrooms
1 tablespoon all-purpose flour
1 teaspoon brown sugar
1 cup beer
about ½ cup beef stock or broth
salt and pepper
1 bouquet garni (3 sprigs parsley,
1 bay leaf and 1 sprig thyme, tied
together)
Dijon-style mustard
6 thick slices buttered French bread

Trim any fat from the meat and cut into 4 cm/1½ inch strips. Heat the oil in
a heavy flameproof casserole and fry the beef strips over a fairly high heat
until browned on both sides. Remove the meat from the casserole.
Reduce the heat to medium and fry the onions and mushrooms until the
onions are soft. Stir in the flour and sugar, cook for 1 minute, then
gradually add the beer. Bring to the boil, add the meat strips and enough
stock to come just to the top of the meat. Season to taste with salt and
pepper and add the bouquet garni. Cover and cook gently for 1 hour.
    Spread mustard on the unbuttered side of the bread slices. Arrange the
slices, buttered side up, on top of the meat and place uncovered in a
preheated moderate oven (160°C/325°F, Gas Mark 3) for 20 or 30
minutes, or until the meat is very tender and the bread is crusty on top.
    Serve immediately with creamed potatoes and a green salad.

# Beef with Noodles

METRIC/IMPERIAL
2 tablespoons oil
350 g/12 oz lean minced beef
2 tablespoons dry sherry
2 tablespoons soy sauce
1 tablespoon cornflour
1 teaspoon sugar
1 clove garlic, crushed
2 slices fresh root ginger, chopped
2 teaspoons Tabasco sauce
120 ml/4 fl oz water
salt
50 g/2 oz egg noodles

AMERICAN
2 tablespoons oil
¾ lb lean ground beef
2 tablespoons dry sherry
2 tablespoons soy sauce
1 tablespoon cornstarch
1 teaspoon sugar
1 clove garlic, crushed
2 slices fresh ginger root, chopped
2 teaspoons hot pepper sauce
½ cup water
salt
2 oz egg noodles

Heat the oil in a wok or heavy frying pan. Add the beef and stir-fry until the meat is brown, breaking up any lumps. Add the sherry, soy sauce, cornflour (cornstarch), sugar, garlic, ginger and Tabasco (hot pepper) sauce. Stir for a minute so everything is well blended, then add the water. Stir again, taste the gravy, and add salt to taste if necessary.

Meanwhile cook the noodles in boiling salted water for 5 minutes, then drain and arrange on a heated serving plate. Pour over the meat mixture.

# Beef Seville

METRIC/IMPERIAL
25 g/1 oz butter
1 tablespoon oil
1 onion, sliced
2 carrots, sliced
500 g/1 lb chuck steak, cubed
1½ tablespoons plain flour
grated rind and juice of 1 orange
250 ml/8 fl oz beef stock
2 tablespoons orange squash
salt and freshly ground pepper
50 g/2 oz dried apricots
watercress to garnish

AMERICAN
2 tablespoons butter
1 tablespoon oil
1 onion, sliced
2 carrots, sliced
1 lb chuck steak, cubed
1½ tablespoons all-purpose flour
grated rind and juice of 1 orange
1 cup beef stock
2 tablespoons orange drink
salt and freshly ground pepper
⅓ cup dried apricots
watercress for garnish

Melt the butter in a pan with the oil and sauté the onion and carrots for 5 minutes. Add the meat and fry, turning frequently, until evenly browned. Sprinkle in the flour and continue to cook for 1 minute. Transfer the meat and vegetables to a 900 ml/1½ pint (3¾ cup) casserole dish.

Stir in the orange rind and juice, stock and orange squash (drink). Add plenty of salt and pepper to taste and the apricots. Cover and cook in a preheated moderate oven (160°C/325°F, Gas Mark 3) for 1 to 1½ hours. Garnish with watercress and serve with long macaroni.

# Old-Fashioned Steak and Mushrooms

METRIC/IMPERIAL
1 kg/2 lb stewing steak
2-3 tablespoons plain flour
50 g/2 oz butter
1 onion, chopped
225 g/8 oz mushrooms
salt and freshly ground pepper
1 tablespoon chopped fresh mixed
   or ½ teaspoon dried herbs
beef stock or water to cover

AMERICAN
2 lb beef for stew
2-3 tablespoons all-purpose flour
¼ cup butter
1 onion, chopped
½ lb mushrooms
salt and freshly ground pepper
1 tablespoon chopped fresh mixed
   or ½ teaspoon dried herbs
beef stock or water to cover

Remove any fat and gristle from the meat and cut into bite-size pieces. Toss the meat in the flour, shaking off any surplus.

Heat the butter in a heavy flameproof casserole or pan and fry the onion until soft. Add the meat and brown over a medium heat. Add the mushrooms and cook for 1 minute. Season with salt and pepper to taste, add the herbs and pour in enough stock or water to come just to the top of the meat. Cover tightly and simmer for about 2 hours until the meat is very tender.

Serve half of the steak and mushrooms with mashed potatoes and green vegetables. Use the rest to make a pie.

VARIATION:
**Steak and Kidney** – cook 100 g/4 oz (¼ lb) chopped lamb's kidney, with the meat. Use as above or in a pie.

# Chinese-Style Steak and Beans

METRIC/IMPERIAL
350 g/12 oz rump steak
4 tablespoons oil
25 g/1 oz whole shelled almonds
225 g/8 oz sliced green beans
250 ml/8 fl oz boiling water
4 spring onions, chopped
1 tablespoon soy sauce
2 teaspoons cornflour
salt and freshly ground pepper

AMERICAN
¾ lb top round steak
¼ cup oil
¼ cup whole shelled almonds
1 cup sliced green beans
1 cup boiling water
4 scallions, chopped
1 tablespoon soy sauce
2 teaspoons cornstarch
salt and freshly ground pepper

Cut the steak into fine strips about 5 cm/2 inches long. Heat the oil in a wok or heavy-based frying pan, add almonds and stir-fry until golden all over. Add the beef and cook, stirring, for 5 minutes. Add beans and boiling water, cover and cook for 5 minutes.

Add spring onions (scallions) and stir in soy sauce mixed with cornflour. Add salt and pepper to taste and cook, stirring, for 3 minutes.

Serve with noodles or plain boiled rice.

# Fricadelles with Piquant Sauce

METRIC/IMPERIAL
*500 g/1 lb lean minced beef*
*salt and freshly ground pepper*
*250 g/1 oz fresh breadcrumbs*
*25 g/1 oz butter, softened*
*1 tablespoon grated horseradish*
*1 tablespoon chopped chives*
*little oil*
*1 tablespoon lemon juice*
*120 ml/4 fl oz beef stock*
*4 tablespoons soured cream*

AMERICAN
*1 lb lean ground beef*
*salt and freshly ground pepper*
*½ cup soft bread crumbs*
*2 tablespoons butter, softened*
*1 tablespoon grated horseradish*
*1 tablespoon chopped chives*
*little oil*
*1 tablespoon lemon juice*
*½ cup beef stock*
*¼ cup sour cream*

Place the meat in a bowl, season with salt and pepper, and mix in the breadcrumbs. Cream together the butter, horseradish and chives and combine gently with the meat. Shape into 4 patties.

Heat enough oil in a heavy-based frying pan to give just a thin film over the base. Cook the fricadelles over a high heat for about 3 minutes on each side, or until well browned outside but still a little pink inside. Transfer to a heated platter and keep warm while you make the sauce.

Add the lemon juice and stock to the pan and stir well to mix in the brown bits from the base of the pan. Cook over a high heat until reduced by about half. Stir in the cream and heat gently, but do not boil. Taste for seasoning, spoon over the patties and serve with Onion Mash (see page 113) and a mixed salad.

VARIATIONS:
**Scandinavian Burgers** – serve fricadelles in warmed baps with slices of large gherkins (dill pickle) and ketchup-flavoured mayonnaise.
**Skewered Fricadelles** – form the mixture into tiny balls 2.5 cm/1 inch in diameter. Roll in a mixture of dry mustard and freshly ground black pepper, then arrange on 2 oiled skewers. Grill (broil) under high heat for 8 to 10 minutes turning frequently and serve with Risotto (see page 165).

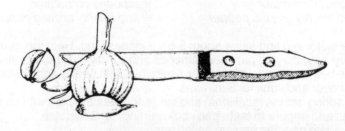

# Roasted Beef and Onions

METRIC/IMPERIAL
1.3 kg/3 lb beef silverside
1 clove garlic, crushed
1 packet French onion soup mix
½ teaspoon dry mustard
salt and pepper

AMERICAN
3 lb boneless rump roast
1 clove garlic, crushed
1 package French onion soup mix
½ teaspoon dry mustard
salt and pepper

Place the meat on a piece of foil large enough to wrap around it. Spread the top with half the garlic and sprinkle with half the soup mix and a little mustard, patting the flavourings in with a broad-bladed knife. Turn over and repeat on the other side.

Wrap the meat loosely in the foil, sealing the edges well, and place in a roasting pan. Roast in a preheated moderately hot oven (190°C/375°F, Gas Mark 5) for 1 hour 40 minutes. Carefully unwrap the meat and transfer to a warmed platter. Pour the juices that have collected back into the pan and add enough hot water to give a good gravy. Reheat, add salt and pepper to taste and pour into a sauceboat.

Carve the meat in thin slices and serve with the gravy, jacket-baked potatoes cooked in the oven at the same time, and green peas.

# Sliced Beef with Green Peppers

METRIC/IMPERIAL
350 g/12 oz fillet or rump steak
4 teaspoons soy sauce
1 teaspoon cornflour
pinch of bicarbonate of soda
2 teaspoons water
pinch of black pepper
5 tablespoons oil
1 large green pepper, cored,
  seeded and cut into thin strips
1 teaspoon salt

AMERICAN
¾ lb sirloin or top round steak
4 teaspoons soy sauce
1 teaspoon cornstarch
pinch of baking soda
2 teaspoons water
pinch of black pepper
⅓ cup oil
1 large green pepper, seeded and
  cut into thin strips
1 teaspoon salt

Cut the beef into thin slices, then into strips a little longer than a match. Mix together 1 teaspoon soy sauce, the cornflour (cornstarch), soda, water and pepper and stir in the beef strips, mixing well.

Heat 2 tablespoons of the oil in a wok or heavy-based frying pan and add the green peppers and salt. Stir-fry for about 2 minutes, until the peppers are tender but still crisp. Remove the peppers with a slotted spoon. Add the remaining 3 tablespoons of oil to the pan and fry the beef for 2 to 3 minutes until golden brown. Return the peppers to the pan with the remaining soy sauce and 2 tablespoons of water. Stir for another minute, then serve with plain boiled rice.

# Provençale Beef Casserole

METRIC/IMPERIAL
2 tablespoons dripping or butter
600 g/1¼ lb chuck steak, cut into
   chunks
3 garlic cloves, crushed
1 tablespoon chopped parsley
1 tablespoon plain flour
250 ml/8 fl oz tomato purée (made
   by puréeing canned tomatoes in
   a blender)
freshly grated nutmeg
salt and pepper
100 g/4 oz button onions
60 ml/2 fl oz Aïoli (see page 154)
1 to 2 tablespoons lukewarm water

AMERICAN
2 tablespoons drippings or butter
1¼ lb stewing beef, cut into chunks
3 garlic cloves, crushed
1 tablespoon chopped parsley
1 tablespoon all-purpose flour
1 cup tomato purée (made by
   puréeing canned tomatoes in a
   blender)
freshly grated nutmeg
salt and pepper
¼ lb pearl onions
¼ cup Aïoli (see page 154)
1 to 2 tablespoons lukewarm water

Melt half the fat in a flameproof casserole, add the beef and fry over moderate heat until juices run. Pour off juices and set aside. Add rest of fat and heat. Finely chop garlic and parsley together, add to casserole and fry briskly for 3 minutes, stirring. Sprinkle in flour, cook for 1 minute, then stir in tomato purée, nutmeg and salt and pepper to taste. Bring to the boil, cover and simmer gently for 1 hour. Add the onions and cook for a further 30 minutes until beef is tender.

Remove beef from casserole with slotted spoon and place in serving dish. Keep hot. Stir Aïoli, warm water and reserved beef juices into casserole, taste and adjust seasoning, then pour into sauceboat. Serve with beef and plain boiled rice.

# Steak and Mushroom Pie

METRIC/IMPERIAL
½ quantity Old-Fashioned Steak
   and Mushrooms (see page 39)
1 x 213 g/7 ½ oz packet frozen puff
   pastry, thawed
1 small egg, beaten

AMERICAN
½ quantity Old-Fashioned Steak
   and Mushrooms (see page 39)
½ lb package frozen puff dough,
   thawed
1 small egg, beaten

Place the cooked steak and mushroom mixture in a small pie dish and leave to cool if necessary. Roll out the pastry (dough) to an oval shape larger than the pie dish. With a sharp knife cut out a pastry lid.

Brush edge of pie dish with water, then cut strips of pastry the same width as rim and arrange on rim. Brush with water, then place pastry lid on top. Knock up and crimp edges, decorate with leaves or tassels made from trimmings. Brush top of pie, not edges, with beaten egg. Cook in a preheated hot oven (220°C/425°F, Gas Mark 7) for 25-30 minutes until well risen and golden.

# Paprika Beef

METRIC/IMPERIAL
1 x 425 g/15 oz can stewed steak
1 onion, sliced
1 clove garlic, crushed
150 ml/¼ pint beer
2 tablespoons paprika pepper
2 tablespoons tomato purée
1 teaspoon sugar
salt and freshly ground pepper
175 g/6 oz pasta shells
15 g/½ oz butter
chopped parsley to garnish

AMERICAN
1 x 1lb can stewed steak
1 onion, sliced
1 clove garlic, crushed
⅔ cup beer
2 tablespoons paprika pepper
2 tablespoons tomato paste
1 teaspoon sugar
salt and freshly ground pepper
1½ cups pasta shells
1 tablespoon butter
chopped parsley for garnish

Place the stewed steak in a pan and break up with a fork. Add the onion, garlic, beer, paprika, tomato purée (paste), sugar and salt and pepper to taste. Gently bring to the boil, cover and simmer for 20 minutes.

Meanwhile cook the pasta shells in plenty of boiling salted water for 15 minutes or until tender. Drain and rinse with hot water. Toss the pasta in the butter then arrange it around the edge of a warmed serving dish. Spoon the meat mixture into the centre. Garnish with parsley and serve with a mixed salad.

# Chilli Con Carne

METRIC/IMPERIAL
275 g/10 oz minced beef
1 onion, finely chopped
½ red pepper, cored, seeded and
    chopped
1 x 227 g/8 oz can tomatoes
2 tablespoons stock
½-1 teaspoon chilli powder
2 tablespoons tomato purée
salt and freshly ground pepper
1 x 396 g/14 oz can red kidney
    beans, drained

AMERICAN
1¼ cups ground beef
1 onion, finely chopped
½ red pepper, seeded and
    chopped
1 x 8 oz can tomatoes
2 tablespoons stock or broth
½-1 teaspoon chili powder
2 tablespoons tomato paste
salt and freshly ground pepper
1 x 14 oz can red kidney beans,
    drained

Heat a frying pan without any fat, add the meat and fry over a moderate heat, turning occasionally until evenly browned. Add the onion and red pepper and fry for 5 minutes.

Stir in the tomatoes and their juice, stock, chilli powder to taste, tomato purée (paste) and salt and pepper to taste. Bring to the boil, stirring, cover and simmer for 35 minutes. Add the kidney beans and continue to cook for a further 15 minutes, uncovered.

Spoon the mixture into two warmed bowls and serve with crusty bread and a crisp salad.

# Tamale Pies

METRIC/IMPERIAL
500 g/1 lb minced beef
1 small onion, chopped
1 green pepper, cored, seeded and
chopped
3 ripe tomatoes, skinned and
chopped
1 x 198 g/7 oz can sweetcorn
kernels, drained
1 teaspoon sugar
½ teaspoon salt
1 teaspoon chilli powder
TOPPING:
50 g/2 oz cornmeal (polenta)
¼ teaspoon salt
250 ml/8 fl oz cold water
25 g/1 oz butter

AMERICAN
1 lb ground beef
1 small onion, chopped
1 green pepper, seeded and
chopped
3 ripe tomatoes, peeled and
chopped
1 x 7 oz can whole kernel corn,
drained
1 teaspoon sugar
½ teaspoon salt
1 teaspoon chili powder
TOPPING:
⅓ cup cornmeal
¼ teaspoon salt
1 cup cold water
2 tablespoons butter

Heat a frying pan, add the beef and stir it until brown, breaking it up with a fork. Add the remaining ingredients, cover and simmer for 20 minutes. Divide between 2 individual ovenproof dishes.

Put the cornmeal, salt and water into a pan. Cook, stirring, for about 10 minutes until thick. Add the butter and spoon over the hot meat in the dishes. Cook in a preheated moderate oven (180°C/350°F, Gas Mark 4) for 40 minutes, or until the topping is firm.

# Gingered Beef and Celery Kebabs

METRIC/IMPERIAL
350 g/12 oz rump or good blade
steak
2 tablespoons soy sauce
1 tablespoon vegetable oil
1 tablespoon honey
1 clove garlic, crushed
1 teaspoon grated fresh root ginger
2 sticks celery, sliced

AMERICAN
¾ lb flank steak or top round
2 tablespoons soy sauce
1 tablespoon vegetable oil
1 tablespoon honey
1 clove garlic, crushed
1 teaspoon grated fresh ginger root
2 stalks celery, sliced

Slice the beef across the grain into 5 mm/¼ inch strips and place in a bowl. Mix the remaining ingredients (except the celery) and pour over, turning the meat to coat evenly. Leave to marinate for 1 hour, turning the meat several times.

Remove the meat strips from the marinade and thread on to skewers, concertina fashion, alternating with slices of celery. Grill (broil) for about 5 minutes turning once and brushing with the marinade. The meat should be rare on the inside. Serve with boiled rice and salad.

# Herb-Stuffed Hamburgers

| METRIC/IMPERIAL | AMERICAN |
|---|---|
| *350 g/12 oz lean minced beef* | *¾ lb lean ground beef* |
| *½ teaspoon Worcestershire sauce* | *½ teaspoon Worcestershire sauce* |
| *½ teaspoon salt* | *½ teasoon salt* |
| *freshly ground pepper* | *freshly ground pepper* |
| *50 g/2 oz butter, melted* | *¼ cup butter, melted* |
| *25 g/1 oz fresh breadcrumbs* | *½ cup soft bread crumbs* |
| *1 small egg, beaten* | *1 small egg, beaten* |
| *1 teaspoon chopped fresh parsley* | *1 teaspoon chopped fresh parsley* |
| *¼ teaspoon chopped fresh thyme* | *¼ teaspoon chopped fresh thyme* |
| *½ teaspoon chopped chives* | *½ teaspoon chopped chives* |
| *salt and pepper* | *salt and pepper* |
| *½ teaspoon grated lemon rind* | *½ teaspoon grated lemon rind* |

Mix the beef, Worcestershire sauce, salt and a good grinding of pepper lightly with a fork. With wet hands, shape into 4 thin patties.

Lightly mix together half the butter and the remaining ingredients with a fork. Spoon on to 2 of the patties, top with the remaining patties and press edges together to seal. Brush the hamburgers with remaining melted butter and grill (broil) on a preheated oiled rack at high heat for about 6 minutes on each side.

VARIATIONS:
**Quick Stuffed Hamburgers** – mix 1 tablespoon poultry stuffing mix (e.g., sage and onion, parsley and thyme) with a little boiling water, add freshly ground pepper and a few drops of brown sauce. Use to stuff hamburgers as above.
**Cheese and Onion Burgers** – place a rounded slice of Gruyère (Swiss) or processed cheese and 2 slices of onion, broken into rings, between the patties. Cook as above.

# Beef with Broccoli

METRIC/IMPERIAL
*350 g/12 oz lean beef, thinly sliced across the grain into bite-size pieces*
*350 g/12 oz brocooli*
*salt*
*3 tablespoons oil*
*2 cloves garlic, crushed*
*3-4 slices root ginger*
*2 teaspoons sugar*
*2 tablespoons soy sauce or oyster sauce*

MARINADE:
*2 teaspoons soy sauce*
*1 tablespoon dry sherry*
*1 tablespoon cornflour*
*1 tablespoon oil*

AMERICAN
*¾ lb flank steak, thinly sliced across the grain into bite-size pieces*
*¾ lb broccoli*
*salt*
*3 tablespoons oil*
*2 cloves garlic, crushed*
*3-4 slices ginger root*
*2 teaspoons sugar*
*2 tablespoons soy sauce or oyster sauce*

MARINADE:
*2 teaspoons soy sauce*
*1 tablespoon pale dry sherry*
*1 tablespoon cornstarch*
*1 tablespoon oil*

Mix together the ingredients for the marinade in a dish. Add the beef and leave to marinate while preparing the broccoli.

Separate the broccoli into florets and slice the stems diagonally. Place in a pan of boiling salted water and cook for 1 minute. Drain and rinse with cold water.

Heat the oil in a pan. Add the garlic and ginger and stir-fry for a few seconds. Add the beef and stir-fry until brown. Add the broccoli, sugar and soy sauce or oyster sauce. Stir-fry for 1 minute.

Serve hot with plain boiled rice or noodles.

# Sliced Beef and Bamboo Shoots

METRIC/IMPERIAL
2 teaspoons dry sherry
5 teaspoons soy sauce
1 egg white
1 tablespoon cornflour
225 g/8 oz beef (rump or topside),
  thinly sliced and cut into bite-
  sized pieces
4 tablespoons oil
100 g/4 oz canned bamboo shoots,
  drained and thinly sliced
4 large dried Chinese mushrooms,
  soaked for 20 minutes, drained,
  stemmed and quartered
½ teaspoon salt
freshly ground pepper
1 spring onion, shredded

AMERICAN
2 teaspoons pale dry sherry
5 teaspoons soy sauce
1 egg white
1 tablespoon cornstarch
½ lb flank steak, thinly sliced and
  cut into bite-sized pieces
¼ cup oil
½ cup thinly sliced canned bamboo
  shoots
4 large dried Chinese mushrooms,
  soaked for 20 minutes, drained,
  stemmed and quartered
½ teaspoon salt
freshly ground pepper
1 scallion, shredded

Using a fork, combine the sherry, 2 teaspoons of the soy sauce, the egg white and cornflour (cornstarch) in a bowl. Add the beef and toss to coat thoroughly.

Heat the oil in a heavy-based frying pan or wok. Add the beef and stir-fry until just brown. Add the bamboo shoots and mushrooms and stir-fry for a few seconds. Stir in the remaining soy sauce, the salt and pepper to taste and cook for 1 minute. Transfer to a serving dish and garnish with the shredded spring onion (scallion).

# Beef Sauté with Onions

METRIC/IMPERIAL
25 g/1 oz dripping or butter
2 large onions, peeled and finely
  sliced into rings
350 g/12 oz cooked beef, thinly
  sliced
salt
freshly ground pepper
2 tablespoons red wine vinegar
3 sprigs parsley, finely chopped
1 clove garlic, finely chopped

AMERICAN
2 tablespoons drippings or butter
2 large onions, peeled and finely
  sliced into rings
¾ lb cooked beef, thinly sliced
salt
freshly ground pepper
2 tablespoons red wine vinegar
3 sprigs parsley, finely chopped
1 clove garlic, finely minced

Melt the fat in a large heavy-based frying pan (skillet). Add the onions and fry gently until tender and lightly coloured, turning mixture frequently. Add the beef, stir well to mix, then cook until heated through. Add salt and pepper, vinegar, parsley and garlic and fry, stirring constantly, for a few minutes. Serve immediately with Buttered Noodles (see page 175).

# Beef in a Cloak

METRIC/IMPERIAL
1 x 213 g/7½ oz frozen puff pastry,
 thawed
1 egg white, lightly beaten
FILLING:
2 tablespoons olive oil
1 small onion, finely chopped
1 tablespoon chopped gherkins, dill
 pickle or capers
1 teaspoon dry mustard
225 g/8 oz cooked beef, minced or
 finely chopped
4 tablespoons single cream or
 evaporated milk
dash of Worcestershire sauce
salt and freshly ground pepper

AMERICAN
½ lb frozen puff pastry, thawed
1 egg white, lightly beaten
FILLING:
2 tablespoons olive oil
1 small onion, finely chopped
1 tablespoon chopped gherkins, dill
 pickle or capers
1 teaspoon dry English mustard
1 cup ground or finely chopped
 cooked beef
¼ cup light cream or evaporated
 milk
dash of Worcestershire sauce
salt and freshly ground pepper

First make the filling: heat the oil in a heavy frying pan and gently fry the onion until soft. Stir in the remaining filling ingredients and leave to cool.

Roll the pastry out thinly to a rectangle about 3 mm/⅛ inch thick. Brush with egg white around the edges. Spoon the meat mixture over half the pastry, leaving a rim of about 1 cm/½ inch. Fold the pastry over the top, pressing the edges together and sealing well. Make a few slashes in the top with a sharp knife and brush with more egg white. Place on a greased baking sheet and cook in a preheated moderately hot oven (200°C/400°F, Gas Mark 6) for about 25 minutes until the pastry is golden brown. Serve the meat, cut into slices, with Fresh Tomato Sauce (see page 144).

VARIATION:
This is a good basic recipe for using up all kinds of leftovers from the refrigerator which can be added to the filling. Apart from onions other 'fresh' foods can be sliced mushrooms, rice, cracked wheat, grated carrot, chopped celery, fresh herbs, chopped spinach, shredded cabbage.

# Beef and Cheese Cake

METRIC/IMPERIAL
*50 g/2 oz butter*
*225 g/8 oz lean minced beef*
*1 onion, finely chopped*
*2 teaspoons dry mustard*
*½ teaspoon cumin powder*
*salt and freshly ground pepper*
*3 eggs*
*3 tablespoons water*
*350 g/12 oz semi-hard cheese,*
*    grated*

AMERICAN
*¼ cup butter*
*½ lb lean ground beef*
*1 onion, finely chopped*
*2 teaspoons dry mustard*
*½ teaspoon cumin powder*
*salt and freshly ground pepper*
*3 eggs*
*3 tablespoons water*
*3 cups grated semi-hard cheese*

Heat the butter and fry the beef briskly until it changes colour, stirring and breaking up the lumps with a fork. Add the onion, mustard and cumin and fry for 3 minutes, adding salt and pepper to taste.

Beat the eggs and water together and add 275 g/10 oz (2½ cups) of the cheese. Stir this mixture into the pan, spread out evenly and press down. Sprinkle the remaining cheese over the top. Put a lid on the pan and cook over a moderate heat for 10 minutes. Remove the lid, put a plate over the pan and turn the meat cake out on to the plate, then reverse on to another plate. Serve cut into wedges, with crusty bread and mixed salad.

# Gratin of Beef

METRIC/IMPERIAL
*65 g/2½ oz butter*
*350 g/12 oz onions, finely chopped*
*1½ tablespoons plain flour*
*2 tablespoons wine vinegar*
*250 ml/8 fl oz beef stock*
*2 tablespoons Fresh Tomato Sauce*
*    (see page 144), or 1 large ripe*
*    tomato, skinned and chopped*
*salt and freshly ground pepper*
*350 g/12 oz cooked beef, cut in thin*
*    slices*
*2 tablespoons dried breadcrumbs*

AMERICAN
*5 tablespoons butter*
*¾ lb onions, finely minced*
*1½ tablespoons all-purpose flour*
*2 tablespoons wine vinegar*
*1 cup beef stock*
*2 tablespoons Fresh Tomato Sauce*
*    (see page 144), or 1 large ripe*
*    tomato peeled and chopped*
*salt and freshly ground pepper*
*¾ lb cooked beef, cut in thin slices*
*2 tablespoons dry bread crumbs*

Melt half the butter in a heavy-based pan. Add the onions and fry gently until tender and lightly coloured. Sprinkle in the flour and cook for 1 minute, then gradually stir in the vinegar and stock. Add the tomato sauce or chopped tomato and salt and pepper to taste. Cook, simmering, for 10 minutes, then add the beef and cook for 10 minutes, turning once.

Turn mixture into flameproof serving dish. Melt the remaining butter, mix with the breadcrumbs, then pour over the beef. Cook under a preheated hot grill (broiler) for a few minutes until crisp and brown. Serve immediately.

# Liver à la Crème

METRIC/IMPERIAL
*50 g/2 oz butter*
*1 tablespoon oil*
*350 g/12 oz calf's liver, cut into thin strips*
*2 medium onions, peeled and sliced into thin rounds*
*150 ml/¼ pint soured cream*
*½ teaspoon finely grated lemon rind*
*1 teaspoon chopped fresh sage or ¼ teaspoon dried sage*
*1 tablespoon chopped parsley*
*salt and freshly ground pepper*

AMERICAN
*¼ cup butter*
*1 tablespoon oil*
*¾ lb calf liver, cut into thin strips*
*2 medium onions, peeled and sliced into thin rounds*
*⅔ cup sour cream*
*½ teaspoon finely grated lemon rind*
*1 teaspoon chopped fresh sage or ¼ teaspoon dried sage*
*1 tablespoon chopped parsley*
*salt and freshly ground pepper*

Heat the butter and oil until butter is frothy, add the liver and cook quickly until brown on all sides. Remove with a slotted spoon and set aside.

Add the onions to the pan and cook gently until tender and lightly coloured. Return liver and any juices from it to the pan, increase heat and stir fry for 1 minute. Reduce heat, stir in cream, lemon rind, sage, parsley and salt and pepper to taste. Cook, stirring gently, until heated through, then serve immediately with plain boiled rice and Minted Peas (page 102).

# Kidney and Beer Stew

METRIC/IMPERIAL
*350 g/12 oz ox kidneys*
*lemon juice*
*50 g/2 oz butter*
*2 tablespoons plain flour*
*120 ml/4 fl oz beef stock*
*120 ml/4 fl oz beer*
*2 tablespoons tomato purée*
*salt and freshly ground pepper*
*chopped parsley to garnish*

AMERICAN
*¾ lb beef kidneys*
*lemon juice*
*¼ cup butter*
*2 tablespoons all-purpose flour*
*½ cup beef stock*
*½ cup beer*
*2 tablespoons tomato paste*
*salt and freshly ground pepper*
*chopped parsley for garnish*

Skin the kidneys and cut out the central cores. Cover with cold water, add a good squeeze of lemon juice and leave for 30 minutes. Drain and pat dry, then cut into wafer thin slices.

Melt the butter in a pan and sauté the kidneys for 3 to 4 minutes, stirring, just until the pink tinge has gone. Remove with a slotted spoon. Stir the flour into the pan drippings, fry for 1 minute, then pour in the stock and beer. Bring to the boil and stir until smooth. Add the tomato purée (paste) and salt and pepper to taste.

Return the kidneys to the pan and stir until heated through. Sprinkle with parsley and serve with boiled rice and a green vegetable.

# Sweetbreads with Mushrooms and Cream

| METRIC/IMPERIAL | AMERICAN |
|---|---|
| 2 calf's sweetbreads | 2 veal sweetbreads |
| 75 g/3 oz butter | 6 tablespoons butter |
| 100 g/4 oz mushrooms, sliced | 1 cup sliced mushrooms |
| 1 tablespoon plain flour | 1 tablespoon all-purpose flour |
| salt | salt |
| freshly ground pepper | freshly ground pepper |
| 2 tablespoons calvados or brandy | 2 tablespoons applejack or brandy |
| 150 ml/¼ pint double cream | ⅔ cup heavy cream |

Soak the sweetbreads in cold water for 3 hours, changing the water 2 or 3 times. Drain and rinse thoroughly, then place in a pan, cover with water and bring slowly to the boil. Simmer for 5 minutes, then drain, rinse and cut away any fatty parts. Place between two plates, weight them down and leave for 1 hour.

Melt half the butter in a frying pan (skillet). Slice the sweetbreads and add to pan. Fry over low heat until lightly coloured on both sides. Toss the mushrooms in the flour until coated. Shake off any excess then add to the pan with salt and pepper to taste. Cover and cook gently for 15 minutes. Remove sweetbreads and mushrooms from pan with slotted spoon and divide between warmed plates. Keep hot.

Stir calvados (applejack) or brandy into the cooking juices, scraping up any sediment. Add cream and simmer until reduced by half. Remove from heat and add remaining butter, a little at a time, whisking vigorously. Taste and adjust seasoning, then pour over the sweetbreads and serve immediately with creamed potatoes and Minted Peas (see page 102).

# Swiss-style Kidneys and Potatoes

METRIC/IMPERIAL
350 g/12 oz potatoes, peeled and
    cut into thin rounds
4 tablespoons oil
40 g/1 ½ oz butter
salt
freshly ground pepper
6 juniper berries
1 clove garlic
2 calf's kidneys, halved with cores
    removed
4 tablespoons medium sherry

AMERICAN
¾ lb potatoes, peeled and cut into
    thin rounds
4 tablespoons oil
3 tablespoons butter
salt
freshly ground pepper
6 juniper berries
1 clove garlic
2 veal kidneys, halved with cores
    removed
4 tablespoons medium sherry

Dry potatoes thoroughly with absorbent paper towels. Heat half the oil in a small, heavy-based frying pan. Melt half the butter. Layer potatoes in the pan, brushing each layer with melted butter and seasoning with salt and pepper. Place small plate on top and weight down. Cook for 10 minutes until underside is golden, then slide cake out on to plate, then return it to pan cooked side up. Replace plate and weight on top and cook until underside is golden.

Meanwhile, pound together juniper berries, garlic and 1 teaspoon salt. Heat the remaining oil and butter in another pan, add the juniper mixture and kidneys and fry over brisk heat for 2 to 3 minutes on each side. Lower the heat, add pepper, cover and cook for 6 to 8 minutes.

Remove the kidneys from the pan with a slotted spoon and slice them. Turn out potato cake and place on warmed serving plate. Arrange kidneys on top. Keep hot.

Add the sherry to the kidney juices in the pan and boil rapidly, stirring up crusty bits from the bottom. Taste and adjust seasoning, then strain over the kidneys. Serve immediately with a mixed salad.

Pork and Bacon Dishes

## *Pork Chop Suey*

METRIC/IMPERIAL
2 tablespoons oil
2 sticks celery, with leaves, cut in
  diagonal slices
3 spring onions, sliced
2 sliced fresh root ginger, finely
  chopped
½ green pepper, cored, seeded
  and sliced
4 mushrooms, sliced
350 g/12 oz cooked pork, cut in
  strips
50 g/2 oz bean sprouts
120 ml/4 fl oz chicken stock
1 tablespoon soy sauce
1 teaspoon sugar
salt and freshly ground pepper
2 teaspoons cornflour, blended with
  1 tablespoon dry sherry

AMERICAN
2 tablespoons oil
2 stalks celery, with leaves, cut in
  diagonal slices
3 scallions, sliced
2 slices fresh ginger root, finely
  chopped
½ green pepper, seeded and sliced
4 mushrooms, sliced
1½ cups cooked pork, cut in strips
1 cup bean sprouts
½ cup chicken stock or broth
1 tablespoon soy sauce
1 teaspoon sugar
salt and freshly ground pepper
2 teaspoons cornstarch, blended
  with 1 tablespoon pale dry sherry

Heat the oil in a large frying pan or wok. Quickly stir-fry the celery, spring onions (scallions), ginger, green pepper and mushrooms for about 3 to 4 minutes until tender-crisp.

Stir in the pork and continue cooking and stirring for a few minutes until the pork is heated through. Add the bean sprouts, stock, soy sauce and sugar, and bring to the boil. Add salt and pepper to taste and the cornflour (cornstarch) mixture and simmer, stirring all the time, until the gravy has thickened and is clear. Serve with boiled rice or buttered noodles.

# Porkburgers with Glazed Pineapple

| METRIC/IMPERIAL | AMERICAN |
|---|---|
| 15 g/½ oz fresh white breadcrumbs | ¼ cup soft white bread crumbs |
| 4 tablespoons milk | ¼ cup milk |
| 350 g/12 oz minced pork | ¾ lb ground pork |
| 1 teaspoon chopped fresh or | 1 teaspoon chopped fresh or |
| ¼ teaspoon dried sage | ¼ teaspoon dried sage |
| 1 small onion, finely chopped | 1 small onion, finely chopped |
| 1 egg, beaten | 1 egg, beaten |
| salt and freshly ground pepper | salt and freshly ground pepper |
| 2 canned pineapple rings, drained | 2 canned pineapple rings, drained |
| 1 teaspoon French mustard | 1 teaspoon Dijon-style mustard |
| 15 g/½ oz butter, melted | 1 tablespoon melted butter |

Put the breadcrumbs into a large bowl, add the milk and leave to soak for a few minutes. Add the pork, sage, onion, egg, salt and a good grinding of pepper and mix lightly. With floured hands, shape the mixture into 2 large or 4 small burgers.

Grill (broil) the porkburgers under a high heat for about 5 minutes on each side. When the first side is done, brush the pineapple slices with a mixture of the mustard and butter and cook for about 2 minutes on each side while the porkburgers finish cooking.

Serve the burgers in baps or with sauté potatoes and mixed salad.

# Pork Chops with Piquant Sauce

| METRIC/IMPERIAL | AMERICAN |
|---|---|
| 2 pork chops | 2 pork chops |
| 15 g/½ oz butter | 1 tablespoon butter |
| 1 small onion, chopped | 1 small onion, chopped |
| 2 teaspoons plain flour | 2 teaspoons all-purpose flour |
| 250 ml/8 fl oz stock | 1 cup stock or broth |
| 2 teaspoons tomato ketchup | 2 teaspoons tomato ketchup |
| 2 teaspoons brown sauce | 2 teaspoons brown sauce |
| 2 midget gherkins, sliced | 2 midget gherkins, sliced |
| salt and freshly ground pepper | salt and freshly ground pepper |

Snip the fat on the chops to prevent curling and cook under a preheated moderate grill (broiler) for 10 to 12 minutes on each side.

Melt the butter in a pan and sauté the onion for 5 minutes. Stir in the flour and cook for 1 minute. Remove from the heat and gradually add the stock, ketchup and brown sauce. Heat, stirring, until the sauce comes to the boil. Add the gherkins and salt and pepper to taste and heat through for 2 minutes.

Place the chops on warmed plates and spoon the sauce over. Serve with rice and green vegetables.

# Pork Fricassée

METRIC/IMPERIAL
500 g/1 lb boned loin of pork, cut
   into 2.5 cm/1 inch cubes
1 large onion, peeled and sliced
2 carrots, scraped and sliced into
   rings
2 cloves garlic, peeled and crushed
1 thyme sprig
1 bay leaf
200 ml/⅓ pint dry white wine
2 tablespoons oil
4 black peppercorns
salt
1 tablespoon pork dripping or butter
1 tablespoon plain flour
250 ml/8 fl oz chicken stock
4 tablespoons double cream
freshly ground pepper
1 tablespoon chopped parsley
croûtes (see page 147), to serve

AMERICAN
1 lb boned loin of pork cut into
   1 inch cubes
1 large onion, peeled and sliced
2 carrots, scraped and sliced into
   rings
2 cloves garlic, peeled and crushed
1 thyme sprig
1 bay leaf
about 1 cup dry white wine
2 tablespoons oil
4 whole black pepper
salt
1 tablespoon pork drippings or
   butter
1 tablespoon all-purpose flour
1 cup chicken stock
4 tablespoons heavy cream
freshly ground pepper
1 tablespoon chopped parsley
croûtes (see page 147), to serve

Put the pork in a bowl with the onion, carrots, garlic, thyme, bay leaf, wine, oil, lightly crushed peppercorns and a little salt. Stir well, cover and leave to marinate overnight.

   The next day remove the pork with a slotted spoon and dry thoroughly on absorbent paper towels. Strain the marinade and reserve. Melt the fat in a flameproof casserole, add the pork and fry over brisk heat until browned all over. Sprinkle the flour over the pork and cook for 1 minute. Gradually stir in the stock and enough marinade to cover the meat. Bring to the boil, lower the heat until liquid simmers, then cover and cook for about 1 hour until the pork is tender.

   Stir in the cream and heat through without boiling. Adjust the seasoning, sprinkle with parsley and serve on freshly cooked croûtes, with side salads.

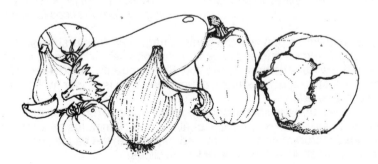

# Pork Chops with Peppercorns

| METRIC/IMPERIAL | AMERICAN |
|---|---|
| 2 pork chops | 2 pork chops |
| salt and freshly ground pepper | salt and freshly ground pepper |
| 1 tablespoon oil | 1 tablespoon oil |
| SAUCE: | SAUCE: |
| 2 teaspoons canned green peppercorns, drained | 2 teaspoons canned green peppercorns, drained |
| 2 teaspoons Dijon mustard | 2 teaspoons Dijon-style mustard |
| 120 ml/4 fl oz single cream | ½ cup light cream |
| chopped parsley to garnish | chopped parsley for garnish |

Season the chops with salt and pepper. Heat the oil in a large frying pan and fry the chops for about 10 minutes on each side, until golden brown and cooked through. Transfer to a warmed serving plate and keep warm.

Pour off any excess fat from the pan. Add the peppercorns and fry for a few seconds, then add the mustard and cream. Stir well to pick up the brown sediment on the bottom of the pan, and continue cooking gently until the sauce thickens. Add salt to taste and spoon the sauce over the pork. Garnish with parsley and serve with French fries and whole green beans.

# Pork Chops with Barbecue Sauce

| METRIC/IMPERIAL | AMERICAN |
|---|---|
| 1 onion, peeled and chopped | 1 onion, peeled and minced |
| 1 garlic clove, crushed | 1 garlic clove, crushed |
| 1½ tablespoons tarragon vinegar | 1½ tablespoons tarragon vinegar |
| 2 teaspoons Worcestershire sauce | 2 teaspoons Worcestershire sauce |
| 25 g/1 oz brown sugar | 2 tablespoons firmly packed light brown sugar |
| grated rind and juice of ½ lemon | grated rind and juice of ½ lemon |
| large pinch of chilli powder | large pinch of chili powder |
| salt and pepper | salt and pepper |
| 5 tablespoons water | 5 tablespoons water |
| 2 large pork chops | 2 large center cut pork chops |
| orange or lemon slices to garnish | orange or lemon slices for garnish |

Put the onion into a pan with the garlic, vinegar, Worcestershire sauce, brown sugar, lemon rind and juice and chilli powder. Add 1 teaspoon of salt and the water and bring to the boil. Simmer gently, uncovered, for 15 minutes, stirring occasionally, or until the onion is tender and the sauce slightly thickened.

Meanwhile, trim the chops, season lightly and grill (broil) under a preheated moderate grill (broiler) for about 8 to 10 minutes on each side or until cooked through and well browned. Serve with the sauce spooned over and garnished with orange or lemon slices.

# Stir-Fried Pork with Celery

| METRIC/IMPERIAL | AMERICAN |
|---|---|
| 350 g/12 oz pork fillet | ¾ lb pork tenderloin |
| 1 clove garlic, crushed | 1 clove garlic, crushed |
| ½ tablespoon sugar | ½ tablespoon sugar |
| 3 tablespoons soy sauce | 3 tablespoons soy sauce |
| 1 tablespoon cornflour | 1 tablespoon cornstarch |
| 4 sticks celery | 4 stalks celery |
| 2-3 tablespoons oil | 2-3 tablespoons oil |

Cut the pork into thin slices. Using a rolling pin, pound the meat lightly to flatten it. Mix together the garlic, sugar, 2 teaspoons soy sauce and cornflour (cornstarch) and mix with the pork. Allow to stand for 30 minutes.

Meanwhile peel any strings from the celery and cut across into diagonal slices about 1 cm/½ inch wide. Blanch in boiling water for 2 minutes, drain and rinse in cold water.

Heat 2 tablespoons of the oil in a wok or large, heavy-based frying pan. Fry the pork slices on both sides until golden brown, adding a little more oil, if necessary, to prevent sticking. This should take 4 to 8 minutes.

When the pork is browned, quickly stir in the remaining soy sauce and celery. Wait a moment until it is heated through, then transfer to a heated serving plate and serve at once with plain boiled rice.

# Spicy Pork Chops

| METRIC/IMPERIAL | AMERICAN |
|---|---|
| 2 pork sparerib chops | 2 country-style pork ribs |
| salt | salt |
| 1 onion, sliced | 1 onion, sliced |
| 1 clove garlic, crushed | 1 clove garlic, crushed |
| 1 x 227 g/8 oz can tomatoes | 1 x 8 oz can tomatoes |
| 1 teaspoon paprika pepper | 1 teaspoon paprika pepper |
| 2 teaspoons Worcestershire sauce | 2 teaspoons Worcestershire sauce |
| 1 tablespoon vinegar | 1 tablespoon vinegar |
| 1 tablespoon brown sugar | 1 tablespoon brown sugar |
| 150 ml/¼ pint dry cider | ⅔ cup hard cider |
| freshly ground black pepper | freshly ground black pepper |

Place the pork in a greased 1.2 litre/2 pint (5 cup) casserole dish. Sprinkle with salt and cook, uncovered, in a preheated moderately hot oven (200°C/400°F, Gas Mark 6) for 15 minutes. Arrange the onion slices over the pork and continue to cook for 10 minutes.

In a blender, combine the garlic, tomatoes with their juice, paprika pepper, Worcestershire sauce, vinegar, sugar, cider and salt and pepper to taste, then pour over the pork and onion. Cover and continue to cook in the oven for 25 minutes or until the pork is tender. Serve with jacket baked potatoes and broccoli.

# Stuffed Pork Chops

METRIC/IMPERIAL
2 pork chops, cut fairly thin
salt and freshly ground pepper
1 small onion, finely chopped
1 stick celery, finely chopped
4 soft dessert prunes, stoned and
 chopped
15 g/½ oz butter, melted
1 tablespoon chopped mixed fresh
 herbs
25 g/1 oz fresh white breadcrumbs
½ teaspoon sugar

AMERICAN
2 pork rib chops, cut fairly thin
salt and freshly ground pepper
1 small onion, finely chopped
1 stalk celery, finely chopped
4 soft prunes, pitted and chopped
1 tablespoon butter, melted
1 tablespoon chopped mixed fresh
 herbs
½ cup soft white bread crumbs
½ teaspoon sugar

Trim excess fat from the chops and snip around the edges with kitchen scissors to prevent curling during cooking. Sprinkle the chops with a little salt and pepper.

Mix all the remaining ingredients together to make a stuffing and add salt and pepper to taste. Place the stuffing on one of the chops, then put the other chop on top to make a "sandwich". Place the stuffed chops in a grill (broiler) pan and add 120 ml/4 fl oz (½ cup) water.

Cook under a preheated moderate grill (broiler) for 15 minutes each side. Cut "sandwich" in half and serve with grilled tomatoes and French fries.


# Marinated Pork Kebabs

METRIC/IMPERIAL
2 tablespoons wine vinegar
1 teaspoon made mustard
salt and pepper
1-2 tablespoons soy sauce
2 tablespoons oil
1 tablespoon finely chopped onion
1 large pork fillet or 350 g/12 oz
 lean leg of pork, cubed
1 green pepper, cored, seeded and
 cut into pieces

AMERICAN
2 tablespoons wine vinegar
1 teaspoon made mustard
salt and pepper
1-2 tablespoons soy sauce
2 tablespoons oil
1 tablespoon finely minced onion
1 large pork tenderloin or ¾ lb lean
 leg of pork, cubed
1 green pepper, cored, seeded and
 cut into pieces

Mix together the vinegar, mustard, salt and pepper to taste, soy sauce, oil and onion in a bowl. Add the pork cubes and allow to marinate for 1 to 2 hours, turning several times. Remove the pork from the marinade and thread on to two long skewers, alternating with pieces of green pepper. Cook under a preheated moderate grill (broiler) for 5 to 8 minutes on each side or until cooked through and well browned, basting with the marinade several times during cooking. Serve on a bed of rice.

# Pork Fillet in Ginger Sauce

METRIC/IMPERIAL
350 g/12 oz pork fillet
2 tablespoons lemon juice
4 slices fresh root ginger chopped
1 tablespoon chopped fresh lemon
   thyme or ½ teaspoon dried
   thyme
salt and freshly ground pepper
1 tablespoon oil
15 g/½ oz butter
1 medium onion, finely chopped
2 tablespoons plain flour
150 ml/¼ pint stock

AMERICAN
¾ lb pork tenderloin
2 tablespoons lemon juice
4 slices fresh ginger root, chopped
1 tablespoon chopped fresh lemon
   thyme or ½ teaspoon dried
   thyme
salt and freshly ground pepper
1 tablespoon oil
1 tablespoon butter
1 medium onion, finely chopped
2 tablespoons all-purpose flour
⅔ cup stock or broth

Cut the pork into 1 cm/½ inch slices. Place between sheets of cling film (plastic wrap) and flatten slightly with a rolling pin. Place in a shallow glass or earthenware dish and sprinkle with the lemon juice, ginger, thyme and salt and pepper to taste. Leave to marinate for 15 minutes.

Heat the oil and butter in frying pan, add the onion and fry gently until golden. Place flour on plate and coat the pork slices. Add the pork to the onions and cook on both sides until brown. Add marinade and stock, bring to boil and cook gently for 5 minutes.

Serve with courgettes (zucchini) and plain rice.

# Braised Pork with Carrots

METRIC/IMPERIAL
1 clove garlic, crushed
1 tablespoon dry sherry
4 tablespoons soy sauce
500 g/1 lb pork fillet, cut into strips
2 tablespoons plain flour
2 tablespoons oil
1 onion, cut into 8 sections
1 tablespoon sugar
2 carrots, cut into chunks
chopped parsley to garnish

AMERICAN
1 clove garlic, crushed
1 tablespoon dry sherry
¼ cup soy sauce
1 lb pork tenderloin, cut into strips
2 tablespoons all-purpose flour
2 tablespoons oil
1 onion, cut into 8 sections
1 tablespoon sugar
2 carrots, cut into chunks
chopped parsley for garnish

Mix together the garlic, sherry and 3 tablespoons of the soy sauce. Add the pork strips and toss to coat well. Leave to marinate for at least 20 minutes, then stir in the flour.

Heat the oil in a pan. Add the onion and meat mixture and stir-fry until the meat is browned. Add the remaining soy sauce, the sugar and just enough water to cover the meat. Bring to the boil. Add the carrots and simmer for 20 minutes or until the meat is tender.

Serve hot, garnished with chopped parsley, with plain boiled rice.

# Pork and Bean Casserole

METRIC/IMPERIAL
*500 g/1 lb sliced belly pork*
*1 tablespoon oil*
*2 cloves garlic, crushed*
*1 pickled chilli, chopped*
*1 onion, chopped*
*1 cooking apple, cored and*
*chopped*
*1 tablespoon black treacle*
*1 tablespoon vinegar*
*1 teaspoon dry mustard*
*2 tablespoons tomato purée*
*150 ml/¼ pint chicken stock*
*sprig of fresh or ½ teaspoon dried*
*thyme*
*salt and freshly ground pepper*
*1 x 396 g/14 oz can red kidney*
*beans, drained*
*1 tablespoon chopped parsley*
*1 large potato, chopped and sautéd*

AMERICAN
*1 lb boneless fresh pork sides,*
*sliced*
*1 tablespoon oil*
*2 cloves garlic, crushed*
*1 pickled chili, chopped*
*1 onion, chopped*
*1 tart apple, cored and chopped*
*1 tablespoon molasses*
*1 tablespoon vinegar*
*1 teaspoon dry mustard*
*2 tablespoons tomato paste*
*⅔ cup chicken stock or broth*
*sprig of fresh or ½ teaspoon dried*
*thyme*
*salt and freshly ground pepper*
*1 x 16 oz can red kidney beans,*
*drained*
*1 tablespoon chopped parsley*
*1 large potato, chopped and sautéd*

Cut the pork into 5 cm/2 inch fingers. Arrange on a rack in a roasting tin and cook towards top of a preheated hot oven (220°C/425°F, Gas Mark 7) for 20 minutes until crisp and browned.

Heat the oil in a flameproof casserole, add the garlic, chilli, onion and apple and fry, stirring, for 3 minutes. Mix together the treacle (molasses), vinegar, mustard, tomato purée (paste) and stock, then pour into the casserole. Add the thyme, pieces of pork, salt and pepper to taste and the beans.

Reduce the oven temperature to moderate (160°C/325°F, Gas Mark 3) and cook the casserole, uncovered, for 20 minutes. Stir in parsley and potatoes and serve immediately with a mixed green salad.

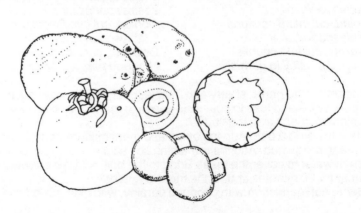

# Spareribs with Barbecue Sauce

METRIC/IMPERIAL
750 g/1 ½ lb pork spareribs in one
    piece
4 tablespoons soy sauce
1 clove garlic, crushed
1 tablespoon honey
1 tablespoon dry sherry
1 tablespoon tomato ketchup

AMERICAN
1 ½ lb pork spareribs in one piece
¼ cup soy sauce
1 clove garlic, crushed
1 tablespoon honey
1 tablespoon dry sherry
1 tablespoon tomato ketchup

Wipe the ribs with damp kitchen paper towels and place on a rack in a shallow roasting pan. Cook in a preheated moderate oven (180°C/350°F, Gas Mark 4) for 45 minutes. Pour off the fat and place the ribs in the pan.

Mix the remaining ingredients together, pour over the ribs and allow to marinate for about 1 hour or refrigerate overnight. Turn the ribs several times.

Cook in preheated moderately hot oven (190°C/375°F, Gas Mark 5) for 25 minutes. Cut into serving pieces and eat with the fingers.

# Stir-Fried Bean Curd with Pork and Cabbage

METRIC/IMPERIAL
1 cake bean curd, cut into 3.5 cm/
    1 ½ inch squares
3 tablespoons oil
225 g/8 oz lean pork, cut into thin
    bite-sized pieces
1 spring onion, chopped
2 slices fresh root ginger, chopped
2 teaspoons salt
1 tablespoon dry sherry
600 ml/1 pint stock
225 g/8 oz Chinese cabbage,
    shredded

AMERICAN
1 cake bean curd, cut into 1 ½ inch
    squares
3 tablespoons oil
½ lb pork butt or loin, cut into thin
    bite-sized pieces
1 scallion, chopped
2 slices fresh ginger root, chopped
2 teaspoons salt
1 tablespoon pale dry sherry
2 ½ cups stock or broth
½ lb Chinese cabbage (bok choy),
    shredded

Freeze the bean curd squares overnight. Thaw in hot water, then drain.

Heat the oil in a pan. Add the pork, spring onion (scallion), ginger and bean curd and stir-fry until the meat is lightly browned. Add the salt, sherry and stock and bring to the boil. Cover and simmer for 10 minutes.

Add the cabbage and simmer for about 10 minutes until it is tender. Serve hot with plain boiled rice.

**Note:** small holes may be left in the bean curd after thawing. These allow the delicious juices to penetrate the bean curd. Do not freeze the bean curd for more than 12 hours or it will toughen.

# Quick-Fried Pork with Bean Sprouts

METRIC/IMPERIAL
350 g/12 oz lean pork, thinly sliced
2 tablespoons soy sauce
4 tablespoons oil
1 teaspoon salt
freshly ground pepper
225 g/8 oz fresh bean sprouts
4 spring onions, cut into 2.5 cm/
   1 inch pieces
1 teaspoon sugar
2 tablespoons boiling water
1½ tablespoons dry sherry
boiled rice to serve

AMERICAN
¾ lb lean pork, thinly sliced
2 tablespoons soy sauce
¼ cup oil
1 teaspoon salt
freshly ground pepper
½ lb fresh bean sprouts
4 scallions, cut into 1 inch pieces
1 teaspoon sugar
2 tablespoons boiling water
1½ tablespoons pale dry sherry
boiled rice to serve

Cut the pork slices into 2.5 cm/1 inch pieces and rub with half the soy sauce and 1 tablespoon of the oil. Sprinkle with the salt and pepper.

Heat the remaining oil in a pan over high heat. Add the pork and stir-fry for 2 minutes, then remove from the pan using a slotted spoon. Add the bean sprouts and chopped spring onions (scallions) to the pan and stir-fry for 1 minute. Sprinkle in the remaining soy sauce, the sugar and water. Stir-fry for 30 seconds. Return the pork to the pan. Add the sherry and stir-fry for a further 1 minute.

To serve, place the cooked rice in a warmed serving dish and arrange the pork and bean sprout mixture on top.

# Fried Bean Sprouts with Pork

METRIC/IMPERIAL
350 g/12 oz minced pork
1 tablespoon dry sherry
1 tablespoon soy sauce
1 teaspoon cornflour
2 tablespoons oil
2 spring onions, chopped
225 g/8 oz fresh bean sprouts,
   rinsed, drained and chopped
1 teaspoon salt
250 ml/8 fl oz water

AMERICAN
¾ lb ground pork
1 tablespoon pale dry sherry
1 tablespoon soy sauce
1 teaspoon cornstarch
2 tablespoons oil
2 scallions, chopped
½ lb fresh bean sprouts, rinsed,
   drained and chopped
1 teaspoon salt
1 cup water

Mix the pork with the sherry, soy sauce and cornflour (cornstarch).

Heat the oil in a pan. Add the meat mixture and stir-fry until brown. Add the spring onions (scallions), bean sprouts and salt and stir-fry for 1 minute. Add the water. Bring to the boil, cover and cook for 15 minutes or until the meat and bean sprouts are tender. Serve hot with noodles.

# Barbecued Pork

METRIC/IMPERIAL
2 tablespoons soy sauce
2 tablespoons dry sherry
2 teaspoons sesame seed oil
1 teaspoon salt
2 teaspoons fresh ginger root,
  finely chopped
2 tablespoons clear honey or
  golden syrup
50 g/2 oz sugar
1-2 cloves garlic, crushed
1 kg/2 lb pork shoulder, cut into 5 x
  5 x 10 cm/2 x 2 x 4 inch chunks

AMERICAN
2 tablespoons soy sauce
2 tablespoons pale dry sherry
2 teaspoons sesame oil
2 teaspoon salt
2 teaspoons finely chopped root
  ginger
2 tablespoons clear honey or corn
  syrup
¼ cup sugar
1-2 cloves garlic, crushed
2 lb pork butt, cut into 2 x 2 x 4 inch
  chunks

Mix together the soy sauce, sherry, oil, salt, ginger, honey or syrup, sugar and garlic in a dish. Add the pork and leave to marinate for at least 6 hours in the refrigerator, turning the meat occasionally.

Place the pork on a wire rack in a roasting pan. Roast in a preheated moderate oven (180°C/350°F, Gas Mark 4) for 40 to 45 minutes or until tender, basting frequently with the pan juices.

Cut into fine slices and arrange on a plate. Serve hot or cold with vegetables, or salad.

# Bacon Steaks with Redcurrant Sauce

METRIC/IMPERIAL
2 bacon steaks
25 g/1 oz butter, melted
50 g/2 oz black pudding
1 dessert apple
2 tablespoons redcurrant jelly
1 teaspoon wine vinegar
1 teaspoon brown sugar
parsley sprigs to garnish

AMERICAN
2 Canadian-style bacon steaks
2 tablespoons melted butter
2 oz blood sausage
1 dessert apple
2 tablespoons redcurrant jelly
1 teaspoon wine vinegar
1 teaspoon brown sugar
parsley sprigs for garnish

Snip the fat edges of the steaks to prevent curling. Brush with the butter and place under a preheated moderate grill (broiler) for 5 minutes.

Slice the black pudding (blood sausage) into 4 pieces. Core the apple and cut into 4 rings. Turn the bacon steaks over and place the apple rings and black pudding (blood sausage) on top. Brush with butter. Continue to grill (broil) for a further 5 minutes, turning the topping once. Transfer to a warmed serving dish and keep hot.

Drain the liquid from the grill (broiler) pan into a pan. Add the redcurrant jelly, wine vinegar and brown sugar. Boil until the mixture is well blended and slightly syrupy. Spoon the sauce over each bacon steak and garnish with a parsley sprig. Serve with mashed potatoes and minted peas.

# Creamy Spinach and Ham Bake

METRIC/IMPERIAL
*225 g/8 oz chopped spinach*
*1 stick celery, diced*
*1 clove garlic, peeled and finely*
  *chopped*
*100 g/4 oz cooked ham, finely*
  *chopped*
*2 parsley sprigs, finely chopped*
*2 thyme sprigs*
*freshly ground pepper*
*15 g/½ oz butter*
*1 tablespoon flour*
*250 ml/8 fl oz milk*
*freshly grated nutmeg*
*salt*
*1 egg yolk*
*2 tablespoons double cream*

AMERICAN
*½ lb chopped spinach*
*1 stalk celery, diced*
*1 clove garlic, peeled and finely*
  *minced*
*½ cup finely chopped cooked ham*
*2 parsley sprigs, finely chopped*
*2 thyme sprigs*
*freshly ground pepper*
*1 tablespoon butter*
*1 tablespoon flour*
*1 cup milk*
*freshly grated nutmeg*
*salt*
*1 egg yolk*
*2 tablespoons heavy cream*

Put the washed and drained spinach in a bowl with celery, garlic, ham and parsley. Remove leaves from thyme and add to bowl with pepper to taste. Mix well.

Heat the butter until frothy in heavy-based pan, add the flour and cook for 1 minute. Gradually stir in the milk and bring slowly to the boil, stirring constantly. Add a generous pinch of nutmeg and salt and pepper to taste, then simmer for 3 to 4 minutes. Remove from heat.

Mix the egg yolk and cream together and stir slowly into the sauce, then fold in the vegetable mixture. Pour into a buttered gratin dish, level the surface, cover and bake in a preheated moderate oven (160°C/325°F, Gas Mark 3) for 20 to 25 minutes. Serve hot, straight from the dish.

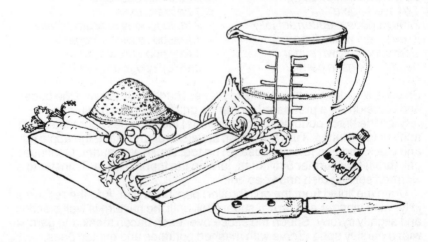

# Boston Baked Beans

METRIC/IMPERIAL
*225 g/8 oz dried haricot beans,*
*soaked overnight*
*2 onions, chopped*
*100 g/4 oz salt pork, cut into small*
*cubes*
*1 tablespoon brown sugar*
*1 tablespoon black treacle*
*2 tablespoons tomato purée*
*1 tablespoon vinegar*
*1 teaspoon dry mustard*
*salt and freshly ground pepper*

AMERICAN
*1 ¼ cups dried navy beans, soaked*
*overnight*
*2 onions, chopped*
*¼ lb salt pork, cut into small cubes*
*1 tablespoon brown sugar*
*1 tablespoon molasses*
*2 tablespoons tomato paste*
*1 tablespoon vinegar*
*1 teaspoon dry English mustard*
*salt and freshly ground pepper*

Drain the soaked beans, rinse and then cover with fresh water. Bring to the boil, boil for 10 minutes, then simmer for 1 to 1 ¼ hours or until tender. Drain, reserving the liquid.

Place the beans in a deep, greased casserole. Mix the remaining ingredients with just enough of the reserved cooking liquid to cover the beans. Cover tightly with a lid or foil and cook in a preheated cool oven (150°C/300°F, Gas Mark 2) for 7 to 8 hours, until the beans are very tender and have absorbed the flavourings. Stir occasionally while they cook, adding a little more bean liquid as necessary. Leave uncovered for the last hour of cooking.

Serve hot from the casserole.

# Ham with Vermouth and Cream

METRIC/IMPERIAL
*50 g/2 oz butter*
*4 thin slices cooked ham*
*100 g/4 oz button mushrooms,*
*sliced*
*120 ml/4 fl oz single cream*
*120 ml/4 fl oz dry vermouth*
*salt and white pepper*

AMERICAN
*¼ cup butter*
*4 thin slices cooked ham*
*1 cup sliced button mushrooms*
*½ cup light cream*
*½ cup dry vermouth*
*salt and white pepper*

Melt the butter in a pan, add the ham slices and heat very gently. Lift out the ham and arrange on a warm serving dish. Cover and keep warm.

Add the mushrooms to the pan, cover, and cook gently for 4 minutes. Remove the lid and stir in the cream and vermouth. Season to taste with salt and pepper and simmer for 3 to 4 minutes until thickened a little. Spoon the sauce over the ham and serve with buttered noodles and salad.

# Sweet and Spicy Ham

| METRIC/IMPERIAL | AMERICAN |
|---|---|
| 2 gammon steaks | 2 ham steaks |
| 15 g/½ oz butter, melted | 1 tablespoon melted butter |
| 4 tablespoons apricot jam, sieved | 4 tablespoons apricot jelly, strained |
| 1 teaspoon dry mustard | 1 teaspoon dry mustard |
| ½ teaspoon ground ginger | ½ teaspoon ground ginger |
| pinch of salt | pinch of salt |
| 1 tablespoon water | 1 tablespoon water |

Make cuts in the rind or fat around the steak at 1 cm/½ inch intervals to stop it curling up in the heat.

Preheat the grill (broiler) and oil the rack. Brush one side of the steaks with butter and grill (broil) on this side for 4 minutes. Mix the remaining ingredients together. Turn the steaks, spread with the mixture and cook for a further 5 minutes, or until the glaze is lightly browned. Serve with sauté potatoes and Peas in Mint Sauce (see page 102).

# Cabbage and Bacon Bake

| METRIC/IMPERIAL | AMERICAN |
|---|---|
| 1 tablespoon olive oil | 1 tablespoon olive oil |
| 1 onion, peeled and thinly sliced | 1 onion, peeled and thinly sliced |
| 50 g/2 oz smoked streaky bacon, derinded and cut into thin strips | ¼ cup smoked fatty bacon, cut into thin strips |
| ¼ white cabbage (about 500 g/ 1 lb), finely shredded | ¼ white cabbage (about 1 lb), finely shredded |
| 1 clove garlic, peeled and crushed | 1 clove garlic, peeled and crushed |
| salt | salt |
| freshly ground pepper | freshly ground pepper |
| 2 eggs | 2 eggs |
| 150 ml/¼ pint milk | ⅔ cup milk |
| 1 tablespoon dried breadcrumbs | 1 tablespoon dried bread crumbs |
| 15 g/½ oz butter | 1 tablespoon butter |

Heat the oil in a large frying pan (skillet), add the onion and fry gently until lightly coloured, stirring occasionally. Add the bacon, cabbage and garlic and a little salt and pepper. Stir well, then fry for 10 to 15 minutes, turning mixture frequently. Transfer to greased gratin dish.

Mix the eggs and milk with a little pepper, then pour over the cabbage. Sprinkle with the breadcrumbs and dot with butter. Bake in a preheated moderate oven (180°C/350°F, Gas Mark 4) for 40 minutes. Serve hot.

# Bacon and Vegetable Ragoût

METRIC/IMPERIAL
*1 tablespoon pork dripping*
*75 g/3 oz streaky bacon in the*
*   piece, derinded and diced*
*2 medium potatoes, peeled and*
*   sliced into rounds*
*500 g/1 lb leeks (white part only),*
*   sliced into rings*
*1½ tablespoons plain flour*
*200 ml/⅓ pint vegetable stock or*
*   water*
*1 clove garlic, peeled and crushed*
*1 bouquet garni*
*salt*
*freshly ground pepper*

AMERICAN
*1 tablespoon pork drippings*
*½ cup thickly diced fatty bacon*
*2 medium potatoes, peeled and*
*   sliced into rounds*
*1 lb leeks (white part only), sliced*
*   into rings*
*1½ tablespoons all-purpose flour*
*1 cup vegetable stock or water*
*1 clove garlic, peeled and minced*
*1 bouquet garni*
*salt*
*freshly ground pepper*

Heat the fat in a heavy-based pan, add the bacon and fry over brisk heat until golden. Reduce heat to medium, add the potatoes and leeks and fry until lightly coloured. Sprinkle in the flour and cook for 1 minute. Gradually stir in the stock or water, then add the garlic, bouquet garni, and salt and pepper to taste. Cover and simmer gently for 20 to 25 minutes until the potatoes are tender. Discard the bouquet garni, taste and adjust seasoning. Serve immediately with Hot Herb Bread (see page 147).

DISHES

# Lamb Dishes

FOR TWO

## French Farmer's Lamb

METRIC/IMPERIAL
*25 g/1 oz butter*
*1 leg of lamb, weighing about*
  *1.75 kg/4 lb*
*3 cloves garlic, cut into thin slivers*
*4 potatoes, thickly sliced*
*salt and freshly ground pepper*
*1 large onion, sliced*
*2 tablespoons chopped parsley*
*450 ml/¾ pint rich chicken stock, or*
  *canned consommé*

AMERICAN
*2 tablespoons butter*
*1 leg of lamb, weighing about 4 lb*
*3 cloves garlic, cut into thin slivers*
*4 potatoes, thickly sliced*
*salt and freshly ground pepper*
*1 large onion, sliced*
*2 tablespoons chopped parsley*
*2 cups rich chicken stock or broth*

Use the butter to generously grease a shallow casserole just wide enough to take the leg of lamb comfortably. Make tiny incisions all over the skin of the lamb and insert half the slivers of garlic.

Arrange the potatoes in overlapping rows in the dish, seasoning well with salt and pepper. Add the onion slices and the remaining garlic, and season again. Sprinkle with the chopped parsley.

Place the lamb on top of the vegetables and pour over the stock. Roast, uncovered, in a preheated moderate oven (160°C/325°F, Gas Mark 3) for 1¾ hours for tender pink lamb, or about 2¼ hours for well done lamb. Baste every 20 minutes with the pan juices while the lamb is cooking.

Remove the lamb to a platter when cooked to your liking and leave it to rest for 20 minutes before carving. (Keep the casserole warm in the oven.)

VARIATION:
**Lamb and Beans** – instead of potatoes, the lamb can be placed on a bed of butter (lima) beans, with the onions and garlic. Use a 450 g/16 oz can and rinse the beans in cold water and drain before adding to dish.

# Middle Eastern Kofta

METRIC/IMPERIAL
*350 g/12 oz minced lean lamb or*
  *beef, or a mixture*
*1 onion, finely chopped*
*1 egg, lightly beaten*
*1 teaspoon salt*
*freshly ground pepper*
*1 tablespoon chopped parsley*
*1 teaspoon ground cumin*
*½ teaspoon coriander seeds,*
  *ground*

AMERICAN
*¾ lb ground lean lamb or beef, or a*
  *mixture*
*1 onion, finely chopped*
*1 egg, lightly beaten*
*1 teaspoon salt*
*freshly ground pepper*
*1 tablespoon chopped parsley*
*1 teaspoon ground cumin*
*½ teaspoon coriander seeds,*
  *ground*

Place all the ingredients in a bowl and pound or knead until very smooth. Divide the mixture in half and mould each portion into a sausage shape around a skewer. Cook at high heat on a preheated oiled grill (broiler) for 7 to 8 minutes, turning several times until browned all over.

Serve on a bed of plain boiled rice or push the meat off the skewers into pockets of warm pitta bread.

VARIATIONS:
**Meatballs and Rice** – form the mixture into small balls, roll in flour to coat, then fry in oil and butter for 20-25 minutes, turning frequently until crisp all over. Serve with rice.
**Spaghetti with Meatballs** – fry meatballs as above and add to Fresh Tomato Sauce (see page 144). Heat through, then toss with freshly cooked spaghetti.

# Marinated Lamb Chops

METRIC/IMPERIAL
*4 lamb loin chops*
*6 tablespoons dry white wine*
*6 tablespoons olive oil*
*2 cloves garlic, finely chopped*
*½ teaspoon ground cumin*
*salt and pepper*

AMERICAN
*4 lamb loin chops*
*6 tablespoons dry white wine*
*6 tablespoons olive oil*
*2 cloves garlic, finely chopped*
*½ teaspoon ground cumin*
*salt and pepper*

Trim the skin and excess fat from the chops. Combine the remaining ingredients and pour over the lamb. Marinate for at least 2 hours, turning the chops occasionally.

Preheat the grill (broiler). Curl the tails of the chops round neatly and secure with small skewers. Brush the rack with oil and grill (broil) the chops at high heat, brushing several times with the marinade. Cook for 4 minutes on each side or until the meat feels soft but springy when pressed. Cook 2 minutes longer on each side if you like chops well done.

Serve with Grilled Mushrooms (see page 117).

# Lamb with Rosemary

METRIC/IMPERIAL
2 lamb steaks or chump chops
25 g/1 oz butter
1 clove garlic, crushed
1 teaspoon chopped fresh or
    ¼ teaspoon dried rosemary
salt and freshly ground pepper
1 tablespoon plain flour
1 teaspoon wine vinegar
120 ml/4 fl oz dry white wine
120 ml/4 fl oz water

AMERICAN
2 lamb steaks or double loin chops
2 tablespoons butter
1 clove garlic, crushed
1 teaspoon chopped fresh or
    ¼ teaspoon dried rosemary
salt and freshly ground pepper
1 tablespoon all-purpose flour
1 teaspoon wine vinegar
½ cup dry white wine
½ cup water

Trim any excess fat from the meat. Heat the butter and, when the foam subsides, brown the lamb well on both sides. Add the garlic, rosemary, salt and pepper to taste and cook gently without a lid for 10 minutes, turning meat once.

Remove the meat and set aside. Add the flour to the pan and cook, stirring, for 2 minutes. Mix the vinegar, wine and water together and stir in gradually. Continue stirring until the mixture boils, then check seasoning. Return the meat to the pan, cover, and simmer for 15 to 20 minutes until tender. Serve with creamed potato and spinach.

# Lamb Cutlets with Lemon Rice

METRIC/IMPERIAL
150 g/5 oz long grain rice
salt and freshly ground black
    pepper
1 lemon
1 clove garlic, crushed
4 lamb cutlets
1 tablespoon oil
GARNISH:
watercress
tomato halves

AMERICAN
¾ cup long grain rice
salt and freshly ground black
    pepper
1 lemon
1 clove garlic
4 lamb rib chops
1 tablespoon oil
GARNISH:
watercress
tomato halves

Cook the rice in plenty of boiling salted water, adding a piece of lemon peel.

Meanwhile rub the garlic into the lamb, sprinkle with salt and pepper and brush with oil. Cook under a preheated moderate grill (broiler) for 15 minutes, turning once.

Grate the rind from the lemon and squeeze the juice. Drain the rice, rinse with hot water and drain. Stir in the grated lemon rind, juice and salt and pepper to taste. Spoon into a warmed serving dish and arrange the lamb on top.

Garnish with watercress and grilled halved tomatoes.

# Turkish Stewed Lamb

METRIC/IMPERIAL
*500 g/1 lb boneless lamb, cut from*
*leg or shoulder*
*1 onion*
*1 small aubergine*
*½ green pepper*
*2 courgettes*
*100 g/4 oz green beans*
*2 ripe tomatoes*
*100 g/4 oz okra (optional)*
*2 tablespoons olive oil*
*about 300 ml/½ pint chicken stock*
*salt and freshly ground pepper*

AMERICAN
*1 lb boneless lamb for stew*
*1 onion*
*1 small eggplant*
*½ green pepper*
*2 zucchini*
*¼ lb green beans*
*2 ripe tomatoes*
*¼ lb okra (optional)*
*2 tablespoons olive oil*
*about 1¼ cups chicken stock or*
*broth*
*salt and freshly ground pepper*

Remove excess fat from the lamb and cut the meat into bite-sized pieces.

Peel and slice the onion. Cut the unpeeled aubergine (eggplant) into cubes; core and seed the pepper and cut into squares. Top and tail the courgettes (zucchini) and beans and cut into slices. Peel the tomatoes and roughly chop. Trim the okra if using by removing the top stem, but leave whole.

Heat the oil in a large, heavy flameproof casserole or pan and slowly brown the meat on all sides. Add the onion and cook until golden, stirring occasionally. Pour in enough stock to come just to the top of the meat, cover and simmer until the meat is almost tender, about 50 minutes. Add all the vegetables to the meat with the remaining stock. Taste the liquid and season well with salt and pepper. Replace the lid and simmer for about 30 minutes until the vegetables are cooked and the meat is very tender. Serve with boiled brown rice.

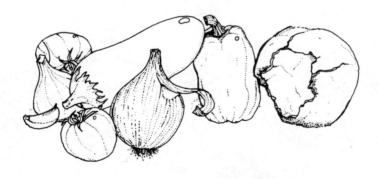

# Pot-Roasted Lamb

METRIC/IMPERIAL
1.5 kg/3 lb boned leg or shoulder of
   lamb
2 tablespoons oil
1 onion, sliced
2 sticks celery, sliced
4 carrots
500 g/1 lb new potatoes, scrubbed
salt and freshly ground pepper
120 ml/4 fl oz white wine or chicken
   stock.
STUFFING:
225 g/8 oz sausagemeat
1 onion, chopped
1 tablespoon chopped parsley
2 teaspoons chopped fresh or
   ½ teaspoon dried oregano
1 clove garlic, crushed

AMERICAN
3 lb boned leg or shoulder of lamb
2 tablespoons oil
1 onion, sliced
2 stalks celery, sliced
4 carrots
1 lb new potatoes, scrubbed
salt and freshly ground pepper
½ cup white wine or chicken stock
   or broth
STUFFING:
½ lb sausagemeat
1 onion, chopped
1 tablespoon chopped parsley
2 teaspoons chopped fresh or
   ½ teaspoon dried oregano
1 clove garlic, crushed

Trim excess fat from the lamb. To make the stuffing, combine the
sausagemeat, onion, parsley, oregano and garlic and stuff the lamb with
the mixture. Secure in place with string or skewers.

Heat the oil in a heavy flameproof casserole or pan and brown the lamb
all over. Add the vegetables, season with salt and pepper to taste, and
pour in the wine or stock. Cover tightly and cook over a low heat for about
2 hours, or until the lamb is very tender. Alternatively the lamb can be
cooked for 2 hours in a preheated moderate oven (180°C/350°F, Gas Mark
4) or in a slow cooker set at the lowest heat for 7 to 8 hours. Serve the
lamb sliced, with the cooking juices poured over and accompanied by the
vegetables.
**Note:** this recipe makes enough for a second meal as well.

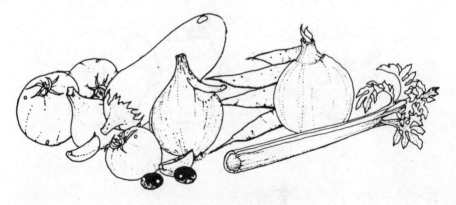

# Persian Roast Lamb

METRIC/IMPERIAL
1.5 kg/3 lb shoulder of lamb, boned
  and rolled
2 tablespoons lemon juice
¼ teaspoon ground cardamom
½ teaspoon ground coriander
120 ml/4 fl oz plain yogurt
freshly ground pepper
25 g/1 oz butter
1 small onion, chopped
¼ teaspoon ground ginger
salt

AMERICAN
3 lb lamb shoulder, boned and
  rolled
2 tablespoons lemon juice
¼ teaspoon ground cardamom
½ teaspoon ground coriander
½ cup plain yoghurt
freshly ground pepper
2 tablespoons butter
1 small onion, chopped
¼ teaspoon ground ginger
salt

Score the surface of the rolled shoulder in a diamond pattern. Place in a glass dish and add the lemon juice, cardamom, coriander, yogurt and pepper to taste. Turn the lamb several times to coat in the mixture, then cover and leave for 1 hour.

Place the lamb and marinating mixture in a roasting pan and roast in a preheated moderate oven (160°C/325°F, Gas Mark 3) for 1 hour.

Melt the butter in a small pan, add the onion and ginger and cook gently until the onion is transparent. Spread on the lamb and roast for a further 30 to 40 minutes, basting occasionally, until lamb is tender.

Skim the fat from the pan juices and scrape up the brown bits from the bottom then season the gravy to taste with salt and pepper. Serve sliced lamb and gravy with Persian Crusty Rice (see page 108) and spinach.

# Honey-Ginger Lamb

METRIC/IMPERIAL
1.5 kg/3 lb shoulder of lamb, boned
  and rolled
500 g/1 lb sweet potatoes
4 tablespoons water
175 g/6 oz clear honey
2 tablespoons lemon juice
1 tablespoon soy sauce
pinch of ground cloves
1 teaspoon ground ginger

AMERICAN
3 lb lamb shoulder, boned and
  rolled
1 lb sweet potatoes
¼ cup water
½ cup clear honey
2 tablespoons lemon juice
1 tablespoon soy sauce
pinch of ground cloves
1 teaspoon ground ginger

Place the meat in a roasting pan and surround with peeled sweet potatoes, cut into serving sizes. Add 4 tablespoons of water and roast in a preheated moderate oven (160°C/325°F, Gas Mark 3) for 45 minutes.

In a small pan, gently warm the honey, lemon juice, soy sauce and spices, then pour over the lamb. Turn the sweet potatoes and roast for a further 45 minutes, turning the lamb frequently.

Serve the meat sliced with the sweet potatoes and gravy.

# Italian Lamb Stew

METRIC/IMPERIAL
1 kg/2 lb boneless lamb, cut from
   leg or shoulder
2 tablespoons oil
100 g/4 oz bacon, diced
1 onion, sliced
2 cloves garlic, crushed
salt and freshly ground pepper
1 teaspoon chopped fresh or
   ½ teaspoon dried marjoram
1 teaspoon chopped fresh sage
120 ml/4 fl oz red wine
2 tablespoons tomato purée

AMERICAN
2 lb boneless lamb for stew
2 tablespoons oil
¼ lb slab bacon, diced
1 onion, sliced
2 cloves garlic, crushed
salt and freshly ground pepper
1 teaspoon chopped fresh or
   ½ teaspoon dried marjoram
1 teaspoon chopped fresh sage
½ cup red wine
2 tablespoons tomato paste

Trim excess fat from the lamb and cut into bite-size pieces. Heat the oil in a large frying pan. Add the bacon, onion and garlic and sauté until golden. Remove and set aside. Add half the meat and brown on all sides, then remove from the pan and brown the remaining meat.

Return all the meat to the pan and season with salt, pepper, marjoram and sage. Stir in all but 2 tablespoons of the red wine and cook gently until the wine reduces to half its original quantity. Add the bacon mixture, tomato purée (paste) and enough water to cover the meat. Cover and simmer for about 1½ hours or until tender. Stir in the reserved wine just before serving. Serve with noodles.

**Note:** this recipe makes enough for a second meal as well.

# Lamb Roll Dijon

METRIC/IMPERIAL
1.5 kg/3 lb boned shoulder of lamb,
   rolled
4 tablespoons Dijon mustard
1 tablespoon soy sauce
¼ teaspoon ground ginger
1 clove garlic, crushed
1 teaspoon dried rosemary
1 tablespoon oil
300 ml/½ pint water

AMERICAN
3 lb boned shoulder of lamb, rolled
¼ cup Dijon-style mustard
1 tablespoon soy sauce
¼ teaspoon ground ginger
1 clove garlic, crushed
1 teaspoon dried rosemary
1 tablespoon oil
1¼ cups water

Place the meat on a rack in a roasting pan. Mix together the remaining ingredients except the water, and spread all over the lamb. Allow to stand for 1 hour at room temperature.

Add the water to the pan and roast the meat in a preheated moderate oven (160°C/325°F, Gas Mark 3) for 1½ to 2 hours. Allow to rest for 20 minutes, then serve the meat cut in thick slices with the heated pan juices.

**Note:** this recipe makes enough for a second meal as well.

# Malayan Curry

METRIC/IMPERIAL
1 tablespoon oil
275 g/10 oz boneless lamb, cut into cubes
1 onion, chopped
2 teaspoons curry powder
½ teaspoon ground cinnamon
pinch of cayenne pepper
salt and freshly ground pepper
200 ml/⅓ pint stock
1 dessert apple, peeled, cored and chopped
150 g/5 oz long grain rice
1 tablespoon desiccated coconut
2 eggs, hard-boiled, to garnish

AMERICAN
1 tablespoon oil
1½ cups cubed boneless lamb for stew
1 onion, chopped
2 teaspoons curry powder
½ teaspoon ground cinnamon
pinch of cayenne
salt and freshly ground pepper
⅞ cup stock
1 dessert apple, peeled, cored and chopped
¾ cup long grain rice
1 tablespoon shredded coconut
2 eggs, hard-cooked, for garnish

Heat the oil in a pan and fry the meat until browned all over. Add the onion and continue to cook for 2 minutes.

Stir in the curry powder, cinnamon, cayenne pepper and salt and pepper to taste. Continue to cook for 1 minute. Add the stock and apple and bring to the boil, cover and simmer for 1 hour. Stir occasionally and add more liquid if necessary.

Cook the rice in plenty of boiling salted water for 15 minutes or until tender. Drain and rinse.

Arrange the rice around the edge of a warmed serving dish and spoon the curry into the centre. Sprinkle with coconut and garnish with halved eggs. Serve immediately.

# Spiced Lamb Bake

METRIC/IMPERIAL
1 orange, sliced
2 lamb leg bone steaks
salt and freshly ground pepper
¼ teaspoon ground ginger
1 teaspoon brown sugar
½ lemon, sliced
150 ml/¼ pint stock
1 teaspoon cornflour
1 tablespoon water
parsley sprigs to garnish

AMERICAN
1 orange, sliced
2 lamb leg bone steaks
salt and freshly ground pepper
¼ teaspoon ground ginger
1 teaspoon brown sugar
½ lemon, sliced
⅔ cup stock
1 teaspoon cornstarch
1 tablespoon water
parsley sprigs for garnish

Cover the bottom of a small roasting dish with the orange slices. Sprinkle the lamb steaks with salt and pepper to place on top.

Mix together the ginger and sugar, then sprinkle over the lamb. Place a slice of lemon on each lamb steak and pour over the stock. Cook, uncovered, in a preheated moderate oven (180°C/350°F, Gas Mark 4) for 1 hour.

Blend the cornflour (cornstarch) with the water. Strain the juices from the dish into a pan and stir in the cornflour (cornstarch) mixture. Heat, stirring, until the sauce has thickened. Arrange the lamb on a warmed serving dish and pour over the sauce. Garnish with parsley and serve with jacket baked potatoes and peas.

# Breton Rack

METRIC/IMPERIAL
1 best end of lamb, chined and
  trimmed
1 clove garlic, crushed
2 tablespoons honey, melted
2 tablespoons fresh breadcrumbs
2 teaspoons chopped parsley
1 teaspoon chopped sage
1 teaspoon crushed rosemary
salt and freshly ground pepper
watercress to garnish

AMERICAN
1 lamb rib roast, chined and
  trimmed
1 clove garlic, crushed
2 tablespoons honey, melted
2 tablespoons soft bread crumbs
2 teaspoons chopped parsley
1 teaspoon chopped sage
1 teaspoon crushed rosemary
salt and freshly ground pepper
watercress for garnish

Cover the bone tips of the lamb with foil. Rub garlic into back of lamb, then spread honey over. Mix together the breadcrumbs, herbs, salt and pepper, then sprinkle them over the honey.

Cook in a preheated moderate oven (180°C/350°F, Gas Mark 4) for 1¼ to 1½ hours, covering lamb with foil after 40 minutes. Transfer to a warmed serving dish, garnish with watercress and serve with roast potatoes and a selection of vegetables.

# Lamb Cutlet Toad with Onion Gravy

METRIC/IMPERIAL
*salt and freshly ground pepper*
*4 very thin lamb cutlets*
*2 tablespoons butter or dripping*
*50 g/2 oz plain flour*
*1 small egg*
*150 ml/¼ pint milk*
*pinch of sugar*
*2 onions, sliced*
*1 tablespoon plain flour*
*150 ml/¼ pint stock*

AMERICAN
*salt and freshly ground pepper*
*4 very thin lamb chops*
*2 tablespoons butter or dripping*
*½ cup all-purpose flour*
*1 small egg*
*½ cup milk*
*pinch of sugar*
*2 onions, sliced*
*1 tablespoon all-purpose flour*
*⅔ cup stock*

Season the lamb on both sides. Heat the butter or dripping in a frying pan and brown meat on both sides. Remove and leave to cool. Reserve frying pan for gravy.

Make a batter by combining flour, egg, a pinch of salt and milk in a blender, then pour into a jug and chill for 30 minutes. Stir before using.

Place a greased shallow ovenproof dish in a preheated hot oven (220°C/425°F, Gas Mark 7) for a few minutes, then place cutlets (chops) on the bottom and pour the batter over. Cook towards the top of the oven for 20 to 25 minutes until well risen.

Meanwhile make the gravy: add the sugar and a little more butter or dripping to the pan if necessary, and fry the onions gently until soft and golden. Just before you're ready to serve, raise the heat and brown the onions quickly.

Stir in the flour and cook for 1 minute. Stir in the stock and cook until thick; pour into sauceboat. Serve with the lamb, creamed potatoes and minted peas.

# Lamb and Vegetable Pie

METRIC/IMPERIAL
*25 g/1 oz butter*
*225 g/8 oz boneless lamb, cut from
    shoulder or leg, cubed*
*1 tablespoon plain flour*
*stock or water to cover*
*1 bay leaf*
*salt and freshly ground pepper*
*1 large tomato, skinned and
    chopped*
*6 button onions, peeled*
*2 carrots, halved*
*½ turnip, diced*
*50 g/2 oz shelled peas*
*1 teaspoon chopped fresh mint*
*1 tablespoon chopped parsley*
*Creamy Mashed Potatoes
    (see page 113)*
*a little extra butter*

AMERICAN
*2 tablespoons butter*
*½ lb boneless lamb for stew, cubed*
*1 tablespoon all-purpose flour*
*stock or water to cover*
*1 bay leaf*
*salt and freshly ground pepper*
*1 large tomato, peeled and
    chopped*
*6 pearl onions, peeled*
*2 carrots, halved*
*½ turnip, diced*
*½ cup shelled peas*
*1 teaspoon chopped fresh mint*
*1 tablespoon chopped parsley*
*Creamy Mashed Potatoes
    (see page 113)*
*1 egg*
*a little extra butter*

Heat the butter in a pan and brown the meat. Sprinkle with the flour, stir well, then cover with stock or water. Add bay leaf, season with salt and pepper, then cover and simmer for 30 minutes. Add the tomato, onions, carrots and turnip. Replace the lid and continue cooking over a low heat for 30 minutes. Stir in the peas, mint and parsley and cook for 10 minutes longer. Pour into a pie dish and leave to cool.

Make Creamy Mashed Potatoes as in recipe and beat in the egg. Pipe or spoon the potato on to the meat, dot with butter and cook in a preheated moderately hot oven (190°C/375°F, Gas Mark 5) for 20 minutes. Serve immediately.

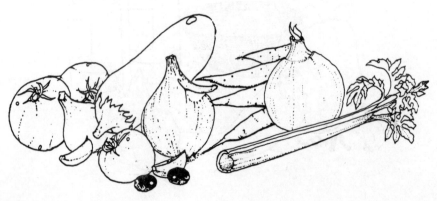

# Lamb with Spring Onions (Scallions)

METRIC/IMPERIAL
2 tablespoons soy sauce
½ teaspoon salt
1 tablespoon dry sherry
4 tablespoons oil
225 g/8 oz lean lamb, very thinly
  sliced
1 tablespoon red wine vinegar
1 tablespoon sesame seed oil
½ teaspoon ground black
  peppercorns
8 spring onions
2 cloves garlic, crushed

AMERICAN
2 tablespoons soy sauce
½ teaspoon salt
1 tablespoon pale dry sherry
¼ cup oil
½ lb lean lamb, very thinly sliced
1 tablespoon red wine vinegar
1 tablespoon sesame oil
½ teaspoon ground black
  peppercorns
8 scallions
2 garlic cloves, crushed

Mix together 1 tablespoon of the soy sauce, salt, sherry and 2 tablespoons of the oil. Add the lamb slices and leave to marinate for 5 minutes. Mix the remaining soy sauce with the vinegar, sesame seed oil and pepper in a small bowl. Shred two of the spring onions (scallions) and set aside for garnish. Cut the remainder into 5 cm (2 inch) pieces.

Heat the remaining oil in a pan. Add the garlic and stir-fry for 10 seconds. Add the meat and stir-fry until browned. Add the spring onion (scallion) pieces to the meat with the vinegar mixture. Stir-fry for a few seconds. Serve hot, garnished with the reserved spring onions (scallions). Serve with rice.

VARIATION:
**Beef with Spring Onions (Scallions)** – simply use 225 g/½ lb very thinly sliced beef instead of the lamb.

# Orange Glazed Lamb

METRIC/IMPERIAL
1.5 kg/3 lb shoulder of lamb, boned
  and rolled
120 ml/4 fl oz orange juice
150 g/5 oz orange marmalade
1 tablespoon lemon juice
freshly ground pepper

AMERICAN
3 lb lamb shoulder, boned and
  rolled
½ cup orange juice
½ cup orange marmalade
1 tablespoon lemon juice
freshly ground pepper

Place lamb in a roasting pan. Mix together the orange juice, marmalade, lemon juice and pepper to taste and spread over the lamb. Cook in a preheated moderate oven (160°C/325°F, Gas Mark 3) for 1½ hours, basting frequently with the pan juices (add a little water if the liquid evaporates too much).

Serve the meat cut into slices, with gravy made from the pan juices. Serve with roast potatoes and a green vegetable.

# Lamb Kebabs with Plum Sauce

METRIC/IMPERIAL
*500 g/1 lb boneless lamb, cut from*
*leg or shoulder*
*salt and freshly ground pepper*
MARINADE:
*1 x 227 g/8 oz can plums*
*1 tablespoon lemon juice*
*1 tablespoon soy sauce*
*1 clove garlic, crushed*
*1 teaspoon sugar*
*¼ teaspoon dried basil*

AMERICAN
*1 lb lamb for kebabs*
*salt and freshly ground pepper*
MARINADE:
*1 x ½ lb can plums*
*1 tablespoon lemon juice*
*1 tablespoon soy sauce*
*1 clove garlic, crushed*
*1 teaspoon sugar*
*¼ teaspoon dried basil*

Remove any fat and skin from the lamb and cut into bite-size cubes. Drain the plums, reserving the syrup. Remove the stones (pits) and rub through a sieve or purée in a blender. Combine the plums and syrup with the remaining marinade ingredients. Pour over the lamb, cover and leave in the refrigerator overnight.

Thread the meat on skewers and season lightly with salt and freshly ground pepper to taste. Grill (broil) on an oiled rack under a preheated grill (broiler) at high heat for about 10 minutes, or until well browned but still springy when pressed. Turn during the cooking time and baste several times with marinade.

When the meat is almost cooked, boil the remaining marinade in a small pan, uncovered, until it is reduced to the consistency of thin gravy, then pour into serving bowl. Serve the kebabs with plain boiled rice or in pitta bread with salad.

VARIATION:
**Pork kebabs** – cubes of lean pork are also excellent marinated in this fruity sauce. Cook at high heat for 2 minutes each side, then turn the heat down to medium and cook for 10 to 15 minutes more.

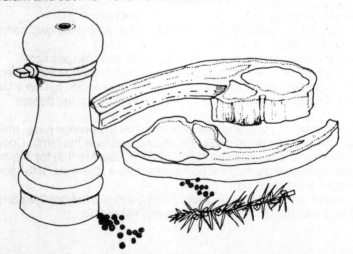

80

# Provençale Lamb Chops

METRIC/IMPERIAL
1 ½ tablespoons olive oil
2 large lamb chops, trimmed of fat
2 potatoes, peeled and sliced into
   thick rounds
2 cloves garlic, peeled and crushed
1 thyme sprig
1 bay leaf
1 rosemary sprig
salt and pepper
about 250 ml/8 fl oz boiling hot beef
   stock
6 black olives, stoned
1 tablespoon chopped parsley

AMERICAN
1 ½ tablespoons olive oil
2 large lamb chops, trimmed of fat
2 potatoes, peeled and sliced into
   thick rounds
2 cloves garlic, peeled and crushed
1 thyme sprig
1 bay leaf
1 rosemary sprig
salt and pepper
about 1 cup boiling hot beef stock
6 ripe olives, pitted
1 tablespoon minced parsley

Heat the oil in a frying pan (skillet), add the chops and fry briskly for 1 to 2 minutes on each side until browned. Remove from pan and set aside. Lower the heat and add potatoes to the pan with the garlic, thyme, bay leaf, rosemary and salt and pepper to taste. Place the chops on top and add enough stock just to cover them.

Cover the pan and cook over moderate heat for 25 to 30 minutes or until the lamb is tender. Check frequently to see that the mixture is not sticking to the bottom of the pan, and press the chops into the potatoes occasionally to crush them to a purée. Just before serving, chop the olives and add to pan with parsley. Heat through for 1 to 2 minutes, then serve.

# Liver au Poivre

METRIC/IMPERIAL
350 g/12 oz lambs' liver
1 tablespoon black peppercorns
2 tablespoons oil
salt
chopped parsley to garnish

AMERICAN
¾ lb lamb liver
1 tablespoon black peppercorns
2 tablespoons oil
salt
chopped parsley for garnish

Remove the outer membrane from the liver and cut into strips about 1 cm/ ½ inch thick, discarding any veins. Crush the peppercorns with a pestle and mortar, or by placing between two sheets of plastic wrap and pounding with a rolling pin. Press the crushed peppercorns on to the liver.

Heat the oil in a frying pan until a faint blue haze rises. Quickly sauté the liver slices, turning until lightly browned on all sides. (The secret of tender liver is not to overcook it.) As soon as the strips have lightly browned and stiffened, without being hard, they are done – about 3 minutes.

Transfer at once to a heated serving plate, sprinkle with a little salt and finely chopped parsley. Serve with French Fried Onion Rings (see page 119) and a green vegetable or salad.

# Stir-Fried Liver

METRIC/IMPERIAL
225 g/8 oz lambs' liver, cut into
5 mm/¼ inch thick slices
300 ml/½ pint water
1 carrot, cut into matchsticks
2 courgettes, diagonally sliced
7 tablespoons oil
1 onion, cut into 8 pieces
2 slices root ginger, shredded
2 tablespoons soy sauce
1 teaspoon sugar
1 tablespoon red wine vinegar
1 tablespoon dry sherry
50 g/2 oz canned water chestnuts,
drained and sliced
1 tablespoon cornflour
MARINADE:
½ teaspoon salt
½ teaspoon freshly ground pepper
2 teaspoons dry sherry
2 teaspoons cornflour
2 teaspoons oil

AMERICAN
½ lb lamb liver, cut into ¼ inch
thick slices
1¼ cups water
1 carrot, cut into matchsticks
2 zucchini, sliced diagonally
7 tablespoons oil
1 onion, cut into 8 pieces
2 slices ginger root, shredded
2 tablespoons soy sauce
1 teaspoon sugar
1 tablespoon red wine vinegar
1 tablespoon pale dry sherry
¼ cup canned water chestnuts,
drained and sliced
1 tablespoon cornstarch
MARINADE:
½ teaspoon salt
½ teaspoon freshly ground pepper
2 teaspoons pale dry sherry
2 teaspoons cornstarch
2 teaspoons oil

Mix the ingredients for the marinade in a bowl. Add the liver slices and leave to marinate for 10 minutes. Bring the water to the boil, add the carrot and courgettes (zucchini) and boil for 3 minutes. Drain, reserving the water. Refresh the vegetables under cold water and reserve.

Heat 5 tablespoons of the oil in a pan over a high heat. Add the liver and stir-fry very rapidly until it changes colour and is firm. Transfer the liver to a plate.

Heat the remaining oil in the pan and stir-fry the onion and ginger for 1 minute. Add the soy sauce, sugar, vinegar and sherry and bring to the boil. Return the liver to the pan with the water chestnuts and vegetables.

Blend the cornflour (cornstarch) with 250 ml/8 fl oz (1 cup) of the reserved cooking liquid and stir into the pan. Simmer, stirring until thickened. Serve immediately with plain boiled rice.

# Crispy Topped Liver

METRIC/IMPERIAL
25 g/1 oz margarine
225 g/8 oz lambs' liver, sliced
1 small onion, chopped
50 g/2 oz mushrooms, chopped
½ red pepper, cored, seeded and
    chopped
40 g/1½ oz fresh breadcrumbs
1 teaspoon dried mixed herbs
1 egg, beaten
salt and freshly ground pepper
parsley sprigs to garnish

AMERICAN
2 tablespoons margarine
½ lb lamb liver, sliced
1 small onion, chopped
½ cup chopped mushrooms
½ red pepper, seeded and
    chopped
¾ cup soft bread crumbs
1 teaspoon dried mixed herbs
1 egg, beaten
salt and freshly ground pepper
parsley sprigs for garnish

Melt the margarine in a frying pan and stir-fry the liver for 6 to 8 minutes, until firm and brown. Remove from the pan with a slotted spoon and keep hot in a shallow flameproof dish.

Add the onion, mushrooms and red pepper to the pan and sauté for 3 minutes. Stir in the breadcrumbs, herbs, beaten egg and salt and pepper to taste. Continue to cook, stirring, for 2 minutes. Spoon the mixture over the liver and cook under a preheated moderate grill (broiler) for 3 to 5 minutes until the topping is crisp and golden brown.

# Liver and Bacon Risotto

METRIC/IMPERIAL
15 g/½ oz butter or margarine
1 teaspoon oil
1 x 1.5 cm/½ inch thick back bacon
    rasher, chopped
1 onion, peeled and sliced
225 g/8 oz lamb's liver, cubed
salt and pepper
6 tablespoons cider
100 g/4 oz long-grain rice, cooked
50 g/2 oz cooked peas
25 g/1 oz salted peanuts
½ teaspoon dried oregano
1 hard-boiled egg, chopped

AMERICAN
1 tablespoon butter or margarine
1 teaspoon oil
1 x ½ inch thick back bacon slice,
    minced
1 onion, peeled and sliced
½ lb lamb's liver, cubed
salt and pepper
6 tablespoons apple cider
¾ cup cooked long-grain rice
4 tablespoons cooked peas
2 tablespoons salted peanuts
½ teaspoon dried oregano
1 hard-cooked egg, minced

Melt the butter or margarine with the oil in a frying pan (skillet) and fry the bacon and onion until lightly coloured. Add the liver and continue cooking until well sealed. Season well with salt and pepper. Stir in the cider and simmer for 3 to 4 minutes or until the liquid has reduced by about half. Add the rice, peas, peanuts and oregano and cook gently until heated through and all the liquid is absorbed. Adjust the seasoning and stir in half the egg. Serve garnished with the remaining egg.

# Fried Liver and Bacon

METRIC/IMPERIAL
4 rashers bacon
50 g/2 oz butter
2 tomatoes, halved
salt and freshly ground pepper
225 g/8 oz lambs' liver
flour for dusting
1 small onion, chopped
4 tablespoons red or white wine or
  stock

AMERICAN
4 slices bacon
¼ cup butter
2 tomatoes, halved
salt and freshly ground pepper
½ lb lamb liver
flour for dusting
1 small onion, chopped
¼ cup red or white wine or stock

Cut each bacon rasher (slice) in half. Place in a cold frying pan and cook until crisp, pouring off and reserving fat as it runs. Remove bacon and keep warm. Return bacon fat to pan, add butter and heat. Fry the tomatoes on both sides and season with salt and pepper.

Meanwhile slice the liver and remove any gristle. Dust with flour on both sides. When the tomatoes are done, remove from the pan and keep warm. Arrange the liver slices in the pan and fry briskly until brown, about 2 minutes on each side. Do not overcook or it will be hard. Season with salt and pepper; remove and keep warm.

Add the onion to the pan and fry, stirring, until golden. Stir in the wine or stock, scraping up all the brown bits from the pan. Bring to the boil, simmer for a minute or two and check for seasoning. Arrange the liver on warm plates surrounded by bacon and tomatoes; pour gravy over.

VARIATIONS:
**Fruity Liver and Bacon** – use 1 tablespoon vermouth and 3 tablespoons orange juice instead of the wine. Just before the liver is cooked, add 4 chopped sage leaves to the pan and stir-fry for 1 minute.
**Piquant Liver and Bacon** – instead of plain flour, coat the liver slices in a mixture of ground black pepper and dry mustard.

# Kidney Kebabs with Barbecue Sauce

| METRIC/IMPERIAL | AMERICAN |
| --- | --- |
| 4 small onions | 4 small onions |
| 4 streaky bacon rashers | 4 fatty bacon slices |
| 4 lambs' kidneys | 4 lamb kidneys |
| 2 chipolata sausages, halved | 2 small sausages, halved |
| BASTE: | BASTE: |
| 1 teaspoon tomato purée | 1 teaspoon tomato paste |
| 1 teaspoon Worcestershire sauce | 1 teaspoon Worcestershire sauce |
| 2 teaspoons oil | 2 teaspoons oil |
| SAUCE: | SAUCE: |
| 15 g/½ oz butter | 1 tablespoon butter |
| ½ small onion, finely chopped | ½ small onion, minced |
| 2 tablespoons tomato ketchup | 2 tablespoons tomato ketchup |
| 1 tablespoon Worcestershire sauce | 1 tablespoon Worcestershire sauce |
| 1 tablespoon clear honey | 1 tablespoon honey |
| 1 tablespoon lemon juice | 1 tablespoon lemon juice |
| salt and freshly ground pepper | salt and freshly ground pepper |

Cook the onions in boiling salted water for 4 minutes, then drain. Remove the rind from the bacon, stretch each rasher (slice) on a board with the back of a knife, then cut in half. Roll up each piece of bacon. Halve the kidneys and remove the cores.

Thread the onions, bacon, kidneys and sausages onto two oiled skewers. Mix the baste ingredients together and brush over the kebabs. Cook under a preheated moderate grill (broiler) for 5 minutes on each side. Brush with the baste while cooking.

To make the sauce: melt the butter in a pan and gently fry the onion for 5 minutes. Add the tomato ketchup, Worcestershire sauce, honey, lemon juice and salt and pepper to taste. Bring to the boil and then simmer for 5 minutes.

Arrange the kebabs on a bed of rice and serve with the sauce and a crisp green salad.

VARIATION:

**Pitta Kidney Kebabs** – shred some crispy lettuce leaves and mix with some chopped onion. Place this salad into pitta bread pockets and top with the kidney kebabs (cooked as in recipe above).

DISHES

**Chicken Dishes**

FOR TWO

## *Chicken Basquaise*

METRIC/IMPERIAL
*2 tablespoons oil*
*40 g/1½ oz butter*
*750 g/1½ lb chicken, cut into 4*
  *pieces*
*1 onion, peeled and finely chopped*
*2 cloves garlic, peeled and crushed*
*1 green pepper, seeded and thinly*
  *sliced*
*2 tomatoes, skinned, chopped and*
  *seeded*
*salt*
*freshly ground pepper*
*90 ml/3 fl oz dry white wine*
GARNISH:
*4 to 6 small spicy sausages*
*100 g/4 oz cooked ham, diced*
*1 tablespoon chopped parsley*

AMERICAN
*2 tablespoons oil*
*3 tablespoons butter*
*1½ lb chicken, cut into 4 serving*
  *pieces*
*1 onion, peeled and finely chopped*
*2 cloves garlic, peeled and crushed*
*1 green pepper, seeded and thinly*
  *sliced*
*2 tomatoes, peeled, chopped and*
  *seeded*
*salt*
*freshly ground pepper*
*⅓ cup dry white wine*
GARNISH:
*4 to 6 small spicy sausages*
*½ cup diced cooked ham*
*1 tablespoon chopped parsley*

Heat the oil and butter in a flameproof casserole, add the chicken pieces and fry over moderate heat, turning frequently, until golden on all sides. Remove with slotted spoon and set aside.

Add the onion to the casserole with the garlic, pepper, tomatoes and salt and pepper to taste. Cook over brisk heat for about 10 minutes, stirring constantly, then add wine and bring to boil. Add chicken, reduce heat, cover and cook gently for 30 to 40 minutes until chicken is tender.

Just before the end of cooking time, fry the sausages, and stir-fry the ham. Arrange the chicken and sauce on warmed plates, garnish with ham, sausages and parsley and serve immediately with plain boiled rice.

# Normandy Chicken

| METRIC/IMPERIAL | AMERICAN |
|---|---|
| 65 g/2½ oz butter | 5 tablespoons butter |
| 750 g/1½ lb chicken, cut into 4 serving pieces | 1½ lb chicken, cut into 4 serving pieces |
| salt | salt |
| freshly ground pepper | freshly ground pepper |
| 225 g/8 oz mushrooms, sliced | ½ lb sliced mushrooms |
| 120 ml/4 fl oz dry cider | ½ cup hard cider |
| 4 tablespoons double cream | ¼ cup heavy cream |

Melt half the butter in a flameproof casserole, add the chicken pieces and fry gently, turning frequently until golden on all sides. Sprinkle with salt and pepper, cover and cook gently for 10 minutes.

Melt the remaining butter in another pan, add the mushrooms and cook until their juices run into the butter. Remove mushrooms with slotted spoon, draining them thoroughly. Pour liquid into the casserole with the cider, cover and simmer gently for 35 minutes or until the chicken is tender.

Remove the chicken pieces and reserve. Stir the cream into the cooking liquid, bring to the boil and simmer until thick, stirring. Return the chicken to the casserole, add the mushrooms and simmer for a few minutes until heated through. Taste and adjust seasoning. Serve immediately with sauté potatoes and Vegetable Ribbon Medley (see page 127).

# Store Cupboard Chicken

| METRIC/IMPERIAL | AMERICAN |
|---|---|
| 1 tablespoon oil | 1 tablespoon oil |
| 1 teaspoon salt | 1 teaspoon salt |
| 2 chicken pieces | 2 chicken pieces |
| 1 x 297 g/10½ oz can sweet and sour sauce | 1 x 10½ oz can sweet and sour sauce |
| 1 x 312 g/11 oz can apricot halves, drained | 1 x 11 oz can apricot halves, drained |
| salt and freshly ground pepper | salt and freshly ground pepper |
| 25 g/1 oz flaked almonds | ¼ cup sliced almonds |

Heat the oil in a frying pan and sprinkle with the salt. Add the chicken pieces and cook for 15 to 20 minutes, turning several times. Drain well and remove all the chicken meat from the bones.

Place the sweet and sour sauce in a pan and add the apricots and chicken meat. Add salt and pepper to taste and bring to the boil. Cover and simmer for 10 to 15 minutes.

Meanwhile toast the almonds. Transfer the chicken to a warmed serving dish and sprinkle with the almonds. Serve with boiled rice and stir-fried vegetables.

# Chicken Paprika

| METRIC/IMPERIAL | AMERICAN |
| --- | --- |
| 25 g/1 oz butter | 2 tablespoons butter |
| 2 tablespoons oil | 2 tablespoons oil |
| 2 large chicken drumsticks | 2 large chicken drumsticks |
| 1 small onion, chopped | 1 small onion, chopped |
| 1 stick celery, chopped | 1 stalk celery, chopped |
| 2 teaspoons paprika pepper | 2 teaspoons paprika |
| 2 tomatoes, skinned and chopped | 2 tomatoes, peeled and chopped |
| 25 g/1 oz mushrooms, sliced | ¼ cup sliced mushrooms |
| 1 green pepper, cored, seeded and cut into rings | 1 green pepper, seeded and cut into rings |
| 150 ml/¼ pint chicken stock | ⅔ cup chicken stock |
| salt and freshly ground pepper | salt and freshly ground pepper |
| 3 tablespoons soured cream | 3 tablespoons sour cream |
| 2 teaspoons plain flour | 2 teaspoons all-purpose flour |
| parsley sprigs to garnish | parsley sprigs for garnish |

Melt the butter in a pan with the oil and fry the chicken until browned all over. Remove from the pan with a slotted spoon and set aside. Sauté the onion and celery for 3 minutes, then add the paprika and cook for 1 minute.

Add the tomatoes, mushrooms, green pepper, stock, and salt and pepper to taste. Bring to the boil, cover and simmer for 45 minutes. Remove the chicken from the sauce and place on a warmed serving dish.

Blend the cream and flour together and add to the sauce. Cook the sauce, stirring, until the sauce thickens. Continue to cook for 1 minute, without boiling, then pour over the chicken. Garnish with parsley and serve with boiled rice and a mixed salad.

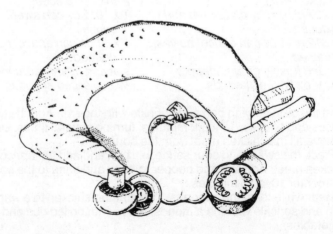

# Devil-Crumbed Chicken

| METRIC/IMPERIAL | AMERICAN |
|---|---|
| 2 half chicken breasts | 2 half chicken breasts |
| 25 g/1 oz butter, melted | 2 tablespoons melted butter |
| DEVIL MIXTURE: | DEVIL MIXTURE: |
| 25 g/1 oz butter, softened | 2 tablespoons softened butter |
| 1 teaspoon dry mustard | 1 teaspoon dry mustard |
| ½ teaspoon salt | ½ teaspoon salt |
| pinch of cayenne pepper | pinch of cayenne |
| 1 teaspoon Worcestershire sauce | 1 teaspoon Worcestershire sauce |
| 25 g/1 oz fresh breadcrumbs | ½ cup soft bread crumbs |

Preheat the grill (broiler) to medium and cover the rack with oiled foil. Brush the chicken breasts with melted butter and cook for 10 minutes with the skin side down, brushing once or twice with butter. Combine the ingredients for the devil mixture.

Remove the chicken from the grill (broiler) and, when it is cool enough to handle, press the crumb mixture firmly over the skin side of each breast. Place the chicken on the rack again, crumb side up, and grill (broil) at medium heat for a further 10 to 12 minutes, until the topping is golden brown and the juices run clear when the flesh is pierced with a fine skewer. (If the crumbs seem to be colouring too much, turn the heat down or move the chicken further away from the heat.)

Serve immediately with Broccoli in Wine (see page 123) and grilled tomato halves.

# Baked Sherried Chicken

| METRIC/IMPERIAL | AMERICAN |
|---|---|
| 4 small chicken pieces | 4 small chicken pieces |
| 2 tablespoons dry sherry | 2 tablespoons pale dry sherry |
| 1 tablespoon soy sauce | 1 tablespoon soy sauce |
| ¼ teaspoon dry mustard | ¼ teaspoon dry mustard |
| ¼ teaspoon ground ginger | ¼ teaspoon ground ginger |
| ½ teaspoon sugar | ½ teaspoon sugar |
| 50 g/2 oz butter, melted | ¼ cup melted butter |

Place the chicken in a bowl and pour over the sherry, soy sauce, mustard, ginger and sugar. Turn the chicken until coated with the marinade. Cover and leave for 2 hours, turning the pieces occasionally.

Place the chicken in a small ovenproof dish and pour over the marinade, then the melted butter. Cook in a preheated moderately hot oven (190°C/375°F, Gas Mark 5), basting frequently with the pan juices, for about 30 minutes or until the juice runs clear when a fine skewer is inserted in the thickest part of the chicken. Serve with sauté potatoes and broccoli.

# Chicken Noodle Bake

METRIC/IMPERIAL
1 small aubergine
salt and freshly ground pepper
50 g/2 oz spaghettini or fine
   noodles
2 tablespoons oil
½ green pepper, cored, seeded
   and chopped
1 small onion, chopped
1 clove garlic, crushed
2 tomatoes, skinned and chopped
100 g/4 oz cooked chicken meat,
   chopped
chopped parsley to garnish
SAUCE:
15 g/½ oz butter
15 g/½ oz plain flour
250 ml/8 fl oz chicken stock
1 egg yolk
TOPPING:
2 tablespoons fresh breadcrumbs
15 g/½ oz butter

AMERICAN
1 small eggplant
salt and freshly ground pepper
½ cup spaghettini or fine noodles
2 tablespoons oil
½ green pepper, seeded and
   chopped
1 small onion, chopped
1 clove garlic, crushed
2 tomatoes, peeled and chopped
½ cup chopped cooked chicken
   meat
chopped parsley for garnish
SAUCE:
1 tablespoon butter
2 tablespoons all-purpose flour
1 cup chicken stock
1 egg yolk
TOPPING:
2 tablespoons soft bread crumbs
1 tablespoon butter

Slice the aubergine (eggplant), place in a colander and sprinkle with salt; leave for 30 minutes.

Meanwhile cook the pasta in plenty of boiling salted water for 10 minutes or until tender. Drain and rinse.

Heat half the oil in a pan and sauté the rinsed and dried aubergine (eggplant) slices until brown. Remove and reserve. Add remaining oil and sauté the green pepper, onion and garlic until soft. Add the tomatoes, chicken and salt and pepper to taste.

Arrange layers of noodles, aubergine (eggplant) and chicken mixture in a greased 900 ml/1½ pints (3¾ cup) ovenproof dish.

To make the sauce: place the butter, flour and stock in a pan and whisk over a moderate heat until the sauce thickens. Continue to cook the sauce, stirring, for 1 minute. Cool slightly and beat in the egg yolk. Pour the sauce over the layers in the dish. Sprinkle with the breadcrumbs and dot with the butter. Cook in a preheated moderate oven (180°C/350°F, Gas Mark 4) for 40 minutes. Serve garnished with parsley.

# Chicken with Almonds

| METRIC/IMPERIAL | AMERICAN |
|---|---|
| *2 boneless chicken pieces* | *2 boneless chicken pieces* |
| *50 g/2 oz butter* | *¼ cup butter* |
| *1 tablespoon dry sherry* | *1 tablespoon pale dry sherry* |
| *1 clove garlic, chopped* | *1 clove garlic, minced* |
| *1 small onion, finely chopped* | *1 small onion, finely chopped* |
| *2 tomatoes, peeled and sliced* | *2 tomatoes, skinned and sliced* |
| *1 tablespoon tomato purée* | *1 tablespoon tomato paste* |
| *1 tablespoon plain flour* | *1 tablespoon all-purpose flour* |
| *250 ml/8 fl oz chicken stock* | *1 cup chicken stock or broth* |
| *1 bay leaf* | *1 bay leaf* |
| *salt and freshly ground pepper* | *salt and freshly ground pepper* |
| *25 g/1 oz flaked almonds* | *¼ cup sliced almonds* |
| *1 teaspoon vinegar* | *1 teaspoon vinegar* |

Cut the chicken into smallish pieces and pat dry with kitchen paper towels.

Heat the butter in a large frying pan and sauté the pieces, turning with 2 spoons so that they brown on all sides. Heat the sherry and pour over the chicken, then remove the chicken to a plate.

Add the garlic and onion to the pan and cook gently for a few minutes. Add one of the sliced tomatoes and cook for 2 to 3 minutes. Remove from the heat and stir in the tomato purée (paste), flour, stock, bay leaf and salt and pepper to taste. Return the chicken to the pan, skin side down. Cover and cook slowly for 25 to 30 minutes, turning the chicken pieces once or twice during cooking.

Arrange the chicken pieces on a serving dish. Add the almonds, vinegar and the remaining sliced tomato to the pan, simmer a few minutes, then spoon over the chicken. Serve with Buttered Noodles (see page 175).

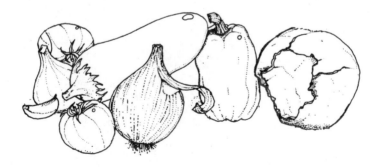

# Chicken and Corn Supper

METRIC/IMPERIAL
2 chicken pieces
6 peppercorns
1 bay leaf
sprig of thyme
15 g/½ oz butter
50 g/2 oz mushrooms, sliced
1 stock cube
25 g/1 oz margarine
25 g/1 oz plain flour
salt and freshly ground pepper
1 x 198 g/7 oz can sweetcorn
watercress to garnish

AMERICAN
2 chicken pieces
6 peppercorns
1 bay leaf
sprig of thyme
1 tablespoon butter
½ cup sliced mushrooms
1 bouillon cube
2 tablespoons margarine
¼ cup all-purpose flour
salt and freshly ground pepper
1 x 7 oz can whole kernel corn
watercress for garnish

Place the chicken pieces in a pan and cover with water. Add the peppercorns, bay leaf and thyme. Bring to the boil, cover and simmer for 20 to 30 minutes until the chicken is tender.

Meanwhile melt the butter in a pan and lightly sauté the mushrooms. Remove the mushrooms and leave on one side.

Remove the chicken from the pan and keep hot. Strain off 300 ml/½ pint (1¼ cups) of the stock and stir in the stock (bouillon) cube. Melt the margarine in a pan and stir in the flour. Cook for 1 minute or until a pale golden colour. Remove from the heat and gradually blend in the stock. Cook the sauce, stirring, until it thickens, then add salt and pepper to taste and the cooked mushrooms.

Heat the corn in the can liquid, then drain. Arrange the chicken on a warmed serving dish and pour over the sauce. Spoon the corn around the chicken and garnish with watercress. Serve with boiled rice.

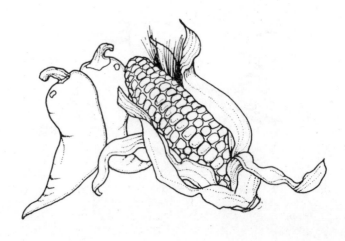

# Chicken with Peppers

METRIC/IMPERIAL
3 tablespoons oil
2 red peppers, cored, seeded and
    sliced into rings
1 teaspoon salt
2 tablespoons water
350 g/12 oz chicken meat, cut into
    2.5 cm/1 inch pieces
15 g/½ oz root ginger, finely
    chopped
pinch of brown sugar
2 teaspoons dry sherry
120 ml/4 fl oz stock
1 teaspoon cornflour
2 teaspoons soy sauce

AMERICAN
3 tablespoons oil
2 red peppers, seeded and sliced
    into rings
1 teaspoon salt
2 tablespoons water
¾ lb chicken meat, cut into 1 inch
    pieces
1 tablespoon finely chopped ginger
    root
pinch of brown sugar
2 teaspoons pale dry sherry
½ cup stock
1 teaspoon cornstarch
2 teaspoons soy sauce

Heat 1 tablespoon of the oil in a pan. Add the pepper rings and salt and
stir-fry for 1 minute. Add the water and simmer until the liquid has
evaporated. Remove the peppers from the pan and set aside.

Heat the remaining oil in the pan. Add the chicken and ginger and stir-fry
for 1 minute. Stir in the sugar, sherry and stock. Cover and simmer for
10 minutes. Blend the cornflour (cornstarch) with the soy sauce and add to
the pan. Simmer, stirring, until thickened. Add the pepper rings and cook
for 1 minute. Serve at once with plain boiled rice.

# Chicken Patties

METRIC/IMPERIAL
15 g/½ oz fresh white breadcrumbs
4 tablespoons evaporated milk
225 g/8 oz minced raw chicken
1 egg
½ teaspoon grated lemon rind
salt and freshly ground pepper
1 tablespoon finely chopped mixed
    fresh herbs (parsley, chives,
    chervil)
15 g/½ oz butter
1 tablespoon oil

AMERICAN
¼ cup soft white bread crumbs
¼ cup evaporated milk
1 cup ground raw chicken
1 egg
½ teaspoon grated lemon rind
salt and freshly ground pepper
1 tablespoon finely chopped mixed
    fresh herbs (parsley, chives,
    chervil)
1 tablespoon butter
1 tablespoon oil

Place the breadcrumbs, milk, chicken, egg, lemon rind, salt and pepper to
taste and herbs in a large bowl and mix lightly with a fork. Turn on to a
lightly floured board and shape into 4 flat patties.

Heat the butter and oil in a frying pan and fry the patties for about 5
minutes on each side. Serve with Fresh Tomato Sauce (page 144).

# Chicken Wings with Oyster Sauce

METRIC/IMPERIAL
500 g/1 lb chicken wings
3 tablespoons oyster sauce
1 tablespoon soy sauce
300 ml/½ pint chicken stock
pinch of salt
1 teaspoon brown sugar
15 g/½ oz root ginger, finely
   chopped
freshly ground black pepper
1 teaspoon coarse salt

AMERICAN
1 lb chicken wings
3 tablespoons oyster sauce
1 tablespoon soy sauce
1¼ cups chicken stock
pinch of salt
1 teaspoon brown sugar
1 tablespoon finely chopped ginger
   root
freshly ground black pepper
1 teaspoon coarse salt

Put the chicken wings in a pan with just enough cold water to cover. Bring to the boil, cover and simmer for 10 minutes. Drain and discard the water.

Put the chicken wings back into the pan and add the oyster sauce, soy sauce, stock, salt and sugar. Bring slowly to the boil, cover and simmer for 20 minutes. Sprinkle over the ginger, pepper and salt and serve.

# Citrus chicken

METRIC/IMPERIAL
2 chicken pieces
flour for dusting
50 g/2 oz butter
1 orange
1 lemon
175 ml/6 fl oz white wine or chicken
   stock
salt and freshly ground pepper
120 ml/4 fl oz single cream
2 tablespoons grated Gruyère
   cheese
lemon slices
little extra butter

AMERICAN
2 chicken pieces
flour for dusting
¼ cup butter
1 orange
1 lemon
¾ cup white wine or chicken stock
   or broth
salt and freshly ground pepper
½ cup light cream
2 tablespoons grated Swiss cheese
lemon slices
little extra butter

Dust the chicken lightly with the flour. Heat the butter in a large frying pan and brown the chicken pieces on all sides. Cover and continue to cook for about 20 to 25 minutes until nearly cooked. Remove to a warm plate.

Grate the rind of the orange and lemon. Stir the white wine or stock, grated rinds and 1 tablespoon lemon juice into the pan and season with salt and pepper. Turn up the heat and stir in the cream slowly. Return the chicken and cook in the cream sauce for a few minutes.

Arrange the chicken on a serving dish, spoon the sauce over and sprinkle with the cheese. Put a slice of lemon on each piece of chicken, dot with butter and brown under a preheated grill (broiler).

# Chicken with Cashew Nuts

METRIC/IMPERIAL
1 egg white
2 tablespoons dry sherry
1 teaspoon salt
freshly ground pepper
1 teaspoon cornflour
1 chicken breast, skinned, boned
 and cut into 2.5 cm/1 inch slices
6 tablespoons oil
50 g/2 oz unsalted cashew nuts
1 spring onion, chopped
½ green pepper, cored, seeded
 and cut into 1 cm/½ inch pieces
100 g/4 oz canned bamboo shoots,
 drained and sliced
1 tablespoon soy sauce
1 teaspoon sugar
1 teaspoon cornflour, blended with
 1 tablespoon water

AMERICAN
1 egg white
2 tablespoons pale dry sherry
1 teaspoon salt
freshly ground pepper
1 teaspoon cornstarch
1 chicken breast, skinned, boned
 and cut into 1 inch slices
6 tablespoons oil
½ cup unsalted cashew nuts
1 scallion, chopped
½ green pepper, seeded and cut
 into ½ inch pieces
1 cup canned sliced bamboo
 shoots, drained and sliced
1 tablespoon soy sauce
1 teaspoon sugar
1 teaspoon cornstarch, blended
 with 1 tablespoon water

Mix together the egg white, 1 tablespoon of the sherry, the salt, pepper and cornflour (cornstarch). Add the chicken and turn to coat with the mixture. Heat 3 tablespoons of the oil in a pan. Add the chicken and stir-fry until golden. Remove from the heat.

Heat 2 tablespoons of the remaining oil in another pan. Add cashew nuts and fry until lightly browned. Remove with a slotted spoon and drain on kitchen paper towels.

Heat the remaining oil in the pan. Add the spring onion (scallion), green pepper and bamboo shoots and stir-fry for 1 minute. Add the remaining sherry, soy sauce, sugar and cornflour (cornstarch) mixture and cook, stirring, until thickened. Add the chicken, turn to coat in the sauce and heat through. Serve hot, sprinkled with the cashew nuts, with plain boiled rice.

# Chinese Chicken with Peppers and Chillies

METRIC/IMPERIAL
1 tablespoon dry sherry
2 tablespoons soy sauce
1 small egg white
2 tablespoons cornflour
500 g/1 lb chicken meat, cut into
　2.5 cm/1 inch cubes
1 tablespoon red wine vinegar
1 teaspoon salt
2 teaspoons sugar
2 teaspoons sesame oil
6 tablespoons olive oil
2 cloves garlic, crushed
2 red chillies, seeded and chopped,
　or 2 teaspoons cayenne pepper
1 large green pepper, cored,
　seeded and cut into 2.5 cm/
　1 inch pieces

AMERICAN
1 tablespoon pale dry sherry
2 tablespoons soy sauce
1 small egg white
2 tablespoons cornstarch
1 lb chicken meat, cut into 1 inch
　cubes
1 tablespoon red wine vinegar
1 teaspoon salt
2 teaspoon sugar
2 teaspoon sesame seed oil
6 tablespoons olive oil
2 cloves garlic, crushed
2 fresh chili peppers, seeded and
　chopped, or 2 teaspoons
　cayenne
1 large green pepper, seeded and
　cut into 1 inch pieces

With a fork, lightly mix together the sherry, soy sauce, egg white and cornflour (cornstarch). Add the chicken cubes and turn to coat well. Leave to marinate for 3 minutes. In a small bowl, mix together the vinegar, salt, sugar and sesame oil.

Heat the olive oil in a wok or heavy-based frying pan. Add the garlic, chilli peppers or cayenne and chicken. Stir-fry until the chicken is golden brown, then add the green pepper and vinegar mixture. Stir-fry until the sauce starts bubbling and thickens. Serve immediately with boiled rice.

# Viennese Chicken Schnitzels

| METRIC/IMPERIAL | AMERICAN |
|---|---|
| 2 half chicken boneless breasts | 2 half chicken boneless breasts |
| salt and freshly ground pepper | salt and freshly ground pepper |
| 2 tablespoons plain flour | 2 tablespoons all-purpose flour |
| 1 egg, beaten | 1 egg, beaten |
| 25 g/1 oz fresh white breadcrumbs | ½ cup soft white bread crumbs |
| 50 g/2 oz butter | ¼ cup butter |
| GARNISH: | GARNISH: |
| 4 lemon wedges | 4 lemon wedges |
| 2 anchovy fillets | 2 anchovy fillets |
| chopped parsley | chopped parsley |

Remove the skin from the chicken breasts. Place between two sheets of cling film (plastic wrap) and pound until thin. Sprinkle each chicken breast with salt and pepper and dredge lightly with the flour. Coat with egg and breadcrumbs, patting lightly to make the crumbs cling. Chill for 20 minutes.

Heat the butter in a large frying pan and fry the chicken for about 6 to 8 minutes until brown on both sides.

Arrange on warmed serving plates and garnish each schnitzel with lemon wedges, a rolled anchovy fillet and a sprinkling of parsley. Serve with boiled potatoes with parsley sauce and a crisp green salad.

# Chicken Pojarski

| METRIC/IMPERIAL | AMERICAN |
|---|---|
| 500 g/1 lb minced chicken | 1 lb ground chicken |
| salt | salt |
| freshly grated nutmeg | freshly grated nutmeg |
| 2 slices white bread | 2 slices white bread |
| 2 tablespoons milk | 2 tablespoons milk |
| 2 tablespoons vodka or dry sherry | 2 tablespoons vodka or dry sherry |
| flour for dusting | flour for dusting |
| 50 g/2 oz butter | ¼ cup butter |
| 50 g/2 oz mushrooms, sliced | ½ cup sliced mushrooms |
| 120 m/4 fl oz single cream | ½ cup light cream |

Place the chicken in a bowl and season with salt and a liberal amount of freshly grated nutmeg. Remove crusts and place bread in the bowl with the milk and half the vodka or sherry. Mix well and shape into 4 patties, then dust lightly with flour. Heat the butter in a large frying pan and cook the patties for 3 to 4 minutes on each side. Transfer to a warm plate.

Sauté the mushrooms in the same pan, adding a little more butter if necessary. Stir in the remaining vodka or sherry and heat through. Add the cream and stir well to pick up the brown bits from the base of the pan, then spoon over the patties. Serve with Steamed New Potatoes (page 108) and Glazed Carrots (page 124).

# Sesame Chicken

METRIC/IMPERIAL
2 chicken pieces
2 tablespoons soy sauce
1 teaspoon sugar
½ teaspoon salt
2 slices fresh root ginger finely
  chopped
15 g/½ oz butter, melted
1 tablespoon toasted sesame
  seeds*

AMERICAN
2 chicken pieces
2 tablespoons soy sauce
1 teaspoon sugar
½ teaspoon salt
2 slices fresh ginger root, finely
  chopped
1 tablespoon melted butter
1 tablespoon toasted sesame
  seeds*

Wipe the chicken with damp kitchen paper towels. Mix the soy sauce, sugar, salt and ginger and marinate the chicken in the mixture for 1 hour.

Remove the chicken from the marinade and grill (broil) until tender about 10 to 15 minutes each side. Mix the melted butter with the remaining marinade and brush the cooked chicken with the mixture, then roll in the toasted sesame seeds. Serve with Stoved Potatoes (see page 114) and Cauliflower in Cream Sauce (see page 157).

*Note: to toast the sesame seeds, spread out on a baking sheet and cook in a moderate oven (180°C/350°F, Gas Mark 4) until lightly browned. Or toast in a frying pan over a medium heat, shaking the pan constantly.

# Chinese Chicken Livers with Prawns (Shrimp) and Broccoli

METRIC/IMPERIAL
350 g/12 oz broccoli cut into small
  florets
225 g/8 oz peeled prawns
1 teaspoon salt
4 tablespoons oil
100 g/4 oz chicken livers
1½ tablespoons soy sauce
2 slices root ginger, shredded
1 teaspoon sugar
2 tablespoons dry sherry

AMERICAN
2 cups broccoli, cut into small
  florets
½ lb shelled shrimp
1 teaspoon salt
¼ cup oil
¼ lb chicken livers
1½ tablespoons soy sauce
2 slices ginger root, shredded
1 teaspoon sugar
2 tablespoons pale dry sherry

Parboil the broccoli for 2 minutes, then drain. Sprinkle the prawns (shrimp) with the salt and 1 tablespoon of the oil. Cut each liver into four pieces. Sprinkle with half the soy sauce and another 1 tablespoon of the oil.

Heat the remaining oil in a pan or wok over high heat. Add the ginger and stir-fry for 20 seconds. Add the prawns (shrimp) and chicken livers and stir-fry for 1½ minutes. Add the broccoli, sugar and sherry and bring to the boil. Sprinkle with remaining soy sauce. Stir-fry for 2 minutes. Serve hot with plain boiled rice.

# Chicken Liver and Aubergine (Eggplant) Casserole

METRIC/IMPERIAL
1 medium aubergine
oil
salt and freshly ground pepper
50 g/2 oz rice, cooked
1 tablespoon chopped parsley
1 medium onion, sliced
100 g/4 oz chicken livers
3 tablespoons soured cream
1 teaspoon paprika pepper
2 tomatoes, sliced

AMERICAN
1 medium-sized eggplant
oil
salt and freshly ground pepper
¼ cup rice, cooked
1 tablespoon chopped parsley
1 medium-size onion, sliced
¼ lb chicken livers
3 tablespoons sour cream
1 teaspoon paprika
2 tomatoes, sliced

Cut the aubergine (eggplant) into 5 mm ¼ inch slices. Brush one side of each slice with a little oil. Sprinkle with salt and pepper, then cook under a low grill (broiler), without turning, until soft and lightly browned.

Arrange a third of the aubergine (eggplant) slices in a 900 ml/1½ pint (3¾ cup) greased casserole dish. Mix the rice with the parsley and spoon into the dish. Cover with another third of the aubergine (eggplant) slices.

Heat a little oil in a pan and sauté the onion until soft. Add the chicken livers and continue to cook for 2 minutes. Stir in the cream, paprika and salt and pepper to taste. Mix well, then pour into the casserole and top with the remaining aubergine (eggplant) slices.

Arrange the tomato slices around the edge and brush with oil. Cook in a preheated moderately hot oven (200°C/400°F, Gas Mark 6) for 25 to 30 minutes. Serve hot.

DISHES

Vegetable
Dishes

FOR TWO

# Lentils with Parsley Butter

| METRIC/IMPERIAL | AMERICAN |
| --- | --- |
| 2 tablespoons olive oil | 2 tablespoons olive oil |
| 1 clove garlic, crushed | 1 clove garlic, crushed |
| 1 small onion, finely chopped | 1 small onion, finely chopped |
| 100 g/4 oz orange lentils | ½ cup orange lentils |
| 400 ml/14 fl oz boiling water | 1¾ cups boiling water |
| salt and freshly ground pepper | salt and freshly ground pepper |
| PARSLEY BUTTER: | PARSLEY BUTTER: |
| 50 g/2 oz softened butter | ¼ cup softened butter |
| 1 tablespoon finely chopped parsley | 1 tablespoon finely chopped parsley |
| lemon juice | lemon juice |

Heat the oil in a large heavy pan and fry the garlic and onion over a medium heat until golden. Stir in the lentils, continuing to stir until they have absorbed the oil. Pour the boiling water over them and simmer for 1 hour, or until the lentils are soft.

Meanwhile cream the butter with a wooden spoon and beat in the parsley, a squeeze of lemon juice and a little salt to taste. Chill until firm.

Season the lentils with salt and pepper to taste. Stir in a little parsley butter and serve with a good knob of butter on top as a garnish.

VARIATION:

**Italian Lentils** – fry 4 chopped rashers (slices) fatty smoked bacon until the fat begins to run, then add the onion and garlic as in recipe above. Use chicken or beef stock instead of the boiling water and stir in 1 tablespoon tomato purée (paste) when the liquid comes back to the boil. Simmer for about 1 hour until the lentils are cooked, then taste and adjust seasoning. Serve hot.

# French-Style Green Peas

METRIC/IMPERIAL
*25 g/1 oz butter*
*1 rasher streaky bacon, diced*
*3 spring onions, finely chopped*
*4 outside lettuce leaves, shredded*
*225 g/8 oz frozen peas*
*1 sprig mint*
*1 teaspoon sugar*
*salt and freshly ground pepper*
*2 tablespoons water*

AMERICAN
*2 tablespoons butter*
*1 slice bacon, diced*
*3 scallions, finely chopped*
*4 outside lettuce leaves, shredded*
*½ lb frozen peas*
*1 sprig mint*
*1 teaspoon sugar*
*salt and freshly ground pepper*
*2 tablespoons water*

Melt the butter in a flameproof casserole and gently fry the bacon and spring onions (scallions) until the onion is soft. Add the lettuce to the casserole, and stir over a low heat until it is bright green. Add the peas with the mint, the sugar and salt and pepper to taste. Pour in the water, cover tightly and cook over a gentle heat for 10 minutes, or until the peas are tender. Garnish with fresh mint, and serve from the casserole.

VARIATIONS:
**Purée of Peas** – cook 225 g/½ lb frozen peas in lightly salted boiling water, then drain. Purée them in a blender with 2 tablespoons of the cooking liquid, salt and pepper to taste, and a chopped sprig of mint if desired. Return to the pan, add a little cream, evaporated milk or a tablespoon of butter and stir over a gentle heat until piping hot.
**Curried Peas and Ham** – cook the peas as usual, then drain. Melt 25 g/1oz (2 tablespoons) butter in the same pan and stir in 1 teaspoon (or more if liked) of curry powder, with 1 crushed clove of garlic. Return the peas to the pan and stir gently until heated through and coated with the curry mixture. Taste, and add extra salt and a pinch of sugar if needed. Sprinkle with finely chopped and cooked ham to serve.
**Peas with Sour Cream and Mushrooms** – cook the peas as usual, then drain. Sauté 50 g/2 oz (½ cup) of sliced mushrooms in 25 g/1 oz (2 tablespoons) butter until tender. Add the peas to the mushrooms in the pan, stir to combine, and season with salt and freshly ground pepper to taste. Stir in 4 tablespoons soured cream and bring to near boiling point. Serve immediately.

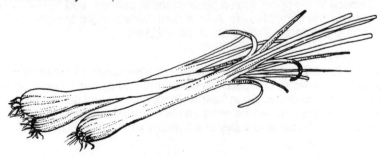

# Fried Mexican Beans (Frijoles)

METRIC/IMPERIAL
1 x 450 g/15 oz can red kidney
  beans
1 onion, chopped
1 clove garlic, crushed
salt
2 tablespoons olive oil
1 teaspoon chilli powder
salt and freshly ground pepper

AMERICAN
1 x 16 oz can red kidney beans
1 onion, chopped
1 clove garlic, crushed
salt
2 tablespoons olive oil
1 teaspoon chili powder
salt and freshly ground pepper

Place the beans and their liquid in a heavy-based pan with half the onion and the garlic. Bring to the boil and simmer for 10 minutes. Drain and leave to cool.

Heat the oil in a heavy frying pan. Gradually add the beans, mashing them as you go with a potato masher. Stir in the chilli powder, adding extra if you like it hotter and spicier. Add salt and pepper at the same time if necessary. Continue stirring over a low heat until the mixture is thick, then spoon into a heated serving bowl and sprinkle with remaining onion.

# Minted Peas

METRIC/IMPERIAL
salt and freshly ground pepper
1 large sprig mint
pinch of sugar
500 g/1 lb fresh peas, shelled
knob of butter
little chopped mint to garnish

AMERICAN
salt and freshly ground pepper
1 large sprig mint
pinch of sugar
1 lb fresh peas, shucked
pat of butter
little chopped mint for garnish

Pour 1 cm/½ inch of water in a pan with a little salt and pepper, the sprig of mint and sugar. Bring the water to the boil, add the peas and cover tightly. Cook over a medium heat for 6 to 8 minutes, or until the peas are tender.

Remove the mint sprig and strain off any liquid. Stir in the butter and a little extra chopped mint and serve.

To cook 225 g (8 oz) frozen peas: place in pan and add ½ teaspoon sugar and 2 to 3 mint leaves. Add enough boiling water to cover, bring to the boil and cook for 2 minutes. Drain and serve.

VARIATIONS:
**Peas in Mint Sauce** – cook the peas as above but do not drain. Stir in 1 teaspoon arrowroot blended with water and 1 teaspoon vinegar and cook gently until thickened. Stir in freshly chopped mint and serve immediately.
**Creamed Peas** – strain the peas and add a few tablespoons of cream with a spoonful of chopped parsley or a few tiny white cocktail onions.

# Mange-Tout (Snow Peas)

METRIC/IMPERIAL
*225 g/8 oz mange-tout peas*
*salt and freshly ground pepper*
*1 spring onion, finely chopped*
*knob of butter*

AMERICAN
*½ lb snow peas*
*salt and freshly ground pepper*
*1 scallion, finely chopped*
*pat of butter*

Top and tail the pods and remove any strings if necessary. Place the peas with salt and pepper to taste in a pan and pour over enough boiling water to barely cover. Sprinkle with the spring onion (scallion), turn the heat down and simmer for 1 to 2 minutes, or until tender but still slightly crisp. Drain the peas, toss with butter and season with extra salt, if required, and freshly ground pepper.

# Beans with Sour Cream

METRIC/IMPERIAL
*225 g/8 oz whole green beans*
*50 g/2 oz butter, melted*
*1 teaspoon lemon juice*
*150 ml/¼ pint boiling beef stock*
*2 tablespoons soured cream*
*sweet paprika powder*

AMERICAN
*½ lb whole green beans*
*¼ cup melted butter*
*1 teaspoon lemon juice*
*⅔ cup boiling beef stock*
*2 tablespoons sour cream*
*sweet paprika powder*

Top and tail the beans, remove the strings, and thinly slice diagonally. Toss the beans in hot butter, then add the lemon juice, salt and pepper to taste, and enough beef stock to cover.

Simmer the beans gently for about 8 minutes until they are almost tender, then boil rapidly and reduce the liquid to a sauce.

Serve topped with the soured cream and a sprinkling of paprika.

# Mixed Beans with Garlic Butter

METRIC/IMPERIAL
*1 x 290 g/10 oz can butter beans*
*50 g/2 oz butter*
*1 clove garlic, crushed*
*100 g/4 oz frozen whole green
  beans*
*salt and freshly ground pepper*

AMERICAN
*1 x 10 oz can lima beans*
*¼ cup butter*
*1 clove garlic, crushed*
*100 g/4 oz frozen whole green
  beans*
*salt and freshly ground pepper*

Drain the butter beans and rinse under cold water. Melt the butter in a frying pan and gently fry the garlic until soft. Add the beans and stir until piping hot – about 8 minutes. Season with salt and pepper to taste and serve immediately.

# Beans with Poulette Sauce

METRIC/IMPERIAL
*225 g/8 oz green beans*
*salt and freshly ground pepper*
*15 g/½ oz butter*
*1 teaspoon plain flour*
*120 ml/4 fl oz chicken stock*
*1 teaspoon chopped fresh savory*
*  or marjoram*
*1 egg yolk*
*1 tablespoon lemon juice*

AMERICAN
*½ lb green beans*
*salt and freshly ground pepper*
*1 tablespoon butter*
*1 teaspoon all-purpose flour*
*½ cup chicken stock or broth*
*1 teaspoon chopped fresh savory*
*  or marjoram*
*1 egg yolk*
*1 tablespoon lemon juice*

Top and tail the beans, and cook in boiling salted water until tender.

Meanwhile make the sauce: melt the butter in a small pan. Stir in the flour, cook for 1 minute, then gradually blend in the stock. Bring the sauce to the boil, stirring constantly. Add salt and pepper to taste and the herbs. Reduce the heat and simmer the sauce for 5 minutes. Beat the egg yolk with the lemon juice. Remove the sauce from the heat, stir in the egg mixture and reheat without boiling.

Drain the beans, arrange in a heated serving dish and pour the sauce over. Serve immediately.

VARIATION:

**Leeks with Poulette Sauce** – choose 4 small leeks with crisp tops. Trim off the roots but leave joined at the root end. Cut off the tops to leave about 5 cm/2 inches of green and remove tough, damaged or discoloured leaves.

Cut two slits at right angles to each other through the green tops down to the white part. Holding the root ends, plunge them up and down in cold water to remove grit. In a wide pan, bring water to boiling point. Salt lightly and place leeks flat in the pan.

Boil the leeks, uncovered, for 15 to 25 minutes, according to size, until tender when tested with a fine skewer. Drain on a cloth or kitchen paper towels. Arrange on a heated serving dish and pour over the hot Poulette Sauce, made as above.

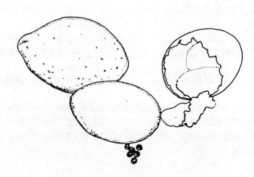

# Broad (Lima) Beans with Bacon

METRIC/IMPERIAL
225 g/8 oz fresh or frozen broad
  beans
4 rashers bacon
15 g/½ oz butter
1 small onion, chopped
2 teaspoons plain flour
salt and freshly ground pepper
1 tablespoon chopped parsley

AMERICAN
½ lb fresh or frozen lima beans
4 slices bacon
1 tablespoon butter
1 small onion, chopped
2 teaspoons all-purpose flour
salt and freshly ground pepper
1 tablespoon chopped parsley

Cook the beans until tender in boiling salted water (15 to 20 minutes if fresh, 5 to 6 minutes if frozen).

Meanwhile cut the bacon into dice. Heat the butter in a pan and fry the bacon and onion for 3 to 4 minutes, or until the onion is soft. Blend in the flour and cook for 1 minute. Drain the beans and add 120 ml/4 fl oz (½ cup) of the cooking liquid to the bacon. Bring to the boil, stirring, add the beans and reheat gently. Add salt and pepper to taste and stir in the chopped parsley.

# Stir-Fried Beans with Almonds

METRIC/IMPERIAL
1½ tablespoons oil
225 g/8 oz frozen sliced or whole
  beans
1 teaspoon sugar
2 tablespoons chicken stock or
  white wine
1 teaspoon cornflour, mixed with
  1 tablespoon soy sauce
salt and freshly ground pepper
25 g/1 oz toasted almonds

AMERICAN
1½ tablespoons oil
½ lb frozen sliced or whole green
  beans
1 teaspoon sugar
2 tablespoons chicken stock or
  white wine
1 teaspoon cornstarch, mixed with
  1 tablespoon soy sauce
salt and freshly ground pepper
¼ cup toasted almonds

Heat the oil in a heavy-based frying pan and add the frozen beans. Stir and cook the beans over a medium heat for 3 minutes, then add the sugar and stock or wine. Simmer the mixture for another 2 minutes, then stir in the cornflour (cornstarch) and soy sauce mixture, and salt and pepper to taste. Use two forks to toss the beans until lightly coated with the sauce. Add the almonds and serve at once.

# Spiced Green Beans

METRIC/IMPERIAL
225 g/8 oz green beans
1 clove garlic, chopped
1 tablespoon lemon juice
½ teaspoon salt
pinch of cayenne pepper
120 ml/4 fl oz vegetable oil
½ teaspoon cumin or coriander
    seeds, crushed

AMERICAN
½ lb green beans
1 clove garlic, chopped
1 tablespoon lemon juice
½ teaspoon salt
pinch of cayenne
½ cup vegetable oil
½ teaspoon cumin or coriander
    seeds, crushed

Top and tail the beans and string if necessary. Cut the beans into 4 cm/
1½ inch lengths. Combine the garlic, lemon juice, salt and cayenne.
    Heat the oil in a frying pan, add the crushed cumin or coriander seeds
and fry for a few seconds. Add the beans and sauté briskly for 1 minute.
Stir in the garlic mixture, cover tightly, and cook over a low heat for
10 minutes or until just tender. Increase the heat, remove the cover and
stir constantly until the liquid has evaporated. Serve immediately.

# Lazy Day Pea Purée

METRIC/IMPERIAL
40 g/1½ oz butter
1 small onion, finely chopped
1 x 290 g/10 oz can condensed
    green pea soup
2 tablespoons single cream
1 teaspoon ground cumin
pinch of cayenne pepper

AMERICAN
3 tablespoons butter
1 small onion, finely chopped
1 x 10 oz can condensed green pea
    soup
2 tablespoons light cream
1 teaspoon ground cumin
pinch of cayenne

Melt the butter in a pan and sauté the onion until soft. Gradually stir in the
remaining ingredients and heat, stirring, until smooth and hot.

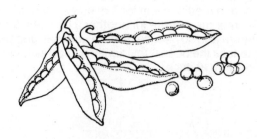

# Tomato and Olive Rice

| METRIC/IMPERIAL | AMERICAN |
|---|---|
| 1 tablespoon oil | 1 tablespoon oil |
| 1 onion, chopped | 1 onion, chopped |
| 1 clove garlic, crushed | 1 clove garlic, crushed |
| 150 g/5 oz long-grain rice | ¾ cup long-grain rice |
| 6 tomatoes, skinned and quartered | 6 tomatoes, peeled and quartered |
| 300 ml/½ pint chicken stock | 1¼ cups chicken stock |
| salt and freshly ground pepper | salt and freshly ground pepper |
| finely grated rind of ½ lemon | finely grated rind of ½ lemon |
| 2 large fresh basil leaves, chopped, or 1 teaspoon dried | 2 large fresh basil leaves, chopped, or 1 teaspoon dried |
| 50 g/2 oz stuffed olives, sliced | ⅓ cup sliced stuffed olives |
| lemon slices to garnish | lemon slices for garnish |

Heat the oil in a pan and sauté the onion and garlic for 3 minutes. Add the rice and continue to fry for 2 minutes. Add the tomatoes, stock, salt and pepper to taste, lemon rind and basil.

Bring to the boil, cover and simmer for 15 to 20 minutes until the rice is cooked and the liquid absorbed.

Stir in the olives, adjust the seasoning and garnish with lemon slices. Serve with grilled meat or fish.

# Sweet-Sour Cracked Wheat

| METRIC/IMPERIAL | AMERICAN |
|---|---|
| 100 g/4 oz cracked wheat | 1 cup cracked wheat |
| 400 ml/⅔ pint beef or chicken stock | 2 cups beef or chicken stock or broth |
| 1 bay leaf | 1 bay leaf |
| 1 teaspoon salt | 1 teaspoon salt |
| 2 cloves garlic, crushed | 2 cloves garlic, crushed |
| freshly grated nutmeg | freshly grated nutmeg |
| 2 tablespoons oil | 2 tablespoons oil |
| 2 tablespoons vinegar | 2 tablespoons vinegar |
| 2 tablespoons brown sugar | 2 tablespoons sugar |
| chopped parsley or spring onions to garnish | chopped parsley or scallions for garnish |

Rinse the wheat in a colander and drain. Bring the stock to the boil with the bay leaf, salt and garlic, and a liberal sprinkling of nutmeg. Add the wheat, turn the heat to low and simmer for 25 to 30 minutes.

Add the oil, vinegar and brown sugar and cook for another 10 minutes or so, stirring often, until quite tender. Turn into a heated serving bowl and sprinkle with chopped parsley or spring onions (scallions).

# Persian Crusty Rice

METRIC/IMPERIAL
*150 g/5 oz long-grain rice*
*50 g/2 oz butter*
*fresh mint to garnish*

AMERICAN
*¾ cup long-grain rice*
*¼ cup butter*
*fresh mint for garnish*

Cook the rice in plenty of boiling salted water for 10 minutes only, then drain and rinse.

Melt half the butter in a heavy-based pan, add the rice piled into a dome, dot with the rest of the butter, then cover and cook over a medium heat for 15 to 20 minutes. Turn into serving dish, scraping up the crusty rice from base of pan. Sprinkle with fresh chopped mint to garnish and serve with cold or hot meats or curried eggs.


# Oven-Cooked New Potatoes

METRIC/IMPERIAL
*500 g/1 lb small new potatoes*
*4 mint leaves, finely chopped*
*1 tablespoon chopped chives or*
  *spring onions*
*40 g/1½ oz butter*
*salt*

AMERICAN
*1 lb small new potatoes*
*4 mint leaves, finely chopped*
*1 tablespoon chopped chives or*
  *scallions*
*3 tablespoons butter*
*salt*

Wash the potatoes, place them in a roasting bag and add the mint and chives or spring onions (scallions). Dot the butter over the potatoes and sprinkle with salt. Close the bag with its twist tie and make 3 or 4 holes in the top as directed.

Place in a baking dish and cook in a preheated moderately hot oven (190°C/375°F, Gas Mark 5) for 30 to 40 minutes, or until tender.

VARIATIONS:
**Steamed New Potatoes** – place washed small new potatoes in the top of a steamer over boiling water. Cover the pan and steam the potatoes for 20 minutes or until tender when pierced with a fork. Transfer to a hot serving dish and sprinkle with a little coarse sea salt.
**Herby New Potatoes** – toss the potatoes in melted butter, then sprinkle with chopped chives, parsley or fresh basil.

# Oven Chips

METRIC/IMPERIAL
*2 medium potatoes*
*1 teaspoon paprika*
*50 g/2 oz butter, melted, or*
  *3 tablespoons oil*
*salt*

AMERICAN
*2 medium potatoes*
*1 teaspoon paprika*
*¼ cup melted butter, or*
  *3 tablespoons oil*
*salt*

Peel the potatoes and cut into sticks about 1 cm/½ inch thick. Dry well on kitchen paper towels. Spread in a single layer in a shallow baking tin and sprinkle with paprika. Pour the butter or oil over and turn the potatoes until they are coated.

Cook the potatoes in a preheated hot oven (230°C/450°F, Gas Mark 8) for 30 to 40 minutes, turning several times, until golden brown and tender. Drain on kitchen paper towels and sprinkle lightly with salt to serve.

# New Potatoes Maître d'Hôtel

METRIC/IMPERIAL
*500 g/1 lb new potatoes*
*25 g/1 oz butter*
*2 spring onions, finely chopped*
*1 tablespoon finely chopped*
  *parsley*
*salt and freshly ground pepper*
*4 tablespoons single cream*

AMERICAN
*1 lb new potatoes*
*2 tablespoons butter*
*2 scallions, finely chopped*
*1 tablespoon finely chopped*
  *parsley*
*salt and freshly ground pepper*
*¼ cup light cream*

Wash the potatoes and boil them in their skins until just tender. Peel the potatoes and cut into fairly thick slices. Melt the butter in a flameproof dish and add the potatoes in layers, seasoning each layer with chopped spring onion (scallion), parsley and salt and pepper to taste.

Heat the cream in a pan to boiling point and pour over the potatoes. Cook the dish in a preheated cool oven (150°C/300°F, Gas Mark 2) for about 20 minutes until the potatoes are heated through. Serve from the dish.

# French-style Creamed Potatoes

METRIC/IMPERIAL
500 g/1 lb floury potatoes, peeled
65 g/2½ oz butter
about 90 ml/3 fl oz hot milk
salt
freshly ground pepper
freshly grated nutmeg
1 large onion, peeled and sliced
  into very thin rings

AMERICAN
1 lb floury potatoes, peeled
5 tablespoons butter
about ⅓ cup hot milk
salt
freshly ground pepper
freshly grated nutmeg
1 large onion, peeled and sliced
  into very thin rings

Steam the potatoes in a pressure cooker, if possible, or cook in a small amount of water until tender, to avoid them becoming too moist. Mash or purée, then beat in one third of the butter, the milk a little at a time, and the salt, pepper and nutmeg to taste.

Melt half the remaining butter in heavy-based frying pan (skillet), add the onion and cook gently until tender and lightly coloured. Add onion to potato purée and cook gently over low heat, turning mixture constantly. Spread mixture in greased gratin dish, dot with remaining butter and brown under a preheated hot grill (broiler). Serve immediately.


# Potato and Cheese Casserole

METRIC/IMPERIAL
750 g/1½ lb potatoes, peeled and
  very thinly sliced
1 large onion, peeled and thinly
  sliced into rounds
225 g/8 oz Cheddar cheese or a
  mixture of Cheddar and blue
  cheese, thinly sliced
25 g/1 oz butter, diced
salt
freshly ground pepper
150 ml/¼ pint milk, preferably
  skimmed
snipped chives, to garnish

AMERICAN
1½ lb potatoes, peeled and very
  thinly sliced
1 large onion, peeled and thinly
  sliced into rounds
½ lb Cheddar cheese, or a mixture
  of Cheddar and blue cheese,
  thinly sliced
2 tablespoons butter, diced
salt
freshly ground pepper
⅔ cup milk, preferably skimmed
snipped chives, for garnish

Place potatoes in cold water for 15 minutes to rinse off some of the starch. Pat dry with absorbent paper towels. Place a layer of potatoes in a buttered 900 ml/1½ pint (3¾ cup) casserole, top with a layer of onions, then a layer of cheese. Dot with half the butter, add salt and pepper, then repeat layers. Bring milk just to the boil, then pour over the layers. Stand the dish on a baking sheet and bake in a preheated fairly hot oven (190°C/375°F, Gas Mark 5) for 40 minutes or until the potatoes are very tender when pierced with a skewer. Garnish and serve immediately.

# Piquant Sauté Potatoes

METRIC/IMPERIAL
*40 g/1½ oz dripping or butter*
*350 g/12 oz waxy potatoes, peeled*
  *and chopped into small pieces*
*1 clove garlic, peeled*
*3 parsley sprigs*
*salt*
*freshly ground pepper*

AMERICAN
*3 tablespoons dripping or butter*
*¾ lb waxy potatoes, peeled and*
  *chopped into small pieces*
*1 clove garlic, peeled*
*3 parsley sprigs*
*salt*
*freshly ground pepper*

Heat the fat in a frying pan (skillet), add the potatoes and cook over medium heat for 15 to 20 minutes until tender. Turn potatoes frequently so they are golden all over.

Meanwhile, chop the garlic and parsley together finely to make an *hachis*. When the potatoes are cooked, sprinkle the *hachis* over them with salt and pepper to taste. Remove from heat, cover and leave for 5 minutes before serving.

# Hash Brown Potatoes

METRIC/IMPERIAL
*4 medium potatoes*
*1 small onion, finely chopped*
*1 tablespoon chopped parsley*
*salt and freshly ground pepper*
*1 teaspoon lemon juice*
*3 tablespoons oil or bacon dripping*
*2 tablespoons single cream*

AMERICAN
*4 medium potatoes*
*1 small onion, finely chopped*
*1 tablespoon chopped parsley*
*salt and freshly ground pepper*
*1 teaspoon lemon juice*
*3 tablespoons oil or bacon fat*
*2 tablespoons light cream*

Wash the potatoes and boil them in their skins until tender. When cooked, peel the potatoes and cut them into small dice. Place the potatoes in a bowl and add the onion, parsley, salt and pepper to taste and lemon juice.

Heat the oil or bacon dripping in a large heavy frying pan (skillet) and press the potato mixture into the pan, shaping it into a broad flat cake. Cook very gently over a low heat, shaking the pan from time to time to prevent sticking. When the bottom is brown, cut the potato cake in half and turn each half with two spatulas to avoid breaking. Pour the cream over the potatoes and continue cooking until the underside is brown. Cut into four pieces, slide on to a heated serving dish and serve at once.

# Potato Pancakes

METRIC/IMPERIAL
*350 g/12 oz potatoes, grated*
*2 eggs, lightly beaten*
*1 tablespoon plain flour*
*½ teaspoon salt*
*¼ teaspoon freshly grated nutmeg*
*oil for frying*

AMERICAN
*1½ cups grated potatoes (about*
*¾ lb)*
*2 eggs, lightly beaten*
*1 tablespoon all-purpose flour*
*½ teaspoon salt*
*¼ teaspoon freshly grated nutmeg*
*oil for frying*

Rinse the grated potatoes, then place them on a tea (dish) towel and wring the towel to extract as much moisture as possible. Place the potatoes in a bowl and stir in the eggs. Sift the flour and salt together and mix into the potatoes with the nutmeg.

Heat enough oil in a heavy frying pan (skillet) to give a depth of about 5 mm/¼ inch. Place half the potato mixture in the hot oil, pressing into a flat pancake shape with the back of a fish slice. Cook over a medium heat until brown and crisp on the bottom, then turn and brown the other side. Drain on kitchen paper towels while you cook the second pancake. Serve hot.

VARIATIONS:

**Rösti** – to make this Swiss special, cook the potatoes for 10 minutes, then drain, cool and peel. Grate into a bowl and add ½ teaspoon salt. Heat 15 g/½ oz (1 tablespoon) butter and 1 tablespoon oil in a heavy-based frying pan and add the potatoes, pressing into a flat cake. Cook over low heat for 10 minutes until the underneath is crisp. Turn out carefully on to a plate. Add 15 g/½ oz (1 tablespoon) butter and 1 tablespoon oil to the pan, heat then slide potato cake, cooked side up, into pan. Cook for about 10 minutes, then serve.

**Potato, bacon and garlic patties** – peel and grate 2 large waxy potatoes. Drain them well in a colander or sieve (strainer), then dry in a clean tea towel (cloth). Place in a bowl with 50 g/2 oz (¼ cup) chopped bacon, and an egg and mix together well. Add chopped parsley and a generous amount of salt and pepper.

Form the mixture into small balls, then flatten them. Heat a little oil in a frying pan (skillet) and fry the patties until golden brown on both sides. Serve with Tomatoes Provençale (see page 116).

# Irish Potato Cakes

METRIC/IMPERIAL
*225 g/8 oz floury potatoes*
*25 g/1 oz butter*
*salt and freshly ground pepper*
*about 50 g/2 oz plain flour*
*butter*

AMERICAN
*½ lb floury potatoes*
*2 tablespoons butter*
*salt and freshly ground pepper*
*about ½ cup all-purpose flour*
*butter*

Peel the potatoes and cook until tender. Drain, and shake the pan over the heat for a moment to dry the potatoes. Mash well, and while still hot, beat in the butter. Season with salt and pepper to taste and work in enough flour to bind to a dough.

Divide the dough in half. Pat or roll each half out into a round, 1 cm/ ½ inch thick, on a floured board, then cut each circle into quarters. Make sure the griddle or frying pan (skillet) is well greased and heated through. Cook the potato cakes for about 5 minutes each side until nicely brown.

Split each potato cake in two, and fill with a slice of butter. Serve very hot with sausages, bacon and tomatoes, or fried eggs, or with golden or maple syrup.

# Creamy Mashed Potatoes

METRIC/IMPERIAL
*500 g/1 lb old potatoes*
*salt and freshly ground pepper*
*25 g/1 oz butter*
*120 ml/4 fl oz milk*

AMERICAN
*1 lb potatoes*
*salt and freshly ground pepper*
*2 tablespoons butter*
*½ cup milk*

Scrub the potatoes well and place them in a pan with enough cold water to cover. Add salt to taste. Bring to the boil and cook with a lid on the pan for about 20 to 25 minutes until the potatoes are easily pierced with a fork. Drain thoroughly.

Hold the potatoes on a fork and strip off the skins with a sharp knife. Return to the pan over a very low heat and mash with a potato masher, or put through a potato ricer. Add the butter and beat the potatoes with a wooden spoon until smooth. Add the milk, pouring in a little at a time and beating until light and fluffy. Remove from the heat, add salt and pepper to taste and serve at once in a heated dish.

VARIATIONS:
**Onion Mash** – add 1 to 2 teaspoons onion flakes with the butter
**Herby Mash** – stir in 1 to 2 tablespoons of finely chopped fresh herbs (parsley, chives, tarragon, chervil).
**Spicy Mash** – stir in ½ teaspoon ground mace and a few drops of Worcestershire sauce. Or crush ¼ teaspoon each of celery and mustard seed and stir in with the butter.

# Potatoes O'Brien

METRIC/IMPERIAL
2 medium potatoes, cooked
½ green pepper, cored, seeded
  and chopped
1 onion, finely chopped
1 tablespoon plain flour
salt
pinch of cayenne pepper
50 g/2 oz mature cheese, grated
120 ml/4 fl oz hot milk
25 g/1 oz dry breadcrumbs
butter

AMERICAN
2 medium potatoes, cooked
½ green pepper, seeded and
  chopped
1 onion, finely chopped
1 tablespoon all-purpose flour
salt
pinch of cayenne
½ cup grated sharp cheese
½ cup hot milk
⅓ cup dry bread crumbs
butter

Peel and slice the potatoes and mix with the green pepper, onion, flour, salt, cayenne, most of the cheese and the milk. Pour into a greased shallow baking dish, sprinkle the breadcrumbs and remaining cheese over the top and dot generously with butter.

Cook in a preheated moderate oven (180°C/350°F, Gas Mark 4) until the top is bubbly and brown.

# Stoved Potatoes with Garlic

METRIC/IMPERIAL
500 g/1 lb even-size new potatoes
1 tablespoon water
40 g/1½ oz butter
2 cloves garlic, finely chopped
salt and freshly ground pepper

AMERICAN
1 lb even-size new potatoes
1 tablespoon water
3 tablespoons butter
2 cloves garlic, finely chopped
salt and freshly ground pepper

Scrub the potatoes well, rubbing off any loose skin. Arrange them in one layer in a large heavy-based frying pan (skillet), or place in an earthenware potato pot. Add the water, dot the butter over the top and sprinkle with the garlic. Season well with salt and pepper.

Place the lid on the pan – it must fit tightly, if it doesn't, cover the pan with foil first. Simmer very gently for about 30 to 40 minutes until the potatoes are cooked. Shake the pan often to prevent sticking, and add just a drop more water if you think it is necessary.

# Sweet Potato Fries

METRIC/IMPERIAL
350 g/12 oz sweet potatoes, peeled
oil for deep frying
1 teaspoon brown sugar
½ teaspoon salt
freshly grated nutmeg

AMERICAN
¾ lb sweet potatoes, peeled
oil for deep frying
1 teaspoon brown sugar
½ teaspoon salt
freshly grated nutmeg

Parboil the potatoes for 10 minutes. Drain and cut into 5 mm/¼ inch thick slices.

Heat the oil to 180°C/350°F (when a cube of bread browns in 25 to 30 seconds) and fry the potato slices until golden brown. Drain on kitchen paper towels, sprinkle with brown sugar, salt and nutmeg and serve immediately.

# Deep-Fried Parsnips

METRIC/IMPERIAL
2 small parsnips
salt and freshly ground pepper
1 egg
2 tablespoons plain flour, seasoned
  with salt and pepper
dry breadcrumbs
oil for deep frying

AMERICAN
2 small parsnips
salt and freshly ground pepper
1 egg
2 tablespoons all-purpose flour,
  seasoned with salt and pepper
dry bread crumbs
oil for deep frying

Peel the parsnips and cut into short sticks about 1 cm/½ inch thick. Parboil in salted water to cover for 8 minutes, then drain and dry and leave to cool.

Beat the egg with a little salt and freshly ground pepper. Dip the parsnip sticks into the seasoned flour and shake off surplus, then dip into the egg, roll in breadcrumbs and chill for 10 minutes to set the coating.

Heat the oil to 180°/350°F (when a cube of bread browns in 25 to 30 seconds) and fry the parsnip sticks until golden brown. Drain on kitchen paper towels and serve at once.

VARIATIONS:
Other vegetables such as cauliflower or broccoli pieces, or artichoke hearts, may be prepared in the same way as parsnips – cooked lightly before coating with flour, egg and breadcrumbs. Aubergine (eggplant), green pepper, courgettes (zucchini) and mushrooms may be coated and deep fried in the same way, but do not need to be parboiled.
**Battered Vegetables** -- mix together 1 egg white and 1 tablespoon arrowroot in a bowl until frothy. Dip the cauliflower or broccoli florets, pieces of green or red pepper, or thick courgettes (zucchini) slices in the batter, then deep-fry as for parsnips above. Serve with lemon wedges or tartare sauce (see page 148).

# Skirlie-Mirlie

METRIC/IMPERIAL
*225 g/8 oz swede, diced*
*350 g/12 oz potatoes*
*salt and freshly ground pepper*
*50 g/2 oz butter or bacon dripping*
*little milk*
*finely chopped parsley to garnish*

AMERICAN
*½ lb rutabaga, diced (about 1 cup)*
*¾ lb potatoes*
*salt and freshly ground pepper*
*¼ cup butter or bacon fat*
*little milk*
*finely chopped parsley for garnish*

Cook the swede (rutabaga) and potatoes separately in boiling salted water; drain well. Heat the fat in a pan, add the swede (rutabaga) and potatoes and mash well, adding enough milk to give a creamy texture. Add salt and freshly ground pepper to taste. Spoon into a heated serving bowl and sprinkle with a finely chopped parsley.

# Buttered Turnips with Mustard

METRIC/IMPERIAL
*225 g/8 oz young turnips*
*25 g/1 oz butter*
*½ teaspoon salt*
*1 tablespoon French mustard*
*1 tablespoon chopped parsley*

AMERICAN
*½ lb young turnips*
*2 tablespoons butter*
*½ teaspoon salt*
*1 tablespoon Dijon-style mustard*
*1 tablespoon chopped parsley*

Cut the turnips into sticks like potato chips (French fries). Drop into boiling salted water and simmer for 10 to 12 minutes, or until just tender. Drain thoroughly.

Heat the butter in a heavy pan and stir in the salt and mustard. Add the turnips and turn gently until they are coated. Fold the chopped parsley through and serve.

# Tomatoes Provençale

METRIC/IMPERIAL
*1 large or 2 small tomatoes*
*1 clove garlic, crushed*
*1 tablespoon chopped parsley*
*2 tablespoons oil*
*25 g/1 oz fresh breadcrumbs*
*salt and freshly ground pepper*

AMERICAN
*1 large or 2 small tomatoes*
*1 clove garlic, crushed*
*1 tablespoon chopped parsley*
*2 tablespoons oil*
*½ cup soft bread crumbs*
*salt and freshly ground pepper*

Halve the tomatoes crosswise in a zig-zag line. Mix together the remaining ingredients with salt and pepper to taste and pile on to the tomatoes. Grill (broil) for about 10 minutes under medium heat, or in a greased shallow dish in a preheated moderate oven (180°C/350°F, Gas Mark 4) for 20 minutes.

# Grilled Mushrooms

METRIC/IMPERIAL
*2 large flat mushrooms*
*1 teaspoon lemon juice*
*salt and freshly ground pepper*
*oil or butter*

AMERICAN
*2 large flat mushrooms*
*1 teaspoon lemon juice*
*salt and freshly ground pepper*
*oil or butter*

Wipe the mushrooms and cut the stalks level with the cups. Sprinkle with lemon juice, salt and pepper and a little oil or butter.

Grill (broil) the mushrooms on a foil-lined rack for about 5 minutes.

VARIATIONS:
**Mushrooms Provençale** – pile the garlic breadcrumb mixture from the Tomatoes Provençale recipe (see opposite page) on to the mushrooms and grill (broil) until crisp.
**Cheesy Mushrooms** – mix 25 g/1 oz (¼ cup) each of grated Cheddar cheese and fresh (soft) breadcrumbs with 1 teaspoon made mustard and spread on mushrooms. Grill until cheese melts and crumbs are crisp.

# Grilled Aubergine (Eggplant)

METRIC/IMPERIAL
*1 small firm aubergine*
*salt*
*1 clove garlic, crushed*
*1 small onion, finely chopped or*
  *grated*
*3 tablespoons olive oil or melted*
  *butter*

AMERICAN
*1 small firm eggplant*
*salt*
*1 clove garlic, crushed*
*1 small onion, finely chopped or*
  *grated*
*3 tablespoons olive oil or melted*
  *butter*

Wash the aubergine (eggplant) and cut off the stalk end. Cut into 2 cm/ ¾ inch thick slices, place in a bowl and sprinkle with salt. Leave for 20 minutes. Mix together the garlic, onion and oil or melted butter.

Rinse the aubergine (eggplant) slices, then pat dry with kitchen paper towels. Arrange on a greased baking sheet and brush with the oil or butter mixture. Grill (broil) the aubergine (eggplant) under medium heat for 5 minutes, basting once, then turn, brush again and cook for 2 to 3 minutes more.

VARIATIONS:
**French-Fried Aubergine (Eggplant)** – salt, rinse and drain the slices as above. Finely chop 50 g/2 oz (½ cup) button mushrooms and 2 spring onions (scallions). Heat 4 tablespoons of oil in a heavy-based frying pan (skillet), add aubergine (eggplant) slices and brown on one side. Turn the slices, sprinkle with mushroom and onion (scallion) mixture and cook for 2 to 3 minutes, basting frequently. Serve hot, sprinkled with freshly ground sea-salt and chopped parsley.

# Provençale Purée of Aubergines (Eggplant)

METRIC/IMPERIAL

1 medium aubergine, sliced into
  thin rounds
salt
3 tablespoons olive oil
1 onion, peeled and thinly sliced
2 tomatoes, skinned, chopped and
  seeded
2 cloves garlic, peeled and finely
  chopped
1 to 2 tablespoons chopped parsley
50 g/2 oz Parmesan cheese, grated

AMERICAN

1 medium eggplant, sliced into thin
  rounds
salt
3 tablespoons olive oil
1 onion, peeled and thinly sliced
2 tomatoes, peeled, chopped and
  seeded
2 cloves garlic, peeled and finely
  minced
1 to 2 tablespoons chopped parsley
½ cup grated Parmesan cheese

Place aubergine (eggplant) slices in a colander and sprinkle generously with salt. Leave for 15 minutes to drain.

Meanwhile, heat the oil in a heavy-based pan, add the onion and fry gently until tender but not coloured. Add the tomatoes and continue to cook gently, pressing tomatoes to break them up.

Drain aubergines (eggplant) and rinse. Dry thoroughly, then add to the pan with the garlic and half the parsley. Stir well, cover and cook gently for 20 to 30 minutes until mixture becomes a purée when pressed with a wooden spoon. Add enough Parmesan, salt, pepper and parsley until taste is to your liking, then serve hot with buttered toast.

# Boiled Onions with Parsley Sauce

METRIC/IMPERIAL

4 small onions
25 g/1 oz butter
1 tablespoon plain flour
120 ml/4 fl oz evaporated milk or
  single cream
salt and freshly ground pepper
1 tablespoon chopped parsley

AMERICAN

4 small onions
2 tablespoons butter
1 tablespoon all-purpose flour
½ cup evaporated milk or light
  cream
salt and freshly ground pepper
1 tablespoon chopped parsley

Cook the onions in boiling salted water for about 30 minutes until tender. Drain and reserve 4 tablespoons of the cooking liquid. Arrange the onions in a serving dish and keep warm.

Melt the butter in a pan, stir in the flour and cook for 1 minute. Gradually add the reserved cooking liquid, stirring constantly, and the milk or cream. Heat the sauce until boiling, season with salt and pepper to taste and stir in the parsley. Pour the sauce over the onions and serve at once.

# Scalloped Onions

METRIC/IMPERIAL
350 g/12 oz onions
salt and freshly ground pepper
1 tablespoon poppy seeds
50 g/2 oz cream cheese
4 tablespoons milk
1 tablespoon chopped parsley

AMERICAN
¾ lb onions
salt and freshly ground pepper
1 tablespoon poppy seeds
¼ cup cream cheese
¼ cup milk
1 tablespoon chopped parsley

Cut the onions into thin slices. Arrange in a shallow baking dish or casserole. Sprinkle the onions with salt, pepper and poppy seeds.

Put the cheese and milk in a small pan and stir over a low heat until smooth. Stir in the parsley. Pour the sauce over the onions, cover the dish, and cook in a preheated moderate oven (180°C/350°F, Gas Mark 4) for 1 hour.

# French-Fried Onion Rings

METRIC/IMPERIAL
1 medium onion
4 tablespoons milk
2 tablespoons plain flour, seasoned
    with salt and pepper
oil for deep frying
salt

AMERICAN
1 medium onion
¼ cup milk
2 tablespoons all-purpose flour,
    seasoned with salt and pepper
oil for deep frying
salt

Peel the onion and cut into 5 mm/¼ inch thick slices. Separate into rings. Dip the rings in milk, then into seasoned flour, shaking off any surplus.

Heat the oil to 190°C/375°F (when a bread cube browns in 25 to 30 seconds). Fry the onion rings for 2 to 3 minutes until crisp and golden. Drain on kitchen paper towels, salt lightly and serve very hot.

# Honeyed Onions

METRIC/IMPERIAL
2 small onions
175 ml/6 fl oz chicken stock
25 g/1 oz butter
2 teaspoons honey
1 teaspoon grated lemon rind
½ teaspoon paprika

AMERICAN
2 small onions
¾ cup chicken stock or broth
2 tablespoons butter
2 teaspoons honey
1 teaspoon grated lemon rind
½ teaspoon paprika

Halve the onions and arrange, cut side up, in a small shallow baking dish. Place the remaining ingredients in a pan and bring to the boil. Pour over the onions, cover and cook in a preheated moderate oven (180°C/350°F, Gas Mark 4) for 45 minutes until tender.

# Brussels Sprout Purée

**METRIC/IMPERIAL**
225 g/8 oz Brussels sprouts
salt and freshly ground pepper
40 g/1½ oz butter
1 medium potato, diced
250 ml/8 fl oz chicken stock
4 tablespoons hot milk
½ teaspoon ground mace

**AMERICAN**
½ lb Brussels sprouts
salt and freshly ground pepper
3 tablespoons butter
1 medium potato, diced
1 cup chicken stock or broth
¼ cup hot milk
½ teaspoon ground mace

Remove any discoloured leaves from the sprouts, trim the stem ends, and parboil for 5 minutes in salted water. Drain well.

Heat the butter in a heavy frying pan (skillet), and toss the sprouts until well coated. Add the potato and stock, bring to the boil, then cover the pan tightly and simmer for 15 to 20 minutes, or until the vegetables are very tender. Cool slightly, then purée in a blender or food processor until smooth. Return the purée to the pan and, over gentle heat, beat in the hot milk, mace, and salt and pepper to taste. Serve at once.

VARIATION:
**Crunchy Brussels Sprout Purée** – grill (broil) 2 rashers (slices), of bacon until crisp. Crumble the bacon into the brussels sprout purée with some croûtons and toasted flaked almonds.


# Buttered Courgettes (Zucchini)

**METRIC/IMPERIAL**
225 g/8 oz courgettes
salt
25 g/1 oz watercress or lettuce,
    shredded
25 g/1 oz butter
freshly ground pepper
freshly grated nutmeg

**AMERICAN**
½ lb zucchini
salt
1 cup shredded watercress or
    lettuce
2 tablespoons butter
freshly ground pepper
freshly grated nutmeg

Wash and trim but do not peel the courgettes (zucchini). Grate the courgettes (zucchini). Toss with a little salt and leave for 30 minutes in a colander or sieve to drain, then rinse under cold water. Fold the watercress or lettuce through the courgettes (zucchini).

Melt the butter in a pan and, when it is foaming, put in the vegetables and toss with two forks over a medium heat. When very hot, season with salt, pepper and nutmeg to taste. Serve immediately.

VARIATION:
If preferred, the courgettes (zucchini) can be cut into wafer thin diagonal slices.

# Spinach Gratin

METRIC/IMPERIAL
3 tablespoons olive oil
750 g/1½ lb chopped spinach
2 cloves garlic, peeled and bruised
salt
freshly ground pepper
1 egg, beaten
25 g/1 oz fresh breadcrumbs
50 g/2 oz Gruyère cheese, grated

AMERICAN
3 tablespoons olive oil
1½ lb chopped spinach
2 cloves garlic, peeled and bruised
salt
freshly ground pepper
1 egg, beaten
½ cup soft bread crumbs
½ cup grated Swiss cheese

Heat 2 tablespoons of the oil in a large heavy pan. Add the washed spinach, garlic and a little salt and pepper. Cook uncovered over brisk heat for 6 to 10 minutes, stirring occasionally, until all the water from the spinach has evaporated. Discard garlic and leave spinach to cool slightly.

Stir in the beaten egg over gentle heat, adding a little more salt and pepper. Spread in an oiled gratin dish and level surface. Mix together breadcrumbs and cheese and sprinkle over the top. Sprinkle with remaining oil, then place under preheated grill (broiler) for 5 minutes or until the topping is golden and bubbling. Serve immediately.

# Oriental Spinach

METRIC/IMPERIAL
225 g/8 oz spinach
2 tablespoons peanut oil
2 spring onions, chopped
1 slice fresh root ginger, finely
  chopped
1 clove garlic, crushed
½ teaspoon salt
1 tablespoon soy sauce
½ teaspoon sugar
1 tablespoon dry sherry .
1 tablespoon sesame seed or
  sunflower oil

AMERICAN
½ lb spinach
2 tablespoons peanut oil
2 scallions, chopped
1 slice fresh ginger root, finely
  chopped
1 clove garlic, crushed
½ teaspoon salt
1 tablespoon soy sauce
½ teaspoon sugar
1 tablespoon pale dry sherry
1 tablespoon sesame seed or
  sunflower oil

Discard any tough white stalks from the spinach, wash thoroughly, and tear into small pieces. Place in a tea (dish) towel and wring out any excess moisture.

Heat the peanut oil in a wok or heavy-based frying pan (skillet) and fry the spring onions (scallions), ginger and garlic for 2 minutes, stirring constantly. Add the spinach and cook for 2 minutes, stirring. Add the remaining ingredients and stir until everything is well blended. Serve at once.

# Asparagus Parmesan

METRIC/IMPERIAL
50 g/2 oz butter, melted
1 x 450 g/15 oz can asparagus
  spears, drained
25 g/1 oz Parmesan cheese, grated
50 g/2 oz Cheddar cheese, grated
salt and freshly ground pepper
25 g/1 oz fresh breadcrumbs

AMERICAN
¼ cup melted butter
1 x 16 oz can asparagus spears,
  drained
¼ cup grated Parmesan cheese
½ cup grated Cheddar cheese
salt and freshly ground pepper
½ cup soft bread crumbs

Pour half the melted butter into a small shallow ovenproof casserole dish.
Arrange the asparagus in the dish and top with the cheeses, adding salt
and pepper to taste. Top with the breadcrumbs and spoon over the
remaining butter.

Cook in a preheated moderate oven (180°C/350°F, Gas Mark 4) for
20 minutes, until piping hot.

# Mixed Vegetable Casserole

METRIC/IMPERIAL
1 kg/2 lb fresh mixed vegetables
  (e.g. carrots, broad and green
  beans)
2 tablespoons oil or butter
6 small pickling onions, peeled
2 tomatoes, skinned and chopped
1 green or red pepper, seeded and
  thinly sliced
about 200 ml/⅓ pint vegetable
  stock
salt
freshly ground pepper
1 tablespoon white wine or cider
  vinegar
3 tablespoons single cream
  (optional)
grated cheese, to serve

AMERICAN
2 lb fresh mixed vegetables (e.g.
  carrots, lima and snap beans)
2 tablespoons oil or butter
6 pearl onions, peeled
2 tomatoes, peeled and chopped
1 green or red pepper, seeded and
  thinly sliced
about 1 cup vegetable stock
salt
freshly ground pepper
1 tablespoon white wine or cider
  vinegar
3 tablespoons light cream
  (optional)
grated cheese, to serve

Prepare the vegetables (peel, top and tail, etc) but leave whole. Melt the oil
or butter in a heavy-based pan, add the onions and fry gently for a few
minutes. Add the vegetables and enough stock just to cover. Add salt and
pepper and bring to the boil. Lower the heat, cover tightly and simmer for
20 minutes. Stir in the wine or vinegar and cream, if using, and cook until
heated through, but do not allow to boil. Serve from the casserole with
grated cheese.

# Broccoli in Wine Sauce

METRIC/IMPERIAL
*300 g/12 oz broccoli*
*2 tablespoons olive oil*
*1 clove garlic, crushed*
*salt and freshly ground pepper*
*175 ml/6 fl oz dry white wine*

AMERICAN
*¾ lb broccoli*
*2 tablespoons olive oil*
*1 clove garlic, crushed*
*salt and freshly ground pepper*
*¾ cup dry white wine*

Remove any tough or wilted leaves and woody ends from the broccoli if necessary. Cut the tender stems into thin slices and separate the heads into florets. Wash and drain.

Heat the oil in a heavy-based pan and sauté the garlic until soft but not brown. Add the broccoli stems and florets, and toss in the hot oil until well coated. Season with salt and pepper to taste, add the wine, and tightly cover the pan. Cook over a low heat for 15 minutes, or until the broccoli is tender, shaking the pan occasionally. Serve with the pan juices.

# Indian Cauliflower

METRIC/IMPERIAL
*1 onion, peeled and quartered*
*2 garlic cloves, peeled*
*1 cm/½ inch piece root ginger*
*4 tablespoons water*
*4 tablespoons oil*
*¼ teaspoon ground turmeric*
*2 tomatoes, skinned and chopped*
*1 teaspoon coriander seeds,*
*    ground*
*1 teaspoon ground cumin*
*¼ teaspoon ground cinnamon*
*2 teaspoons salt*
*freshly ground pepper*
*2 tablespoons lemon juice*
*1 medium cauliflower, washed and*
*    divided into florets*
*plain yogurt, to serve*

AMERICAN
*1 onion, peeled and quartered*
*2 garlic cloves, peeled*
*½ inch piece ginger root*
*¼ cup water*
*¼ cup oil*
*¼ teaspoon ground turmeric*
*2 tomatoes, peeled and chopped*
*1 teaspoon coriander seeds,*
*    ground*
*1 teaspoon ground cumin*
*¼ teaspoon ground cinnamon*
*2 teaspoons salt*
*freshly ground pepper* .
*2 tablespoons lemon juice*
*1 medium cauliflower, washed and*
*    divided into florets*
*plain yogurt, to serve*

Put the onion, garlic, ginger and water in an electric blender and process until smooth. Heat the oil in a shallow pan, add the contents of the blender and all the other ingredients except the cauliflower and yogurt. Cook gently for 5 minutes, adding a little water if the mixture becomes too thick and begins to stick to the bottom of the pan.

Add the cauliflower and stir well, turning the florets until coated with the sauce. Cover and cook gently for 15 to 20 minutes until the florets are just tender. Serve hot with a side dish of yogurt.

# Glazed Carrots

METRIC/IMPERIAL
*225 g/8 oz carrots*
*175 ml/6 fl oz boiling chicken stock*
*25 g/1 oz butter*
*1½ tablespoons sugar*
*salt and freshly ground pepper*
*chopped mint or parsley to garnish*

AMERICAN
*½ lb carrots*
*¾ cup boiling chicken stock or broth*
*2 tablespoons butter*
*1½ tablespoons sugar*
*salt and freshly ground pepper*
*chopped mint or parsley for garnish*

Cut the carrots into rounds or fingers, or leave them whole if tiny. Place the carrots in a pan with the stock, butter and sugar, cover and simmer gently for 20 minutes. Remove the lid and continue cooking over a high heat until the liquid is thick and syrupy. Stir carefully from time to time to stop the carrots sticking to the pan.

When the carrots are bright and glistening and the liquid has almost evaporated, add salt and pepper to taste, pile into a hot serving dish and garnish with mint or parsley.

VARIATION:
**Vichy Carrots** – cook carrots in the same way, using water instead of stock, for 12 to 20 minutes (this will vary according to the age of the carrots).

Remove the lid, raise the heat and boil rapidly until nearly all the liquid has evaporated. Stir in 1 tablespoon of chopped parsley and 1 tablespoon of double (heavy) cream, turn until heated through, then serve.

# Vermouth Carrots with Grapes

METRIC/IMPERIAL
*225 g/8 oz young carrots*
*25 g/1 oz butter*
*1 teaspoon sugar*
*1 tablespoon dry vermouth*
*2 tablespoons water*
*salt and freshly ground pepper*
*50 g/2 oz black grapes, seeded*

AMERICAN
*½ lb young carrots*
*2 tablespoons butter*
*1 teaspoon sugar*
*1 tablespoon dry vermouth*
*2 tablespoons water*
*salt and freshly ground pepper*
*½ cup purple grapes, seeded*

Cut the carrots into diagonal slices. Heat the butter in a heavy frying pan (skillet) and stir in the carrots until well coated, then sprinkle with sugar. Cook for 1 minute without stirring.

Add the vermouth and water and cook the carrots until almost tender, stirring all the time. Add salt and pepper to taste and lightly stir in the grapes. Cook for a further 20 seconds. Serve with grilled or poached white fish.

# Austrian Red Cabbage

METRIC/IMPERIAL
*500 g/1 lb red cabbage, washed,*
*trimmed and finely sliced*
*1 medium onion, peeled and thinly*
*sliced*
*1 medium cooking apple, peeled,*
*cored and chopped*
*2 teaspoons sugar*
*2 cloves*
*salt*
*freshly ground pepper*
*3 tablespoons chicken stock*
*1½ tablespoons wine or cider*
*vinegar*
*chopped parsley, to garnish*

AMERICAN
*1 lb red cabbage, washed, trimmed*
*and finely sliced*
*1 medium onion, peeled and thinly*
*sliced*
*1 medium tart apple, peeled, cored*
*and chopped*
*2 teaspoons sugar*
*2 whole cloves*
*salt*
*freshly ground pepper*
*3 tablespoons chicken stock*
*1½ tablespoons wine or cider*
*vinegar*
*chopped parsley, for garnish*

Put the cabbage, onion and apple in a non-metal ovenproof casserole. Add the sugar, cloves, salt and pepper to taste, chicken stock and vinegar and mix well. Cover with a lid or buttered aluminium foil and bake in a moderate oven (180°C/350°F, Gas Mark 4) for 45 minutes to 1 hour or until the cabbage is very tender. Serve immediately, or leave to cool, then chill before serving, garnished with parsley.

# Bubble and Squeak

METRIC/IMPERIAL
*50 g/2 oz butter, oil or beef or*
*bacon dripping*
*1 small onion, finely chopped*
*100 g/4 oz shredded cabbage,*
*cooked*
*leftover potatoes*
*leftover roast meat, finely chopped*
*salt and freshly ground pepper*

AMERICAN
*¼ cup butter, oil or beef or bacon*
*dripping*
*1 small onion, finely chopped*
*1 cup shredded cabbage, cooked*
*leftover potatoes*
*leftover roast meat, finely chopped*
*salt and freshly ground pepper*

Heat the butter, oil or dripping in a large heavy frying pan (skillet). Fry the onion over medium heat until golden brown, then add the remaining ingredients (chop or slice the potatoes if not mashed or creamed). Stir well.

Cook, without stirring, until a brown crust forms on the bottom. Turn the bubble and squeak over with a spatula (it will be easier to do if you cut it in half or quarters first) and cook the other side until crisp and brown. Serve very hot.

VARIATION:
Omit the meat and serve the Bubble and Squeak simply as a vegetable or with cooked bacon as a main course.

# Cabbage Surprise

METRIC/IMPERIAL
50 g/2 oz streaky bacon, derinded
   and finely chopped
2 tablespoons red wine vinegar
350 g/12 oz white cabbage, cored
   and shredded
salt
freshly ground pepper

AMERICAN
¼ cup finely chopped fatty bacon
2 tablespoons red wine vinegar
¾ lb white cabbage, cored and
   shredded
salt
freshly ground pepper

Put the bacon in heavy-based pan and cook until the fat runs. Add the
wine vinegar, cabbage and salt and pepper to taste and fry over a high
heat for 3 to 4 minutes, turning mixture frequently. Serve immediately.


# Cabbage with Soured Cream and Paprika

METRIC/IMPERIAL
350 g/12 oz white cabbage
50 g/2 oz butter
1 small onion, chopped
1½ teaspoons paprika
salt and freshly ground pepper
120 ml/4 fl oz soured cream

AMERICAN
about ¾ lb white cabbage
¼ cup butter
1 small onion, chopped
1½ teaspoons paprika
salt and freshly ground pepper
½ cup soured cream

Remove any coarse outer leaves from the cabbage. Cut into quarters,
discard the tough stalk, and shred the cabbage finely. Wash under cold
running water, and drain.
   Heat the butter in a flameproof casserole or pan and gently fry the onion
until soft. Stir in the cabbage and continue cooking and stirring over a low
heat for about 2 minutes until the cabbage is beginning to soften. Stir in the
paprika and salt and pepper to taste. Mix well together, cover with a lid,
and cook over a low heat for 8 to 10 minutes, or until the cabbage is
cooked. Stir in the cream and heat through without boiling.

VARIATION:
**Rich Creamy Cabbage** – cook the cabbage in butter until almost tender,
then remove from heat and beat in salt and pepper to taste, ½ teaspoon
cumin powder and 1 egg. Turn cabbage until coated, sprinkle with
chopped chives and serve.

# Vegetable Ribbon Medley

| METRIC/IMPERIAL | AMERICAN |
|---|---|
| 1 carrot | 1 carrot |
| 1 courgette | 1 zucchini |
| ½ white turnip | ½ white turnip |
| 1 small parsnip | 1 small parsnip |
| 50 g/2 oz butter | ¼ cup butter |
| ½ teaspoon sugar | ½ teaspoon sugar |
| 1 tablespoon water | 1 tablespoon water |
| salt and freshly ground pepper | salt and freshly ground pepper |
| 1 tablespoon chopped parsley, mint or thyme, to garnish | 1 tablespoon chopped parsley, mint or thyme for garnish |

Chill the washed vegetables and cut lengthwise into thin ribbons with a vegetable peeler with a swivel blade.

Melt the butter in a heavy pan and add the sugar. While the butter is still foaming, add the vegetable ribbons and toss gently until coated. Add the water, place a piece of greaseproof (waxed) paper or foil over the pan and cover tightly with a lid.

Cook the vegetables over a high heat for 2 minutes, then turn the heat to low and cook a few minutes more, shaking the pan frequently, until the ribbons are tender-crisp. Season with salt and pepper to taste and sprinkle with herbs. Serve immediately.

# Chicory (Belgian Endive) with Lemon

| METRIC/IMPERIAL | AMERICAN |
|---|---|
| 500 g/1 lb chicory (4 small heads) | 1 lb Belgian endive (4 small heads) |
| 75 g/3 oz butter | ⅓ cup butter |
| 1 tablespoon sugar | 1 tablespoon sugar |
| salt | salt |
| freshly ground pepper or coriander | freshly ground pepper or coriander |
| juice of 1 lemon (3 tablespoons) | juice of 1 lemon (3 tablespoons) |

Cut off any damaged outer leaves from chicory (endive). Slit one side of each head with stainless steel knife. Wash thoroughly, drain upside down in a colander, then dry with absorbent paper towels.

Heat half the butter in a shallow ovenproof casserole until frothy, remove from heat and add chicory heads in a single layer. Add sugar, salt, pepper or coriander and lemon juice. Cover with sheet of buttered greaseproof (waxed) paper and cook in a preheated moderate oven (180°C/350°F, Gas Mark 4) for 30 minutes or until the chicory is tender. Melt the remaining butter and when quite hot but not browned, pour over the chicory. Serve immediately.

# Chicory (Endive) au Gratin

METRIC/IMPERIAL
2 heads chicory
2 teaspoons lemon juice
salt and freshly ground white
  pepper
25 g/1 oz butter
1 tablespoon plain flour
120 ml/4 fl oz milk
freshly grated nutmeg
2 slices cooked ham
3 tablespoons grated cheese
2 tablespoons fresh breadcrumbs

AMERICAN
2 heads Belgian endive
2 teaspoons lemon juice
salt and freshly ground white
  pepper
2 tablespoons butter
1 tablespoon all-purpose flour
½ cup milk
freshly grated nutmeg
2 slices cooked ham
3 tablespoons grated cheese
2 tablespoons soft bread crumbs

Remove any damaged leaves from the chicory (endive), trim the bases
and cut out the bottom of the cores with a pointed knife. Cover with cold
water in a pan. Add the lemon juice and a little salt, and bring to the boil.
Cook for 5 minutes, then drain.

Melt half the butter in a small pan, stir in the flour and cook for 1 minute.
Gradually add the milk, nutmeg, salt and pepper to taste and cook, stirring,
until thick.

Roll each head of chicory (endive) in a slice of ham and arrange in a
buttered shallow ovenproof dish. Pour the sauce over and sprinkle with the
cheese.

Melt the remaining butter in a pan, add breadcrumbs and toss, then
scatter over the dish. Cook in a preheated moderate oven (180°C/350°F,
Gas Mark 4) for 20 to 30 minutes, until the chicory (endive) is tender and
the top is golden.


# Broccoli with Lemon Butter

METRIC/IMPERIAL
350 g/12 oz broccoli spears
40 g/1½ oz butter
1 tablespoon lemon juice
salt and freshly ground pepper
2 tablespoons grated Parmesan
  cheese

AMERICAN
¾ lb broccoli spears
3 tablespoons butter
1 tablespoon lemon juice
salt and freshly ground pepper
2 tablespoons grated Parmesan
  cheese

Trim any tough ends from the broccoli stalks and discard coarse leaves.
Place the broccoli in a wide pan and cover with boiling salted water. Cook
for about 10 to 12 minutes until just tender.

Drain the broccoli, and place in a heated flameproof serving dish. Heat
the butter in a small pan, stir in the lemon juice and salt and pepper to
taste, and pour over the broccoli. Sprinkle with the cheese and cook under
a preheated grill (broiler) for 1 to 2 minutes.

# Stuffed Peppers

METRIC/IMPERIAL
*2 green peppers*
*2 tomatoes, skinned and chopped*
*50 g/2 oz fresh breadcrumbs*
*½ dessert apple, cored and*
  *chopped*
*50 g/2 oz Edam cheese, finely*
  *grated*
*40 g/1½ oz garlic sausage, finely*
  *chopped*
*½ teaspoon French mustard*
*salt and freshly ground pepper*

AMERICAN
*2 green peppers*
*2 tomatoes, peeled and chopped*
*1 cup soft bread crumbs*
*½ apple, cored and chopped*
*½ cup finely grated Edam cheese*
*⅓ cup finely chopped garlic*
  *sausage*
*½ teaspoon Dijon-style mustard*
*salt and freshly ground pepper*

Cut the tops off the peppers and reserve; discard the seeds and cores. Blanch in boiling salted water for 4 minutes, then drain.

Place the tomatoes in a bowl with the breadcrumbs, apple, cheese, garlic sausage, mustard and salt and pepper to taste. Mix well and spoon the mixture into the peppers. Replace the lids and place in a greased small, shallow ovenproof dish. Cook in a preheated moderately hot oven (190°C/375°F, Gas Mark 5) for 20 minutes. Serve hot as a starter or with cold meats and salad.

VARIATIONS:
Here are some other ideas for stuffings for peppers. Add salt and pepper to taste to all the stuffings.
**Red Peppers** – 100 g/4 oz leftover cooked chicken; 50 g/2 oz sweetcorn kernels and 50 g/2 oz cooked long grain rice.
**Red Peppers** – 100 g/4 oz chopped salami; 50 g/2 oz wholewheat breadcrumbs and 50 g/2 oz cooked minted peas.
**Green Peppers** – 225 g/8 oz leftover boiled potato, diced; 2 tomatoes skinned and chopped; 4 spring onions (scallions), chopped and 50 g/2 oz strong cheese, grated.

DISHES

**Salads and Sauces**

FOR TWO

# *Cucumber and Yogurt Salad*

METRIC/IMPERIAL
½ cucumber, finely sliced
1 teaspoon sugar
1 teaspoon wine or cider vinegar
2 spring onions, chopped
½ teaspoon salt
freshly ground pepper
150 ml/¼ pint plain yogurt
¼ teaspoon cumin seeds, ground

AMERICAN
½ cucumber, finely sliced
1 teaspoon sugar
1 teaspoon wine or cider vinegar
2 scallions, chopped
½ teaspoon salt
freshly ground pepper
½ cup plain yogurt
¼ teaspoon cumin seeds, ground

Place the cucumber in a glass bowl with the sugar and vinegar. Turn the cucumber until coated, then leave, covered, for 10 minutes.

Rinse the cucumber slices under cold water, then drain. Place in a salad bowl with the spring onions (scallions). Mix together the salt, pepper to taste, yogurt and cumin, then pour over the cucumber. Mix gently then chill for 2 hours (or more) before serving.

VARIATIONS:
**Spiced Cucumber and Yogurt Salad** – add ½ teaspoon ground coriander seeds and a few drops Tabasco (hot pepper) sauce to the salad above. This mixture also makes a good dressing for tiny meatballs.
**Piquant Cucumber Salad** – mix 1 finely chopped small gherkin and 1 chopped pickled onion into the salad above.
**Balkan Salad** – use only half the amount of yogurt and mix it with 25 g/ 1 oz cream cheese, 1 crushed clove garlic and ½ green chilli, seeded and finely chopped. Place the sliced cucumber in a bowl and sprinkle with salt. Leave for 15 minutes to drain then rinse and drain again. Mix with the cream cheese dressing plus freshly ground white pepper to taste. Chill for 30 minutes before serving.

# Potato, Celery and Mushroom Salad

METRIC/IMPERIAL
500 g/1 lb waxy potatoes
salt
120 ml/4 fl oz double cream
1 tablespoon cider vinegar or
   lemon juice
freshly ground black pepper
4 sticks celery, trimmed and cut into
   1 cm/½ inch pieces
100 g/4 oz button mushrooms,
   sliced
1 small banana, peeled and
   chopped
2 tablespoons chopped parsley

AMERICAN
1 lb waxy potatoes
salt
½ cup heavy cream
1 tablespoon cider vinegar or
   lemon juice
freshly ground black pepper
4 stalks celery, trimmed and cut
   into ½ inch pieces
1 cup sliced button mushrooms
1 small banana, chopped
2 tablespoons chopped parsley

Cook the potatoes in their skins in boiling salted water for about
20 minutes until just tender. Drain, then peel while still hot. Slice thinly and
place in salad bowl.
   Whip the cream lightly until just fluffy, then whip in the vinegar or lemon
juice and generous salt and pepper. Add the celery, mushrooms, banana
and parsley to the potatoes and gently fold in the cream dressing. Serve
as soon as possible with wholemeal (wholewheat) bread.


# Herb and Bean Salad

METRIC/IMPERIAL
1 x 450 g/15 oz can red kidney
   beans
1 Spanish onion, chopped
1 carrot, grated
1 stick celery, chopped
salt and freshly ground pepper
1 clove garlic, crushed
3 tablespoons olive oil
1 tablespoon white wine vinegar
2 tablespoons chopped chervil
1 tablespoon chopped chives
1 teaspoon chopped lovage
1 teaspoon chopped summer
   savory

AMERICAN
1 x 16 oz can red kidney beans
1 Bermuda onion, chopped
1 carrot, grated
1 stalk celery, chopped
salt and freshly ground pepper
1 clove garlic, crushed
3 tablespoons olive oil
1 tablespoon white wine vinegar
2 tablespoons chopped chervil
1 tablespoon chopped chives
1 teaspoon chopped lovage
1 teaspoon chopped summer
   savory

Drain the beans, rinse and then place in a serving bowl with the remaining
ingredients. Serve the salad at room temperature.

# Curly Endive and Apple Salad

METRIC/IMPERIAL
*6 leaves curly endive*
*1 red dessert apple*
*lemon juice*
*2 celery sticks, chopped*
*Sour Cream Salad Dressing (see*
*    page 148)*
*walnut halves to garnish*

AMERICAN
*6 leaves curly endive*
*1 red-skinned apple*
*lemon juice*
*2 stalks celery chopped*
*Sour Cream Salad Dressing (see*
*    page 148)*
*walnut halves for garnish*

Wash and dry the curly endive and tear into pieces. Place in a salad bowl. Cut the apple into fine slices, discarding the core, and sprinkle with lemon juice. Add the apple to the bowl with the celery and the dressing and toss gently. Garnish with walnuts and serve.

# Spinach and Bacon Salad

METRIC/IMPERIAL
*100 g/4 oz fatty bacon, sliced*
*225 g/8 oz fresh spinach*
*1 tablespoon oil*
*15 g/½ oz butter*
*1 slice white bread, diced*

AMERICAN
*¼ lb sliced fatty bacon*
*½ lb fresh spinach*
*1 tablespoon oil*
*1 tablespoon butter*
*1 slice white bread, diced*

Finely chop the bacon and place in a heavy-based frying pan (skillet) over a low heat. Cook slowly until the fat begins to run and bacon pieces are crisp.

Meanwhile wash and drain the spinach, removing white stalks and tearing the green part into smallish pieces. Place in a serving bowl. Heat the oil and butter in another pan and when foam subsides, cook the bread, turning frequently, until crisp.

When the salad is ready to serve, add the croûtons to the spinach then pour on the hot bacon and fat. Quickly toss and serve.

VARIATIONS:
**Blue Cheese and Spinach Salad** – crumble in 50 g/2 oz blue cheese instead of adding croûtons to the above salad.
**Hot Orange and Spinach Salad** – remove peel and pith from one juicy orange and chop the flesh into fine pieces. Mix in with the spinach and coarsely ground sea-salt, then pour in the hot bacon dressing.
**Cold Orange and Spinach Salad** – prepare the spinach, then shred and place in a salad bowl. Remove the peel and pith from a juicy orange and chop the flesh into fine pieces. Make a dressing by combining 2 teaspoons orange juice, 2 tablespoons olive oil, coarsely ground sea-salt and freshly ground pepper. Add more orange juice or seasoning to taste, then pour the dressing over salad and toss. Serve.

# Chicory Niçoise

METRIC/IMPERIAL
1 medium head of chicory
leftover boiled potatoes, chopped
2 tablespoons mayonnaise
1 x 99 g/3½ oz can tuna fish,
    drained
100 g/4 oz French beans, sliced
    and cooked
2 tomatoes, quartered
10 black olives
2 hard-boiled eggs, shelled and
    quartered
chopped parsley to garnish

AMERICAN
1 medium head of Belgian endive
leftover boiled potatoes, chopped
2 tablespoons mayonnaise
1 x 3½ oz can tuna fish, drained
¼ lb green beans, sliced and
    cooked
2 tomatoes, quartered
10 ripe olives
2 hard-cooked eggs, shelled and
    quartered
chopped parsley for garnish

Separate the chicory (endive) leaves and wash and dry. Arrange the chicory (endive) around the edge of a serving plate.

Mix the chopped potatoes and mayonnaise and place in the middle. Mix together the tuna, beans, tomatoes and olives and arrange around the potatoes. Garnish with egg quarters and chopped parsley and serve with Garlic Bread (see page 147).

# Sausage Salad

METRIC/IMPERIAL
225 g/8 oz sausages, cooked and
    sliced
3 spring onions, chopped
50 g/2 oz cooked peas
100 g/4 oz shredded cabbage
1 carrot, grated
juice of 1 lemon
1 orange, peeled and segmented
25 g/1 oz seedless raisins
4 tablespoons plain yogurt
salt and freshly ground pepper

AMERICAN
½ lb sausages, cooked and sliced
3 scallions, chopped
½ cup cooked peas
1 cup shredded cabbage
1 carrot, grated
juice of 1 lemon
1 orange, peeled and segmented
3 tablespoons seedless raisins
¼ cup plain yogurt
salt and freshly ground pepper

Place the sliced sausages in a bowl and add the spring onions (scallions) and peas. Mix the cabbage and carrot with the lemon juice and leave for 15 minutes, then add to the sausages. Add the orange and raisins, stir in the yogurt and mix well. Add salt and pepper to taste. Serve in warm pitta bread.

# Thai Hot-Cold Salad

METRIC/IMPERIAL
1 large navel orange
2 crisp lettuce leaves
1 tablespoon oil
1 clove garlic, crushed
350 g/12 oz cooked cold pork
   minced
1 tablespoon finely chopped
   peanuts
1 teaspoon sugar
1 tablespoon soy sauce
1 tablespoon water
salt
pinch of cayenne pepper
coriander sprigs to garnish

AMERICAN
1 large navel orange
2 crisp lettuce leaves
1 tablespoon oil
1 clove garlic, crushed
¾ lb ground cooked cold pork
1 tablespoon finely chopped
   peanuts
1 teaspoon sugar
1 tablespoon soy sauce
1 tablespoon water
salt
pinch of cayenne
coriander sprigs for garnish

Peel the orange, removing the pith and white membrane, and cut into thin slices. Line 2 plates with lettuce, arrange the orange slices on top and chill. Heat the oil in a frying pan (skillet) and fry the garlic until golden. Add the pork and stir until brown and cooked through – about 5 minutes. Add the peanuts, sugar, soy sauce, water, salt and cayenne to the pan and mix well. Pour the hot pork mixture over the oranges and garnish with coriander. Serve immediately.


# Warm Beetroot (Beet) Salad

METRIC/IMPERIAL
1 freshly cooked large beetroot,
   skinned
salt and freshly ground pepper
good pinch of ground allspice
1 tablespoon olive oil
1 teaspoon wine vinegar
1 tablespoon chopped parsley

AMERICAN
1 freshly cooked large beet, peeled
salt and freshly ground pepper
good pinch of ground allspice
1 tablespoon olive oil
1 teaspoon wine vinegar
1 tablespoon chopped parsley

Cut the beetroot into cubes while warm and sprinkle with salt, pepper and allspice to taste. Whisk the oil little by little into the vinegar; pour over the beetroot, add the parsley and toss gently. Serve immediately.

# Mixed French Salad

METRIC/IMPERIAL
3 leaves crisp lettuce
2 leaves curly endive
watercress sprigs (optional)
1 ripe tomato, quartered
2 radishes, thinly sliced
½ small cucumber, peeled and cut
  into chunks
French Dressing (see page 148)
finely chopped spring onion to
  garnish

AMERICAN
3 leaves Romaine or iceberg
  lettuce
2 leaves chicory
watercress sprigs (optional)
1 ripe tomato, quartered
2 radishes, thinly sliced
½ small cucumber, peeled and cut
  into chunks
Vinaigrette Dressing (see page 148)
finely chopped scallion for garnish

Wash and dry the salad greens. If the lettuce leaves are large, tear them into pieces with the fingers, do not slice. Combine all the ingredients in a salad bowl, toss with the dressing and sprinkle with spring onion (scallion).

# Turkish Barley Salad

METRIC/IMPERIAL
100 g/4 oz barley
salt and freshly ground pepper
2 tablespoons lemon juice
½ teaspoon salt
6 tablespoons olive oil
½ small cucumber, peeled, seeded
  and chopped
4 radishes, thinly sliced
2 spring onions, shredded into
  matchstick lengths
15 g/½ oz parsley, chopped
chopped fresh mint

AMERICAN
½ cup barley
salt and freshly ground pepper
2 tablespoons lemon juice
½ teaspoon salt
6 tablespoons olive oil
½ small cucumber, peeled, seeded
  and chopped
4 radishes, thinly sliced
2 scallions, shredded into
  matchstick lengths
¼ cup chopped parsley
chopped fresh mint

Cover the barley with cold water and bring to the boil. Remove from the heat, cover and leave to soak for 1 hour. Drain, cover again with salted cold water, bring to the boil and simmer for 1 to 1½ hours until tender.

Meanwhile make the dressing: put the lemon juice and salt in a bowl and gradually whisk in the oil. Drain the barley, and toss gently with the dressing. (This can be done several hours ahead of serving.)

Toss the barley with the chilled vegetables and herbs and season to taste. Serve with kebabs or spoon inside pitta bread.

# Beefsteak Tomatoes with Basil

METRIC/IMPERIAL
1 large ripe tomato
1 teaspoon wine vinegar
1 tablespoon olive oil
salt and freshly ground pepper
1 tablespoon chopped fresh basil

AMERICAN
1 large ripe beefsteak tomato
1 teaspoon wine vinegar
1 tablespoon olive oil
salt and freshly ground pepper
1 tablespoon chopped fresh basil

Cut the tomato into thin slices and arrange on a glass serving plate.
Combine the remaining ingredients in a screw-top jar. Pour the dressing
over the tomato slices just before serving.

# Chilled Beans and Tomatoes

METRIC/IMPERIAL
120 ml/4 fl oz olive oil
1 clove garlic, crushed
1 onion, finely chopped
2 ripe tomatoes, skinned and
 chopped
15 g/½ oz parsley, chopped
½ teaspoon sugar
350 g/12 oz butter beans, cooked
1 tablespoon wine vinegar
salt and freshly ground pepper
3 springs onions, finely chopped
 (including green tops)

AMERICAN
½ cup olive oil
1 clove garlic, crushed
1 onion, finely chopped
2 ripe tomatoes, peeled and
 chopped
¼ cup chopped parsley
½ teaspoon sugar
¾ lb baby lima beans, cooked
1 tablespoon wine vinegar
salt and freshly ground pepper
3 scallions, finely chopped
 (including green tops)

Heat half the oil in a pan and gently fry the garlic and onion until soft,
stirring often. Do not let them brown. Add the tomatoes, parsley and sugar
to the pan and continue cooking and stirring until the tomatoes are soft,
about 5 minutes.

Mix the beans with the tomato mixture, turn into a serving bowl, cool and
chill. Just before serving, whisk together the remaining oil and vinegar with
salt and pepper to taste and add to the beans. Sprinkle with the chopped
spring onions (scallions) and serve.

VARIATION:
**Tuscany Beans** – instead of the parsley add 2 sprigs sage. Heat the
beans with the tomato mixture and cook, uncovered, for 10 minutes.
Adjust seasoning and serve hot.

# Pineapple Salad

METRIC/IMPERIAL
225 g/8 oz cottage cheese
25 g/1 oz walnuts, chopped
25 g/1 oz sultanas
225 g/8 oz leftover chicken or lamb,
  cut into strips
salt and freshly ground pepper
iceberg lettuce leaves
2 slices pineapple
cucumber slices
parsley sprigs to garnish

AMERICAN
1 cup cottage cheese
¼ cup chopped walnuts
3 tablespoons seedless raisins
1 cup leftover chicken or lamb, cut
  into strips
salt and freshly ground pepper
iceberg lettuce leaves
2 slices pineapple
cucumber slices
parsley sprigs for garnish

Place the cottage cheese in a bowl and add the walnuts, sultanas (raisins) meat and salt and pepper to taste. Mix well.

Arrange the washed and drained lettuce leaves on two serving plates. Place a pineapple slice in the centre and spoon the cottage cheese mixture on top. Arrange the cucumber slices around the edge and garnish each dish with parsley sprigs. Serve with Hot Garlic Bread (see page 147).

# Salad Niçoise

METRIC/IMPERIAL
2 ripe tomatoes, skinned and
  quartered
1 green pepper, cored, seeded and
  sliced
1 large onion, thinly sliced
2 lettuce leaves, shredded
1 x 99 g/3½ oz can tuna in oil
1 small can anchovy fillets
French Dressing (see page 148)
100 g/4 oz green beans, cooked
8 black olives, stoned
2 hard-boiled eggs, quartered

AMERICAN
2 ripe tomatoes, peeled and
  quartered
1 green pepper, seeded and sliced
1 large onion, thinly sliced
2 lettuce leaves, shredded
1 x 3½ oz can tuna in oil
1 small can anchovy fillets
Vinaigrette Dressing (see page 148)
¼ lb green beans, cooked
8 ripe olives, pitted
2 hard-cooked eggs, quartered

Place the tomatoes and green pepper in a salad bowl. Separate the onion into rings. Wash and dry the lettuce. Drain and flake the tuna. Cut the anchovy fillets in half.

Add half the dressing to the salad bowl with the lettuce and beans. Toss until well coated. Arrange the tuna on top with the onion rings, olives, eggs and anchovy fillets, and sprinkle the remaining dressing over. Serve at room temperature (do not chill).

# Chicken and Fruit Salad

METRIC/IMPERIAL
½ honeydew melon
1 firm banana, sliced
50 g/2 oz seedless green grapes
25 g/1 oz stoned dates, chopped
50 g/2 oz walnuts, chopped
225 g/8 oz cooked chicken, cut into
  strips
2 tablespoons mayonnaise
2 tablespoons plain yogurt
salt and freshly ground pepper
crisp lettuce leaves, to serve
chopped parsley to garnish

AMERICAN
½ honeydew melon
1 firm banana, sliced
½ cup seedless white grapes
3 tablespoons pitted and chopped
  dates
½ cup chopped walnuts
½ lb cooked chicken, cut into strips
2 tablespoons mayonnaise
2 tablespoons plain yogurt
salt and freshly ground pepper
crisp lettuce leaves, to serve
chopped parsley for garnish

Remove the seeds from the melon. Scoop out the flesh and cut into dice. Place in a bowl with the banana, grapes, dates and walnuts.

Add the chicken to the fruit with the mayonnaise and yogurt. Mix well and add salt and pepper to taste. Spoon on to lettuce arranged on serving plates and garnish and serve at once.

# Chinese Spinach Salad

METRIC/IMPERIAL
350 g/12 oz spinach
salt
1 tablespoon sesame seed oil
1 teaspoon sugar
1 tablespoon red wine vinegar
2 tablespoon soy sauce
1 teaspoon made mustard

AMERICAN
¾ lb spinach
salt
1 tablespoon sesame seed oil
1 teaspoon sugar
1 tablespoon red wine vinegar
2 tablespoons soy sauce
1 teaspoon prepared mustard

Trim the spinach, leaving in central stalks, and wash thoroughly in cold water. Cook in a little boiling salted water until just tender. Drain well, then refresh under cold running water. Drain the spinach again, squeezing out all the water, then cut each leaf into 3 or 4 pieces and place in a salad bowl. Allow to cool.

Combine the sesame seed oil, sugar, vinegar, soy sauce and mustard in a screw-topped jar. Pour the dressing over the spinach and toss well. Chill before serving.

# Herby Egg Salad

| METRIC/IMPERIAL | AMERICAN |
|---|---|
| 4 hard-boiled eggs | 4 hard-cooked eggs |
| heart of 1 Cos lettuce | heart of 1 Romaine lettuce |
| 2 tablespoons toasted sesame | 2 tablespoons toasted sesame |
| seeds | seeds |
| 1 tablespoon chopped dill weed | 1 tablespoon chopped dill weed |
| 1 tablespoon chopped chervil or | 1 tablespoon chopped chervil or |
| parsley | parsley |
| 120 ml/4 fl oz single cream | ½ cup light cream |
| 2 tablespoons lemon juice | 2 tablespoons lemon juice |
| salt and freshly ground pepper | salt and freshly ground pepper |

Shell the eggs when cold. Wash and dry the lettuce, and cut it in strips. Lay the shredded lettuce on a flat dish with the eggs on top.

Stir the sesame seeds and herbs into the cream; add the lemon juice and a little salt and black pepper to taste. Spoon the sauce over the eggs and serve with hot buttered toast.


# Frankfurter Salad

| METRIC/IMPERIAL | AMERICAN |
|---|---|
| 100 g/4 oz long-grain rice, cooked | ½ cup long-grain rice, cooked |
| 3 tablespoons canned sweetcorn | 3 tablespoons canned whole kernel |
| 25 g/1 oz unsalted peanuts | corn |
| 4 canned frankfurters | 2 tablespoons unsalted peanuts |
| 1 dessert apple, cored and | 4 canned frankfurters |
| chopped | 1 dessert apple, cored and |
| lemon juice | chopped |
| 3 tablespoons French dressing | lemon juice |
| (see page 148) | 3 tablespoons vinaigrette dressing |
| sea-salt and freshly ground pepper | (see page 148) |
|  | sea-salt and freshly ground pepper |

Place the rice in a bowl and add the corn and peanuts. Slice the frankfurters and add to the bowl. Mix the apple with some lemon juice and stir into the rice mixture with the French (vinaigrette) dressing. Mix well and add salt and pepper to taste.

Serve in shallow individual dishes with wholewheat rolls and butter.

# Rice with Chick Peas

METRIC/IMPERIAL
1 x 200 g/7 oz can chick peas,
    drained
150 g/5 oz long-grain rice, freshly
    cooked
100 g/4 oz Spanish onion, finely
    chopped
salt and pepper
3 tablespoons olive oil
3 tablespoons lemon juice
2 tablespoons chopped chervil

AMERICAN
1 x 8 oz can chick peas
    (garbanzos), drained
¾ cup long-grain rice, freshly
    cooked
1 cup chopped Bermuda onion
salt and pepper
3 tablespoons olive oil
3 tablespoons lemon juice
2 tablespoons chopped chervil

Place the chick peas in serving bowl with the still-hot, cooked rice. Stir in the finely sliced onion with salt and black pepper to taste. Stir in the olive oil, lemon juice and the chopped chervil. Leave to cool completely before serving at room temperature (do not chill).

# Cauliflower and Seafood Salad

METRIC/IMPERIAL
225 g/8 oz cauliflower, broken into
    florets
salt and freshly ground pepper
1 x 90 g/3½ oz can crabmeat,
    salmon or tuna
100 g/4 oz cooked peeled prawns,
    scallops or firm white fish chunks
    (or a combination)
2 spring onions, finely chopped
1 teaspoon chopped fresh or
    ¼ teaspoon dried tarragon
120 ml/4 fl oz mayonnaise
1 tablespoon vinegar
lettuce leaves
chopped parsley
4 tiny tomatoes, halved

AMERICAN
½ lb cauliflower, broken into florets
salt and freshly ground pepper
1 x 3½ oz can crabmeat, salmon or
    tuna
¼ lb cooked shelled shrimp,
    scallops or firm white fish chunks
    (or a combination)
2 scallions, finely chopped
1 teaspoon chopped fresh or
    ¼ teaspoon dried tarragon
½ cup mayonnaise
1 tablespoon vinegar
lettuce leaves
chopped parsley
4 cherry tomatoes, halved

Drop the cauliflower florets into boiling salted water and cook for 2 minutes. Drain, cool under running water, and drain again. Place in a large bowl.

Drain the canned fish, remove any bones and break into lumps. Add to the cauliflower with the other seafood, onions, herbs, salt and pepper to taste, mayonnaise and vinegar. Fold lightly together.

Serve on a bed of lettuce, sprinkled with parsley and garnished with tomatoes.

# Mussel and Potato Salad

METRIC/IMPERIAL
1½ litres/2¾ pints fresh mussels
1 onion, peeled and chopped
1 bouquet garni
150 ml/¼ pint water
350 g/12 oz waxy potatoes
120 ml/4 fl oz dry white wine
juice of ½ lemon
4 tablespoons single cream
salt
2 tablespoons olive oil
few chives, snipped
2 chervil sprigs, chopped
2 gherkins, thinly sliced
freshly ground pepper

AMERICAN
3¼ pints/6½ cups fresh mussels
1 onion, peeled and chopped
1 bouquet garni
⅔ cup water
¾ lb waxy potatoes
½ cup dry white wine
juice of ½ lemon
4 tablespoons light cream
salt
2 tablespoons olive oil
few chives, snipped
2 chervil sprigs, chopped
2 small sweet dill pickles, thinly
    sliced
freshly ground pepper

Scrub the mussel shells clean and discard any that are open or will not close when tapped. Put mussels in large pan with onion, bouquet garni and water. Cover and cook over high heat for 5 to 7 minutes, shaking the pan from time to time, until the shells open. Discard any closed mussels. Remove mussels from shells and reserve.

Cook the potatoes in their skins in boiling salted water until tender (about 20 minutes). Peel off skins while still hot, cut into 1 cm/½ inch thick slices. Place in a bowl, sprinkle with wine.

In another bowl mix lemon juice, cream and salt to taste. Gradually stir in the oil, a little at a time. When absorbed, add the herbs, gherkins (dill pickles) and pepper to taste.

Divide potatoes between two serving bowls. Top with mussels, then the sauce. Serve immediately with Hot Garlic Bread (see page 147).

# Smoked Mackerel, Potato and Egg Salad

| METRIC/IMPERIAL | AMERICAN |
|---|---|
| *500 g/1 lb waxy potatoes* | *1 lb waxy potatoes* |
| *salt* | *salt* |
| *2 hard-boiled eggs, thinly sliced* | *2 hard-cooked eggs, thinly sliced* |
| *1 onion, peeled and very thinly sliced* | *1 onion, peeled and very thinly sliced* |
| *1 shallot, peeled and very thinly sliced* | *1 shallot, peeled and very thinly sliced* |
| *few sprigs each parsley, tarragon and chervil* | *few sprigs each parsley, tarragon and chervil* |
| *freshly ground pepper* | *freshly ground pepper* |
| *1 smoked mackerel fillet* | *1 smoked mackerel fillet* |
| *3 tablespoons oil* | *3 tablespoons oil* |
| *1½ tablespoons vinegar* | *1½ tablespoons vinegar* |
| *1 tablespoon single cream* | *1 tablespoon light cream* |

Cook the potatoes in their skins in boiling salted water for about 20 minutes, until just tender. Drain and peel while hot and slice thinly. Place in salad bowl with the eggs, onion, shallot, herbs and salt and pepper to taste. Flake the mackerel into bite-size pieces, discarding skin and any bones, and add to the bowl. Mix the oil, vinegar and cream together with a fork, pour over the mixture in the bowl and fold in gently, taking care not to break the potatoes and eggs. Serve immediately

VARIATION:
**Smoked Fish and Potato Salad** – place 500 g/1 lb freshly cooked new potatoes in a salad bowl. Place 100 g/4 oz of smoked fish with a large chopped onion in just enough water to cover and bring almost to boiling point. Drain and flake the fish, discarding skin and bones. Add to the potatoes with the onion.

Blend 2 tablespoons of plain yogurt with 1 tablespoon of capers and 1 tablespoon of grated horseradish, and toss lightly with the potatoes and fish. Season well with pepper and sprinkle with chopped parsley. Serve warm.

# Crunchy Edam Salad

METRIC/IMPERIAL
few lettuce leaves
175 g/6 oz Edam cheese, cubed
1 dessert apple, cored and diced
1 small red pepper, cored, seeded
  and chopped
1 stick celery, chopped
2 bananas, sliced
lemon juice
salt and freshly ground pepper
chopped parsley to garnish
Croûtons (see page 147)
French dressing (see page 148)

AMERICAN
few lettuce leaves
1 cup diced Edam cheese
1 apple, cored and diced
1 small red pepper, seeded and
  chopped
1 stalk celery, chopped
2 bananas, sliced
lemon juice
salt and freshly ground pepper
chopped parsley for garnish
Croûtons (see page 147)
vinaigrette dressing (see page 148)

Arrange the lettuce leaves on a serving dish. Place the cheese in a bowl with the apple, red pepper and celery. Dip the banana slices in lemon juice and add to the other ingredients. Mix well and add salt and pepper to taste.

Spoon on to the lettuce and garnish with parsley and Croûtons. Serve with French (vinaigrette) dressing.

# Fresh Tomato Juice

METRIC/IMPERIAL
12 medium ripe tomatoes
120 ml/4 fl oz water
1 medium onion, sliced
2 sticks celery (with leaves), sliced
1 bay leaf
3 sprigs parsley
1 teaspoon Worcestershire sauce
1 teaspoon sugar
salt and freshly ground pepper

AMERICAN
12 medium ripe tomatoes
½ cup water
1 medium onion, sliced
2 stalks celery (with leaves), sliced
1 bay leaf
3 sprigs parsley
1 teaspoon Worcestershire sauce
1 teaspoon sugar
salt and freshly ground pepper

Chop the tomatoes coarsely and bring to the boil with the water, onion, celery, bay leaf and parsley. Simmer for 15 minutes, then strain and add the remaining ingredients. Cool and chill before serving.

VARIATION:
Fresh tomato juice makes a delicious Bloody Mary! Mix 1 part vodka with 4 parts fresh tomato juice and crushed ice.

# Avocado and Corn Salad

METRIC/IMPERIAL
1 avocado
1 teaspoon orange juice
1 tablespoon mayonnaise
1 x 198 g/7 oz can sweetcorn,
    drained
25 g/1 oz blue cheese, crumbled
50 g/2 oz ham, finely chopped
sea-salt and freshly ground black
    pepper

AMERICAN
1 avocado
1 teaspoon orange juice
1 tablespoon mayonnaise
1 x 7 oz can whole kernel corn,
    drained
¼ cup crumbled blue cheese
½ cup finely chopped ham
sea-salt and freshly ground black
    pepper

Cut the avocado in half lengthwise, remove the stone (seed) and scoop out the flesh. Reserve the shells. Place the avocado flesh in a bowl with the orange juice and mayonnaise and mash together with a fork.

Stir in half the corn, the cheese and ham. Add salt and pepper to taste. Pile the mixture back into the avocado shells. Place on two serving dishes and arrange the remaining corn around the edge. Serve with thinly sliced wholemeal bread and butter.

# Fresh Tomato Sauce

METRIC/IMPERIAL
2 teaspoons olive oil
4 ripe tomatoes, skinned, seeded
    and roughly chopped
1 clove garlic, crushed
2 teaspoons tomato purée
1 tablespoon chopped fresh or
    ½ teaspoon dried herbs
    (parsley, basil or oregano)
150 ml/¼ pint chicken stock
salt and freshly ground pepper

AMERICAN
2 teaspoons olive oil
4 ripe tomatoes, peeled, seeded
    and roughly chopped
1 clove garlic, crushed
2 teaspoons tomato paste
1 tablespoon chopped fresh or
    ½ teaspoon dried herbs
    (parsley, basil or oregano)
⅔ cup chicken stock or broth
salt and freshly ground pepper

Heat the oil in a pan and cook the tomatoes and garlic for about 4 minutes until the tomatoes are soft. Add the tomato purée (paste), herbs and stock and bring to the boil and simmer for 5 minutes.

Add salt and pepper to taste, then rub the sauce through a sieve or purée in a blender. If the sauce is too thin, reduce by rapid boiling. Serve hot or cold.

# Cumberland-Style Sauce

METRIC/IMPERIAL
1 small onion, finely chopped
4 tablespoons boiling water
2 tablespoons fine-cut marmalade
2 tablespoons port
salt
pinch of cayenne pepper

AMERICAN
1 small onion, finely chopped
¼ cup boiling water
2 tablespoons fine-cut marmalade
2 tablespoons port
salt
pinch of cayenne

Cook the onion in the boiling water for 3 minutes, then stir in remaining ingredients, adding salt and pepper to taste. Stir over medium heat until blended. Cool the sauce and serve cold with ham or other cold meats, grilled (broiled) gammon ham steaks, roast venison or duck.

# Gooseberry Sauce

METRIC/IMPERIAL
100 g/4 oz gooseberries
1 tablespoon water
25 g/1 oz butter
sugar to taste

AMERICAN
¼ lb gooseberries
1 tablespoon water
2 tablespoons butter
sugar to taste

Top and tail the gooseberries. Place them in a small heavy pan with the water, cover and cook gently until soft. Remove the lid, beat the fruit with a wooden spoon until smooth and continue cooking over a very low heat to form a thick purée. Stir in the butter and sugar to taste.

Serve the sauce hot or cold with grilled (broiled) mackerel and other oily fish, and with pork chops.

# Baked Rhubarb

METRIC/IMPERIAL
500 g/1 lb rhubarb
grated rind and juice of 1 medium
    orange
50 g/2 oz sugar
½ teaspoon ground ginger

AMERICAN
1 lb rhubarb
grated rind and juice of 1 medium
    orange
¼ cup sugar
½ teaspoon ground ginger

Wash the rhubarb and cut into 5 cm/2 inch lengths. Place in a buttered baking dish with the remaining ingredients and cook in a preheated moderate oven (180°C/350°F, Gas Mark 4) for 20 minutes or until tender.

Baked Rhubarb is delicious with hot or cold pork.

# Apple Sauce

METRIC/IMPERIAL
*350 g/12 oz cooking apples*
*25 g/1 oz butter*
*sugar to taste*

AMERICAN
*¾ lb baking apples*
*2 tablespoons butter*
*sugar to taste*

Peel, core and slice the apples. Put into a small heavy pan with the butter; cover and cook gently until soft. Remove the lid, beat the apples with a wooden spoon until smooth and continue cooking over a very low heat until thickened. Add sugar to taste and beat until melted.

Serve the sauce hot or cold with roast duck, roast pork or pork sausages.

# Bercy Butter

METRIC/IMPERIAL
*2 teaspoons finely chopped spring onions*
*175 ml/6 fl oz dry white wine*
*50 g/2 oz butter, softened*
*2 teaspoons finely chopped parsley*
*salt and freshly ground pepper*

AMERICAN
*2 teaspoons finely chopped scallions*
*¾ cup dry white wine*
*¼ cup softened butter*
*2 teaspoons finely chopped parsley*
*salt and freshly ground pepper*

Place the spring onions (scallions) and wine in a small pan and boil until reduced to 1 tablespoon. Strain and cool, then blend into the softened butter with the remaining ingredients. Serve with grilled (broiled) meats.

# Parsley Butter

METRIC/IMPERIAL
*50 g/2 oz butter, softened*
*1 tablespoon finely chopped parsley*
*2 teaspoons lemon juice*
*salt and freshly ground pepper*

AMERICAN
*¼ cup softened butter*
*1 tablespoon finely chopped parsley*
*2 teaspoons lemon juice*
*salt and freshly ground pepper*

Mix all the ingredients together and mould into a roll. Wrap in foil and chill. Cut into slices and serve on grilled (broiled) meats, fish or vegetables.

# Garlic Butter

METRIC/IMPERIAL
*2 cloves garlic*
*50 g/2 oz butter, softened*
*2 teaspoons oil*
*salt and freshly ground pepper*

AMERICAN
*2 cloves garlic*
*¼ cup softened butter*
*2 teaspoons oil*
*salt and freshly ground pepper*

Simmer the peeled garlic in a little water for 5 minutes. Drain and crush.
    Mash the garlic with the butter, oil and salt and pepper to taste.
    Use for garlic bread, garlic croûtons, or as a flavouring for meats and vegetables.

### Croûtons
Allow 1 slice of bread per person, remove crusts and cut into 1 cm/½ inch dice. Sauté until crisp in a mixture of hot butter and oil.

### Garlic Croûtons
Heat the Garlic Butter (see recipe above) in a frying pan, add the diced bread and fry until crisp all over.

### Croûtes
Cut bread into large round or square shapes. Brush both sides with oil or butter them. Cook on baking sheet in a preheated moderately hot oven (190°C/375°F, Gas Mark 5) for 20 minutes until crisp and golden.

### Garlic Bread
Use half a French loaf or a short Italian loaf. Cut into diagonal 2.5 cm/ 1 inch slices without cutting right the way through. Spread garlic butter in the cuts and on the top and ends of the loaf. Wrap well in foil and cook in a preheated moderately hot oven (190°C/375°F, Gas Mark 5) for 20 minutes.

### Herb Bread
Use half a French loaf or a short Italian loaf. Cut into diagonal 2.5 cm/ 1 inch slices without cutting right the way through. Make Parsley Butter (see opposite) and double the quantity of herbs or add an equal amount of chives or chervil. Spread into the cuts and on the top and ends of the loaf. Wrap well in foil and cook in a preheated moderately hot oven (190°C/375°F, Gas Mark 5) for 20 minutes.

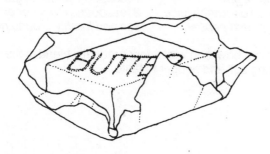

# Quick Tartare Sauce

METRIC/IMPERIAL
4 capers, drained and finely
   chopped
1 small gherkin, finely chopped
2 green olives, stoned and finely
   chopped
1 teaspoon chopped fresh herbs
   (parsley, chives, tarragon)
120 ml/4 oz mayonnaise

AMERICAN
4 capers, drained and finely
   chopped
1 small dill pickle, finely chopped
2 green olives, pitted and finely
   chopped
1 teaspoon chopped fresh herbs
   (parsley, chives, tarragon)
½ cup mayonnaise

Place all ingredients together in a bowl and stir well. Cover and leave to stand for 15 minutes at room temperature before serving.

# French (Vinaigrette) Dressing

METRIC/IMPERIAL
1 teaspoon French mustard
1 tablespoon cider, wine vinegar or
   lemon juice
3 tablespoons olive oil
sea-salt and freshly ground pepper
pinch of sugar

AMERICAN
1 teaspoon Dijon-style mustard
1 tablespoon cider, wine vinegar or
   lemon juice
3 tablespoons olive oil
sea-salt and freshly ground pepper
pinch of sugar

Place all the ingredients in a screw-topped jar and shake until thick and creamy. Taste and adjust seasoning.

# Sour Cream Salad Dressing

METRIC/IMPERIAL
4 tablespoons soured cream
½ teaspoon French mustard
1 teaspoon caster sugar
2 teaspoons lemon or orange juice
salt and freshly ground pepper

AMERICAN
¼ cup sour cream
½ teaspoon Dijon-style mustard
1 teaspoon caster sugar
2 teaspoons lemon or orange juice
salt and freshly ground pepper

Place the cream in a bowl and with a fork gradually blend in the remaining ingredients, adding salt and pepper to taste.

# Onion Sauce

| METRIC/IMPERIAL | AMERICAN |
|---|---|
| 1 large onion | 1 large onion |
| 15 g/½ oz butter | 1 tablespoon butter |
| 1 tablespoon plain flour | 1 tablespoon all-purpose flour |
| 120 ml/4 fl oz warm milk | ½ cup warm milk |
| salt and freshly ground pepper | salt and freshly ground pepper |
| freshly grated nutmeg | freshly grated nutmeg |

Chop the onion and simmer in salted water to cover until tender. Drain, reserving the liquid.

Melt the butter in a pan, remove from the heat and stir in the flour. Return to a low heat and stir for 1 minute. Blend in the milk and 2 tablespoons of the cooking liquid. Season with salt, pepper and nutmeg to taste. Stir until boiling and thickening, then add the onion. Serve with hot or cold meats, or vegetables.


# Horseradish Cream

| METRIC/IMPERIAL | AMERICAN |
|---|---|
| 1 tablespoon grated horseradish | 1 tablespoon grated horseradish |
| 4 tablespoons soured cream | ¼ cup sour cream |
| ½ teaspoon French mustard | ½ teaspoon Dijon-style mustard |
| ½ teaspoon caster sugar | ½ teaspoon sugar |
| salt and freshly ground pepper | salt and freshly ground pepper |

Mix all the ingredients together. Serve with roast and boiled beef, smoked trout, mackerel, eel, or as a dressing for jacket baked potatoes (see page 152).

DISHES

FOR TWO

Meatless
Dishes

# Three Bean Bake

| METRIC/IMPERIAL | AMERICAN |
|---|---|
| *50 g/2 oz dried chick peas* | *⅓ cup dried chick peas* |
| *50 g/2 oz dried butter beans* | *⅓ cup dried butter beans* |
| *50 g/2 oz dried red kidney beans* | *⅓ cup dried red kidney beans* |
| *1 clove garlic, crushed* | *1 clove garlic, crushed* |
| *1 onion, chopped* | *1 onion, chopped* |
| *1 x 396 g/14 oz can tomatoes* | *1 x 16 oz can tomatoes* |
| *1 green pepper, cored, seeded and* | *1 green pepper, seeded and* |
| *chopped* | *chopped* |
| *½ teaspoon ground ginger* | *½ teaspoon ground ginger* |
| *¼ teaspoon ground cloves* | *¼ teaspoon ground cloves* |
| *150 ml/¼ pint stock* | *⅔ cup stock* |
| *salt and freshly ground pepper* | *salt and freshly ground pepper* |
| *chopped parsley to garnish* | *chopped parsley for garnish* |

Place the chick peas, butter beans and kidney beans in a bowl and cover with cold water. Leave to soak overnight.

Drain the peas and beans, rinse, then place in a pan and cover with fresh cold water. Bring to the boil, boil for 10 minutes, then simmer for 40 to 45 minutes or until tender. Drain and rinse under cold water.

Return the beans to the pan and add the garlic, onion, tomatoes with their juice, green pepper, ginger, cloves, stock and salt and pepper to taste. Bring to the boil, cover and simmer for 1 hour, adding water if the mixture becomes too dry. Add salt and pepper to taste, then transfer to a warmed serving dish.

Garnish with parsley. Serve with cheese and crusty rolls.

# Corn and Bean Dinner

METRIC/IMPERIAL
1 x 198 g/7 oz can sweetcorn
  kernels, drained
225 g/8 oz cooked beans
1 x 227 g/8 oz can tomatoes
salt and freshly ground pepper
1 medium onion, finely chopped
1 teaspoon brown sugar
100 g/4 oz unsalted roasted
  peanuts, finely chopped
100 g/4 oz mature cheese, grated

AMERICAN
1 x 7 oz can whole kernel corn,
  drained
½ lb cooked beans
1 x 8 oz can tomatoes
salt and freshly ground pepper
1 medium-sized onion, finely
  chopped
1 teaspoon brown sugar
1 cup finely chopped unsalted
  roasted peanuts
1 cup grated sharp cheese

Mix together the corn, beans, tomatoes with their juice, salt and pepper to taste, onion, sugar and peanuts and spoon into a greased baking dish. Sprinkle with the cheese and cook in a preheated moderate oven (180°C/350°F, Gas Mark 4) for 30 minutes. Serve with thickly sliced wholewheat bread.


# Potatoes Garbo

METRIC/IMPERIAL
2 large potatoes
15 g/½ oz butter, melted
salt and freshly ground pepper
25 g/1 oz parsley or watercress,
  chopped

AMERICAN
2 large baking potatoes
1 tablespoon melted butter
salt and freshly ground pepper
1 cup chopped parsley or
  watercress

Scrub and dry the potatoes and bake in a preheated moderate oven (190°C/375°F, Gas Mark 5) for 50 minutes.

Cut each potato in half and scoop out the flesh, leaving a shell about 1 cm/½ inch thick. Brush the insides with melted butter and season with salt and pepper. Return the shells to the oven and cook for 10 minutes.

Serve the shells sprinkled liberally with chopped parsley or watercress.

VARIATION:
**Swiss-Style Potato Cake** – use the scooped-out flesh from Potatoes Garbo. Mash the potato with 1 small chopped onion and salt and pepper to taste. Heat a thin film of oil in a small frying pan (skillet) and add the potato, pressing it down into a firm cake. Cook over a medium heat until brown and crusty on the bottom, then turn and brown the other side. Serve topped with scrambled egg.

# Special Potato Bakes

METRIC/IMPERIAL
*2 large old potatoes*
*oil*
*salt*
*filling (see below)*

AMERICAN
*2 large potatoes*
*oil*
*salt*
*filling (see below)*

Scrub the potatoes well, dry, then prick all over with a fork. Rub each potato with cooking oil and salt. Place on a baking sheet or directly onto the oven shelf and cook in a preheated moderately hot oven (190°C/ 375°F, Gas Mark 5) for 50 minutes to 1 hour. While the potatoes are cooking, prepare one of the fillings below.

   When the potatoes are cooked, make a crosswise cut in each and push in the sides to open it up. Add the filling as directed. Serve with a green or mixed salad.

FILLINGS:
**Creamy Prawn** – mix together 50 g/2 oz (½ cup) cream cheese, 1 teaspoon onion flakes, salt and pepper to taste, 100 g/4 oz (⅔ cup) peeled prawns (shelled shrimp) and 1 tablespoon lemon juice. Spoon out some of the flesh from the cooked potato and stir it into the filling. Pile the filling back into the potatoes and return to the oven for 10 minutes. Serve immediately.

**Crispy Tuna** – mix a drained 99 g/3½ oz can tuna with 50 g/2 oz (½ cup) cottage cheese, ½ teaspoon ground mace, salt and pepper to taste and ½ green pepper, seeded and finely chopped. Stir in some of the cooked potato, then pile back into the potatoes and return to the oven for 10 minutes to heat through.

**Herby Mackerel** – remove the skin from 175 g/6 oz fillet of smoked mackerel and flake flesh into a bowl. Stir in 2 tablespoons soured cream, salt and pepper to taste and 1 tablespoon each of chopped parsley, chives and chervil (or tarragon). Pile the filling on to the cooked potatoes and serve immediately.

**Ratatouille** – make the vegetable mixture as for Spaghetti Provençale (see page 175). Pile the filling into cross-cuts on the potatoes, then serve sprinkled with grated Parmesan cheese.

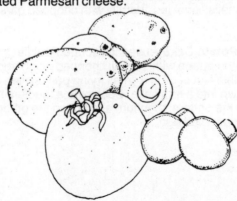

# Surprise Baked Potatoes

METRIC/IMPERIAL
*2 medium potatoes*
*4 tablespoons single cream, or*
  *50 g/2 oz butter*
*1 egg yolk*
*salt and freshly ground pepper*
*100 g/4 oz cooked green peas*
*1 tablespoon chopped chives*
*2 tablespoons grated cheese*

AMERICAN
*2 medium potatoes*
*¼ cup light cream, or ¼ cup butter*
*1 egg yolk*
*salt and freshly ground pepper*
*½ cup cooked, green peas*
*1 tablespoon chopped chives*
*2 tablespoons grated cheese*

Scrub and dry the potatoes and bake in a preheated moderately hot oven (190°C/375°F, Gas Mark 5) for 1 hour.

Cut a slice from the top of each potato, scoop out the flesh and mash. Stir in the cream or butter, egg yolk and salt and pepper to taste. Half fill each potato shell with the mixture. Mix the peas with the chives and divide equally between the potatoes. Pile the rest of the potato on top, sprinkle with cheese, and return to the oven for 12 minutes until heated through and browned on top.

# Broccoli Grill (Broil)

METRIC/IMPERIAL
*40 g/1½ oz butter*
*350 g/12 oz fresh or frozen broccoli*
*salt and freshly ground pepper*
*25 g/1 oz plain flour*
*300 ml/½ pint milk*
*75 g/3 oz mature cheese, grated*
*½ teaspoon made mustard*
*2 tomatoes, quartered*
*25 g/1 oz dry breadcrumbs*

AMERICAN
*3 tablespoons butter*
*¾ lb fresh or frozen broccoli*
*salt and freshly ground pepper*
*¼ cup all-purpose flour*
*1¼ cups milk*
*¾ cup grated sharp cheese*
*½ teaspoon prepared mustard*
*2 tomatoes, quartered*
*¼ cup dry bread crumbs*

Use 15 g/½ oz (1 tablespoon) of the butter to grease a shallow ovenproof dish. Cook the broccoli in boiling, salted water for 5 to 8 minutes. Drain and arrange in the dish.

To make the sauce, melt the remaining butter in a pan, stir in the flour and cook for 1 minute. Remove from the heat and gradually blend in the milk. Cook the sauce, stirring, until it thickens. Stir in the grated cheese, mustard and salt and pepper to taste.

Pour the sauce over the broccoli, arrange the tomatoes around the edge and sprinkle with breadcrumbs. Cook under a preheated moderate grill (broiler) for 10 minutes until the top is golden and bubbling. Serve with wholewheat bread.

# German Vegetable Platter

METRIC/IMPERIAL

| METRIC/IMPERIAL | AMERICAN |
|---|---|
| 100 g/4 oz green beans | ¼ lb green beans |
| 100 g/4 oz shelled peas | ¼ lb shelled peas |
| 175 g/6 oz cauliflower florets | 1 cup cauliflower florets |
| 8 small young carrots | 8 small young carrots |
| 40 g/1½ oz butter | 3 tablespoons butter |
| 50 g/2 oz mushrooms, sliced | ½ cup sliced mushrooms |
| 1 tablespoon plain flour | 1 tablespoon all-purpose flour |
| salt and freshly ground pepper | salt and freshly ground pepper |
| 1 tablespoon chopped fresh or | 1 tablespoon chopped fresh or |
| 1 teaspoon dried herbs | 1 teaspoon dried herbs |
| 4 tablespoons single cream | ¼ cup light cream |
| 1 tablespoon lemon juice | 1 tablespoon lemon juice |
| chopped parsley to garnish | chopped parsley for garnish |

Prepare the vegetables and cook separately in boiling salted water for 3 to 5 minutes until just tender – be careful not to overcook. Drain the vegetables, reserving 250 ml/8 fl oz (1 cup) cooking liquid, and arrange on a serving platter. Keep warm.

To make the sauce, melt the butter in a heavy frying pan (skillet) and sauté the mushrooms for about 3 minutes until just tender. Stir in the flour, then gradually add the reserved vegetable liquid. Bring the sauce to the boil, stirring all the time, and add salt and pepper to taste. Stir in the herbs and cream and then the lemon juice and reheat gently.

Spoon the sauce over the vegetables and sprinkle with parsley. Serve with slices of black or rye bread.

VARIATIONS:

**Provençale Platter** – serve the vegetables with aïoli made in a blender. Put 4 peeled cloves of garlic in a blender with a good pinch of salt and 1 egg yolk and blend until smooth, then gradually drizzle in 120 ml/4 fl oz (½ cup) olive oil and 2 teaspoons lemon juice. Pour the thick, creamy sauce into a bowl to serve.

**Italian Vegetable Platter** – arrange an assortment of fresh vegetables, such as cucumber sticks, quarters of seeded green and red peppers, carrot sticks and celery on a plate and serve with warm anchovy sauce into which the vegetables can be dipped like a fondue. Make the anchovy sauce by gently frying 2 crushed cloves garlic in 50 g/2 oz (¼ cup) butter until golden. Mash the contents of 1 small can of anchovies to a paste, then stir into the garlic with 5 tablespoons olive oil. Heat through, stirring, for 5 minutes, then serve the sauce warm. Serve sliced crusty bread as well to mop up the juices.

# Vegetable Layer

METRIC/IMPERIAL
1 small aubergine, sliced
1 tablespoon oil
1 onion, sliced
1 large leek, sliced
3 courgettes, sliced
75 g/3 oz cheese grated
1 teaspoon dried oregano
salt and freshly ground pepper
150 ml/¼ pint tomato juice

AMERICAN
1 small eggplant, sliced
1 tablespoon oil
1 onion, sliced
1 large leek, sliced
3 zucchini, sliced
¾ cup grated cheese
1 teaspoon dried oregano
salt and freshly ground pepper
⅔ cup tomato juice

Blanch the aubergine (eggplant) in boiling water for 2 minutes, drain and pat dry. Heat the oil in a pan and sauté the aubergine (eggplant) and onion for 5 minutes.

In a greased 1.2 litre/2 pint (5 cup) casserole dish, layer the aubergine (eggplant) and onion with the leek and courgettes (zucchini). Sprinkle each layer with cheese, oregano and plenty of salt and pepper. Pour over the tomato juice.

Cover tightly and cook in a preheated oven (180°C/350°F, Gas Mark 4) for 45 minutes to 1 hour until the vegetables are tender. Serve hot with plain boiled rice.

# Chinese Courgettes (Zucchini) with Tomatoes

METRIC/IMPERIAL
350 g/12 oz courgettes
6 tablespoons oil
1 teaspoon salt
2 large firm tomatoes, skinned and
    quartered
250 ml/8 fl oz stock
1 tablespoon cornflour, blended
    with 2 tablespoons water

AMERICAN
¾ lb zucchini
6 tablespoons oil
1 teaspoon salt
2 large firm tomatoes, peeled and
    quartered
1 cup stock or broth
1 tablespoon cornstarch, blended
    with 2 tablespoons water

Cut the courgettes (zucchini) lengthwise into quarters, and then crosswise into 1 cm/½ inch pieces. Heat 3 tablespoons of the oil in a pan. Add the courgettes (zucchini) and half the salt and stir-fry over a high heat until slightly softened. Transfer to a plate and keep hot. Heat the remaining oil in the pan and stir-fry the tomatoes for 30 seconds. Add to the courgettes.

Add the stock to the pan with the remaining salt and bring to the boil. Stir in the cornflour (cornstarch) mixture and simmer the sauce, stirring, until thickened. Place the courgettes (zucchini) in the centre of a warmed serving plate and arrange the tomatoes around them. Pour the stock over the courgettes (zucchini) and serve hot with boiled brown rice.

# Courgette (Zucchini) Scallop

METRIC/IMPERIAL
*350 g/12 oz courgettes*
*salt and freshly ground pepper*
*100 g/4 oz Gruyère cheese, grated*
*40 g/1½ oz butter*

AMERICAN
*¾ lb zucchini*
*salt and freshly ground pepper*
*1 cup grated Swiss cheese*
*3 tablespoons butter*

Cut the courgettes (zucchini) in halves lengthwise if large, then cut into 5 cm/2 inch lengths. Cook for 1 minute in boiling salted water and drain well.

Butter a shallow ovenproof dish and arrange half the courgettes (zucchini) in it. Sprinkle with half the grated cheese and season with salt and pepper. Repeat the layers. Cut the butter into small pieces, dot over the top and cook in a preheated moderately hot oven (200°C/400°F, Gas Mark 6) for about 40 minutes until golden brown.

# Cheese Soufflé

METRIC/IMPERIAL
*50 g/2 oz butter*
*25 g/1 oz plain flour*
*250 ml/8 fl oz milk*
*2 tablespoons cream*
*salt*
*freshly ground pepper*
*freshly grated nutmeg*
*3 eggs, separated*
*100 g/4 oz Gruyère cheese, grated*

AMERICAN
*¼ cup butter*
*¼ cup all-purpose flour*
*1 cup milk*
*2 tablespoons cream*
*salt*
*freshly ground pepper*
*freshly grated nutmeg*
*3 eggs, separated*
*1 cup grated Swiss cheese*

Melt the butter in a heavy-based pan, and when frothy add the flour and cook for 1 minute. Gradually stir in the milk and cook, stirring, for 5 to 10 minutes until sauce thickens. Remove from heat and stir in cream and salt, pepper and nutmeg to taste. Add egg yolks one at a time, beating well between additions, then add the cheese. Leave to cool slightly.

Whisk the egg whites until stiff, then fold quickly but gently into the sauce with a large metal spoon. Pour the mixture into a well buttered 900 ml/1½ pints (3¾ cups) soufflé dish and bake in a preheated moderate oven (180°C/350°F, Gas Mark 4) for 15 minutes. Increase the heat to moderately hot (200°C/400°F, Gas Mark 6) and bake for further 15 to 20 minutes. Serve immediately with salad of choice.

# Beans Greek Style

METRIC/IMPERIAL
*500 g/1 lb green beans*
*4 tablespoons olive oil*
*1 medium onion, thinly sliced*
*1 clove garlic, crushed*
*1 large ripe tomato, skinned and*
  *chopped*
*2 tablespoons chopped parsley*
*1 teaspoon chopped fresh or*
  *½ teaspoon dried oregano*
*salt and freshly ground pepper*
*½ teaspoon sugar*
*1 teaspoon ground cumin*

AMERICAN
*1 lb green beans*
*¼ cup olive oil*
*1 medium-sized onion, thinly sliced*
*1 clove garlic, crushed*
*1 large ripe tomato, peeled and*
  *chopped*
*2 tablepsoons chopped parsley*
*1 teaspoon chopped fresh or*
  *½ teaspoon dried oregano*
*salt and freshly ground pepper*
*½ teaspoon sugar*
*1 teaspoon ground cumin*

Top and tail the beans and cut in half if very long; leave whole if the beans are small and young. Heat the oil in a large pan and gently fry the onion and garlic until they soften and turn a pale golden colour. Place the beans on top of the onions, then the tomato and half the parsley. Sprinkle with the oregano, salt and pepper to taste and sugar.

Cover the pan tightly and simmer over a gentle heat for about 20 minutes until the beans are tender. Check the liquid from time to time, and add a little water if it seems to be evaporating too much. You should have a thick sauce at the end of the cooking time. Stir in the cumin and sprinkle with the remaining parsley. Serve hot or allow to cool, then cover and chill.

# Cauliflower with Cream Sauce

METRIC/IMPERIAL
*1 small cauliflower*
*salt and freshly ground pepper*
*150 ml/¼ pint soured cream*
*50 g/2 oz cream cheese, softened*
*2 tablespoons lemon juice*
*2 spring onions, finely chopped*

AMERICAN
*1 small cauliflower*
*salt and freshly ground pepper*
*⅔ cup sour cream*
*¼ cup softened cream cheese*
*2 tablespoons lemon juice*
*2 scallions, finely chopped*

Trim off the outside green leaves and wash the cauliflower. Place stalk side down in boiling salted water, cover and simmer for 15 minutes, or until just tender when tested with a skewer – be sure not to overcook. Drain and place in a heated serving bowl.

To make the sauce, heat the sour cream and softened cream cheese over a gentle heat, stirring, until combined. Add the lemon juice, spring onions (scallions) and salt and pepper to taste and bring to near boiling, then pour over the cauliflower.

# Creamy Onion Mini Quiches

METRIC/IMPERIAL
*100 g/4 oz shortcrust pastry*
*25 g/1 oz butter*
*225 g/8 oz chopped onion*
*pinch ground mace*
*2 tablespoons milk*
*2 tablespoons double cream*
*2 eggs*
*freshly grated nutmeg*
*salt*
*freshly ground pepper*

AMERICAN
*¼ lb pie dough*
*2 tablespoons butter*
*½ lb chopped onion*
*pinch ground mace*
*2 tablespoons milk*
*2 tablespoons heavy cream*
*2 eggs*
*freshly grated nutmeg*
*salt*
*freshly ground pepper*

Roll out pastry dough thinly and use to line two 13 cm/5 inch fluted tartlet tins. Prick bases, then chill in refrigerator.

Heat the butter in a heavy-based pan, add the onions and mace and cook gently for 6 to 10 minutes, stirring occasionally, without browning the onions. In a bowl mix together the milk, cream, and eggs, and add nutmeg and salt and pepper to taste.

Spread the onions in the pastry-lined tins, then pour over the egg mixture. Bake in a preheated moderately hot oven (220°C/400°F, Gas Mark 6) for about 20 minutes until pastry is golden and filling is just set. Serve hot or cold with a crisp mixed salad.

# Beans with Cheese and Herbs

METRIC/IMPERIAL
*25 g/1 oz butter*
*1 tablespoon oil*
*2 tablespoons chopped parsley*
*1 tablespoon chopped chives*
*1 clove garlic, crushed*
*350 g/12 oz frozen green beans*
*salt and freshly ground pepper*
*freshly grated nutmeg*
*2 tablespoons grated Parmesan*
  *cheese*

AMERICAN
*2 tablespoons butter*
*1 tablespoon oil*
*2 tablespoons chopped parsley*
*1 tablespoon chopped chives*
*1 clove garlic, crushed*
*¾ lb frozen green beans*
*salt and freshly ground pepper*
*freshly grated nutmeg*
*2 tablespoons grated Parmesan*
  *cheese*

Heat the butter and oil in a pan, stir in half the parsley, the chives and the garlic. Cook for 1 minute, stirring, then add the beans and season to taste with salt, pepper and nutmeg. Stir for 3 minutes over a gentle heat until the beans are piping hot, then add the grated cheese and lightly stir through. Sprinkle with remaining parsley and serve.

# Vegetables Vinaigrette

| METRIC/IMPERIAL | AMERICAN |
|---|---|
| 100 g/4 oz young green beans | ¼ lb young green beans |
| 100 g/4 oz courgettes | ¼ lb zucchini |
| 100 g/4 oz button mushrooms | 1 cup button mushrooms |
| salt and freshly ground pepper | salt and freshly ground pepper |
| 2 hard-boiled eggs, quartered | 2 hard-cooked eggs, quartered |
| 2 tablespoons olive oil | 2 tablespoons olive oil |
| juice of ½ lemon | juice of ½ lemon |
| chopped fresh herbs (parsley, chives, marjoram, oregano) | chopped fresh herbs (parsley, chives, marjoram, oregano) |
| 1 lemon, quartered, to garnish | 1 lemon, quartered, for garnish |

Top and tail the beans; thickly slice the courgettes (zucchini); cut the mushroom stems level with the caps. Cook each vegetable separately in 250 ml/8 fl oz (1 cup) boiling salted water, without a lid, until just tender-crisp. As each vegetable is cooked, refresh under cold running water. Drain well and pat dry.

Arrange the vegetables on a plate with the eggs. Combine the oil and lemon juice, season with salt and pepper to taste and beat with a whisk or fork until thick and creamy. Spoon over the vegetables and sprinkle with herbs. Garnish with lemon wedges and serve at room temperature.


# Spinach and Cheese Dumplings

| METRIC/IMPERIAL | AMERICAN |
|---|---|
| 225 g/8 oz spinach | ½ lb spinach |
| 100 g/4 oz ricotta cheese | ¼ lb ricotta cheese |
| salt and freshly ground pepper | salt and freshly ground pepper |
| freshly grated nutmeg | freshly grated nutmeg |
| 2 egg yolks | 2 egg yolks |
| 4 tablespoons grated Parmesan cheese | 4 tablespoons grated Parmesan cheese |
| flour for coating | flour for coating |
| 50 g/2 oz butter | ¼ cup melted butter |

Wash the spinach and finely chop the leaves, discarding the stalks. Cook the spinach without added water until just tender, drain well, and process in a blender or food processor, or push through a sieve. Mix together the spinach, ricotta cheese, salt and pepper and nutmeg to taste, egg yolks and half the Parmesan cheese.

Drop spoonfuls of the mixture into a little flour spread on greaseproof (waxed) paper. Shape into small balls. Bring a large saucepan of lightly salted water to the boil, add the dumplings and cover tightly. Simmer for 5 minutes, then remove with a slotted spoon to hot serving plates. Pour the melted butter over and sprinkle with the remaining Parmesan cheese.

# Winter Gougère

METRIC/IMPERIAL
*300 ml/½ pint water*
*100 g/4 oz butter*
*salt*
*150 g/5 oz plain flour*
*3 eggs, beaten*
*50 g/2 oz Gruyère cheese, diced*
*½ teaspoon dry mustard*
*1 small carrot, grated*
*1 small parsnip, grated*
*1 tablespoon chopped parsley*
*freshly ground pepper*

AMERICAN
*1¼ cups water*
*8 tablespoons (1 stick) butter*
*salt*
*1¼ cups all-purpose flour*
*3 eggs, beaten*
*½ cup diced Swiss cheese*
*½ teaspoon mustard powder*
*1 small carrot, grated*
*1 small parsnip, grated*
*1 tablespoon chopped parsley*
*freshly ground pepper*

Put the water, butter and a pinch of salt in a large heavy-based pan and bring slowly to the boil – the butter should melt before the water boils. Add the flour all at once and beat vigorously with a wooden spoon over gentle heat until the mixture forms a smooth dough which leaves the sides of the pan clean. Remove the pan from the heat and beat in the eggs a little at a time, incorporating each addition before adding any more. Add only as much as the dough will absorb; it should be thick and shiny, not liquid. Reserve a little beaten egg for the glaze.

Beat in the cheese, mustard, vegetables, parsley, salt and pepper to taste. Place large dollops of the dough in a well-buttered 23 cm/9 inch circular baking dish, arranging them side by side to fill the dish.

Brush top with reserved egg. Bake in a preheated moderately hot oven (200°C/400°F, Gas Mark 6) for 35 to 40 minutes until golden brown. Serve immediately.

# Brown Rice with Vegetables

| METRIC/IMPERIAL | AMERICAN |
|---|---|
| 150 g/5 oz brown rice | ¾ cup brown rice |
| 600 ml/1 pint water or stock | 2½ cups water or stock |
| salt | salt |
| 1 bay leaf | 1 bay leaf |
| 2 tablespoons oil | 2 tablespoons oil |
| 1 clove garlic, crushed | 1 clove garlic, crushed |
| 1 onion, finely chopped | 1 onion, finely chopped |
| 2 sticks celery, thinly sliced | 2 stalks celery, thinly sliced |
| 1 green pepper, cored, seeded and thinly sliced | 1 green pepper, seeded and thinly sliced |
| ½ teaspoon dried basil | ½ teaspoon dried basil |
| freshly ground pepper | freshly ground pepper |
| 2 large tomatoes, thinly sliced | 2 large tomatoes, thinly sliced |
| 50 g/2 oz mature cheese, grated | ½ cup grated sharp cheese |
| chopped parsley to garnish | chopped parsley for garnish |

Place the rice in a colander and rinse in cold running water. Turn into a bowl, cover with cold water, and allow to soak for 30 minutes. Drain, and place in a pan with the water or stock, 1 teaspoon salt and bay leaf. Bring to the boil, then cover the pan and simmer over a gentle heat for 40 to 45 minutes, or until the rice is tender and liquid absorbed.

Fifteen minutes before the rice is cooked, heat the oil in a large frying pan. Gently fry the garlic, onion, celery and green pepper until they are soft but not browned. Stir in the basil and rice and season well with salt and pepper. Toss lightly with a fork until heated through.

Spoon the mixture into a shallow flameproof casserole dish and arrange the tomato slices on top. Sprinkle with grated cheese and place under a hot grill (broiler) for 2 to 3 minutes until the cheese is golden and bubbly. Sprinkle with chopped parsley and serve.

# Jambalaya

METRIC/IMPERIAL

*40 g/1½ oz butter*
*½ green pepper, cored, seeded*
  *and diced*
*1 stick celery, finely chopped*
*1 small onion, finely chopped*
*1 clove garlic, crushed*
*1 x 227 g/8 oz can tomatoes*
*½ teaspoon dried oregano*
*salt and freshly ground pepper*
*100 g/4 oz cooked ham, diced*
*100 g/4 oz peeled prawns*
*200 g/7 oz long-grain rice, cooked*
*chopped parsley, to garnish*

AMERICAN

*3 tablespoons butter*
*½ green pepper, seeded and diced*
*1 stalk celery, finely chopped*
*1 small onion, finely chopped*
*1 clove garlic, crushed*
*1 x 8 oz can tomatoes*
*½ teaspoon dried oregano*
*salt and freshly ground pepper*
*½ cup diced cooked ham*
*¼ lb shelled shrimp*
*1 cup long-grain rice, cooked*
*chopped parsley for garnish*

Heat the butter in a chafing dish or a heavy-based frying pan (skillet) over medium heat. Sauté the pepper, celery, onion and garlic for about 3 minutes until soft but not brown. Stir in the tomatoes with their juice and heat to boiling point. Add the oregano, salt and pepper to taste, ham and prawns (shrimp). Add the rice and heat through, stirring gently, so the rice does not stick to the bottom. Serve in deep bowls sprinkled with parsley.

VARIATION:
**Spicy Jambalaya** – add 50 g/2 oz (¼ cup) chopped spicy sausage when frying the vegetables, add a pinch of cayenne pepper with the rice, and use cooked crayfish instead of prawns (shrimp).

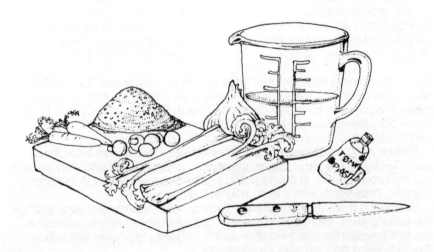

# Ham and Rice Rolls

METRIC/IMPERIAL
*4 thin slices cooked ham*
*Dijon mustard*
*50 g/2 oz rice, cooked*
*25 g/1 oz raisins, chopped*
*1 egg, beaten*
*1 stick celery, finely chopped*
*½ teaspoon dried basil*
*25 g/1 oz Cheddar cheese, grated*
*120 ml/4 fl oz single cream or*
  *evaporated milk*

AMERICAN
*4 thin slices cooked ham*
*Dijon-style mustard*
*½ cup cooked rice*
*3 tablespoons chopped raisins*
*1 egg, beaten*
*1 stalk celery, finely chopped*
*½ teaspoon dried basil*
*¼ cup grated Cheddar cheese*
*½ cup light cream or evaporated*
  *milk*

Spread the ham slices lightly with mustard. Combine the rice, raisins, egg, celery and basil and divide equally between the ham slices. Roll up and secure with wooden cocktail sticks (toothpicks).

Place the rolls, seam side down, in a small shallow greased baking dish. Heat the cheese and cream or evaporated milk in a small pan until the cheese melts. Spoon the sauce over the rolls and cook in a preheated moderate oven (180°C/350°F, Gas Mark 4) for 20 minutes.

# Kedgeree

METRIC/IMPERIAL
*150 g/5 oz long-grain rice*
*225 g/8 oz smoked cod or haddock*
*2 hard-boiled eggs*
*50 g/2 oz butter*
*1 teaspoon curry powder*
*1 small onion, chopped*
*½ green pepper, cored, seeded*
  *and chopped*
*1 tablespoon chopped parsley*
*1 tablespoon lemon juice*
*salt and freshly ground pepper*

AMERICAN
*¾ cup long grain rice*
*½ lb smoked cod or haddock*
  *(finnan haddie)*
*2 hard-cooked eggs*
*¼ cup butter*
*1 teaspoon curry powder*
*1 small onion, chopped*
*½ green pepper, seeded and*
  *chopped*
*1 tablespoon chopped parsley*
*1 tablespoon lemon juice*
*salt and freshly ground pepper*

Cook the rice in plenty of boiling salted water for about 15 to 20 minutes.

Meanwhile place the fish in a pan of cold water and bring slowly to the boil. Remove from the heat and drain and flake the fish, discarding any skin and bones. Shell the eggs and chop roughly. When the rice is cooked, drain into a colander and pour boiling water through to separate grains. Leave to drain.

Melt the butter in a pan and add curry powder, onion and green pepper. Cover and cook gently for 3 minutes. Add the cooked rice, parsley, lemon juice and salt and pepper to taste. Stir in the flaked fish and chopped eggs and heat through gently. Serve immediately.

163

# Continental Kedgeree

METRIC/IMPERIAL
3 bratwurst sausages
25 g/1 oz butter
1 tablespoon oil
½ teaspoon ground coriander
   seeds
1 onion, finely chopped
1 clove garlic, crushed
2 sticks celery, chopped
½ teaspoon turmeric
150 g/5 oz long-grain rice, cooked
salt and freshly ground pepper
chopped parsley to garnish

AMERICAN
3 bratwurst sausages
2 tablespoons butter
1 tablespoon oil
½ teaspoon ground coriander
   seeds
1 onion, finely chopped
1 clove garlic, crushed
2 stalks celery, chopped
½ teaspoon turmeric
¾ cup long-grain rice, cooked
salt and freshly ground pepper
chopped parsley for garnish

Cook the sausages under a preheated moderate grill (broiler) for 8 to 10 minutes until cooked through. Meanwhile heat the butter and oil in a pan, add the coriander seeds, onion, garlic, celery and turmeric. Cover and cook for 3 minutes. Add the rice, season with salt and pepper and cook gently, stirring, until the rice is hot and lightly coloured.

Pile the rice into the centre of a warmed serving dish. Slice the sausages and arrange around the edge. Garnish with parsley and serve immediately with hot buttered toast.

# Chicken Pilaff

METRIC/IMPERIAL
25 g/1 oz butter
1 tablespoon oil
1 small onion, finely chopped
200 g/7 oz long-grain rice
400 ml/⅔ pint hot chicken stock
salt and freshly ground pepper
225 g/8 oz leftover chicken, cut into
   strips
½ red pepper, cored, seeded and
   chopped
2 tablespoons single cream

AMERICAN
2 tablespoons butter
1 tablespoon oil
1 small onion, finely chopped
1 cup long-grain rice
1¾ cups hot chicken stock or broth
salt and freshly ground pepper
1 cup leftover cooked chicken, cut
   into strips
½ red pepper, seeded and
   chopped
2 tablespoons light cream

Melt the butter in a large heavy-based pan, add the oil and onion and fry until soft but not brown. Stir in the rice and cook, stirring, for 2 minutes until the grains are coated. Add the stock a little at a time, waiting until the liquid in the pan comes to the boil before adding the rest. Add ½ teaspoon salt and pepper to taste, reduce the heat so that the liquid simmers, then cover and cook for 15 minutes until the liquid is absorbed.

Remove from the heat, fluff with a fork and stir in the chicken strips, red pepper and cream. Cook, stirring, over a gentle heat until heated through.

# Risotto with Cabbage and Beans

METRIC/IMPERIAL
*100 g/4 oz broad beans, fresh or
  frozen*
*175 g/6 oz cabbage, shredded*
*150 g/5 oz short-grain rice*
*salt*
*50 g/2 oz butter*
*few sage leaves, chopped*
*25 g/1 oz grated Parmesan cheese*
*freshly ground pepper*

AMERICAN
*½ cup lima beans, fresh or frozen*
*2 cups shredded cabbage*
*¾ cup short-grain rice*
*salt*
*¼ cup butter*
*few sage leaves, chopped*
*¼ cup grated Parmesan cheese*
*freshly ground pepper*

Parboil the beans if fresh for 2 to 3 minutes, then drain. Put the cabbage, rice and 1 tablespoon salt in a large pan with plenty of boiling water and simmer for 10 minutes. Add the beans and cook for a further 10 minutes.

Drain and pile the mixture into a warmed serving dish. Melt the butter in a small pan with the sage, then pour over the rice. Sprinkle the Parmesan cheese over and a little pepper and fold gently to mix. Serve immediately.

# Baked Risotto

METRIC/IMPERIAL
*50 g/2 oz butter*
*1 small onion, chopped*
*100 g/4 oz salami, diced*
*50 g/2 oz shelled peas*
*2 artichoke hearts, chopped*
*25 g/1 oz mushrooms, chopped*
*250 ml/8 fl oz beef stock*
*salt and freshly ground pepper*
*150 g/5 oz short-grain rice*
*400 ml/⅔ pint boiling water*
*40 g/1½ oz grated Parmesan
  cheese*

AMERICAN
*¼ cup butter*
*1 small onion, chopped*
*¼ lb salami, diced*
*⅓ cup shelled peas*
*2 artichoke hearts, chopped*
*¼ cup chopped mushrooms*
*1 cup beef stock*
*salt and freshly ground pepper*
*¾ cup short-grain rice*
*1¾ cups boiling water*
*⅓ cup grated Parmesan cheese*

Melt half the butter in a flameproof casserole, add the onions and fry gently until golden. Stir in the salami, peas, artichokes, mushrooms, stock and salt and pepper to taste. Cook gently for 20 minutes.

Meanwhile place the rice and water in a separate pan with salt to taste and boil for 5 minutes. Drain, then stir into the salami mixture with the Parmesan cheese and remaining butter.

Cook in a preheated moderately hot oven (200°C/400°F, Gas Mark 6) for 20 minutes or until a golden brown crust forms on top. Serve immediately with a mixed salad and crusty bread.

# Spanish Risotto

METRIC/IMPERIAL
4 tablespoons olive oil
1 small onion, sliced
1 clove garlic, crushed
150 g/5 oz long-grain rice
300 ml/½ pint chicken or beef stock
300 ml/½ pint tomato juice
½ teaspoon dried thyme or
  oregano
½ teaspoon ground mace
50 g/2 oz mature cheese, grated
1 tablespoon lemon juice or cider
  vinegar
salt and freshly ground pepper
flavouring of choice (see below)

AMERICAN
¼ cup olive oil
1 small onion, sliced
1 clove garlic, crushed
¾ cup long-grain rice
1¼ cups chicken or beef stock
1¼ cups tomato juice
½ teaspoon dried thyme or
  oregano
½ teaspoon ground mace
½ cup grated sharp cheese
1 tablespoon lemon juice or cider
  vinegar
salt and freshly ground pepper
flavorings of choice (see below)

Heat the oil in a heavy-based frying pan (skillet) and gently fry the onion and garlic until soft but not brown, stirring constantly. Add the unwashed rice and continue cooking and stirring over a medium heat until the grains are coated. Add the stock and tomato juice and cook, stirring, until the liquid begins to boil. Reduce the heat and simmer the mixture for 20 minutes. The liquid should then have been absorbed; if it is too wet, raise the heat a little and cook until the liquid has evaporated.

Remove the pan from the heat and add the herbs, cheese, lemon juice or vinegar and salt and pepper to taste. Serve as an accompaniment to jacket baked potatoes and cold meats, or add one of the flavourings below, heat through, and serve.

**Flavourings for Risotto:**
100 g/4 oz of either: peeled prawns (shelled shrimp); chopped cooked chicken; cooked cubed ham; diced salami-type sausage; drained canned tuna or salmon. Add crunch to the risotto with ½ green or red pepper, seeded, blanched and chopped, or flaked almonds or pine nuts, toasted until golden; or finely chopped walnuts.

# Caribbean Rice

METRIC/IMPERIAL
2 lean bacon rashers, chopped
1 onion, sliced
2 tablespoons oil
½ red pepper, seeded and
  chopped
150 g/5 oz long-grain rice
salt and freshly ground pepper
2 ripe tomatoes, chopped
300 ml/½ pint tomato juice
300 ml/½ pint fish stock
few drops Tabasco sauce
100 g/4 oz peeled prawns

AMERICAN
2 slices lean bacon, chopped
1 onion, sliced
2 tablespoons oil
½ red pepper, seeded and
  chopped
¾ cup long-grain rice
salt and freshly ground pepper
2 ripe tomatoes, chopped
1 ¼ cups tomato juice
1 ¼ cups fish stock
few drops hot pepper sauce
⅔ cup shelled shrimp

Sauté the bacon and onion in the oil for 5 minutes without browning. Add chopped pepper and rice and cook gently, stirring, for 2 minutes until grains are coated. Add salt and pepper, tomatoes, tomato juice, stock and Tabasco (hot pepper) sauce and bring to the boil, stirring occasionally. Cover tightly and simmer for 15 minutes.

Remove the lid and if there is too much liquid, cook uncovered for a few minutes more. Stir in prawns (shrimp) and cook over a low heat for 3 minutes. Adjust seasoning, then serve immediately with side dishes of cucumber in yogurt and banana slices sprinkled with desiccated (shredded) coconut.

# Spanish Rice and Eggs

METRIC/IMPERIAL
150 g/5 oz cooked rice
25 g/1 oz butter, melted
1 tablespoon chopped parsley or
  chives
salt and pepper
50 g/2 oz mature cheese, grated
4 eggs
2 grilled bacon rashers, to serve

AMERICAN
¾ cup rice, cooked
2 tablespoons melted butter
1 tablespoon chopped parsley or
  chives
salt and pepper
½ cup grated sharp cheese
4 eggs
2 broiled slices bacon to serve

Mix together the rice, melted butter, herbs, salt and pepper to taste and half the cheese, then spread in a small shallow ovenproof greased dish. Make 4 hollows in the rice with the back of a spoon and break an egg into each nest. Season lightly, then sprinkle the remaining cheese over.

Cook in a preheated moderately hot oven (190°C/375°F, Gas Mark 5) for about 12 minutes until the eggs are set and the cheese melted. Divide between serving plates and top with grilled (broiled) bacon.

# Rice Salad

METRIC/IMPERIAL
200 g/7 oz long-grain rice, cooked
2 spring onions, chopped
1 stick celery, finely chopped
½ red or green pepper, thinly sliced
2 teaspoons French mustard
1 teaspoon salt
½ teaspoon sugar
½ teaspoon coriander seeds,
  ground
1 tablespoon lemon juice or cider
  vinegar
3 tablespoons olive oil
freshly ground pepper

AMERICAN
1 cup rice, cooked
2 scallions, chopped
1 stalk celery, finely chopped
½ red or green pepper, thinly sliced
2 teaspoons Dijon-style mustard
1 teaspoon salt
½ teaspoon sugar
½ teaspoon coriander seeds,
  ground
1 tablespoon lemon juice or cider
  vinegar
3 tablespoons olive oil
freshly ground pepper

Place the warm rice in a salad bowl and stir in the onions (scallions), celery and red or green pepper.

In a screw-top jar, mix together the mustard, salt, sugar, coriander, lemon juice or vinegar, oil and pepper to taste. Shake well, then pour over the rice and toss gently.

Serve this rice salad as an accompaniment or add one of the variations below to make a main dish.

VARIATIONS:

**Chicken and Rice Salad** – lightly poach half a chicken breast and cut into bite-size pieces. Make the rice salad as above and add the chicken and 50 g/2 oz canned pineapple pieces.

**Pork and Bean Sprout Rice Salad** – shred 100 g/4 oz cooked pork and marinate in 1 tablespoon soy sauce and 1 tablespoon dry sherry. Make the rice salad as above and add the pork and marinade and 50 g/2 oz (1 cup) bean sprouts.

**Mackerel Rice Salad** – make the rice salad as above and add 225 g/8 oz flaked smoked mackerel and 50 g/2 oz canned sweetcorn.

**Tuna Rice Salad** – make the rice salad as above and add 25 g/1 oz finely diced cucumber, 25 g/1 oz cooked peas and drained chunks of tuna from a 99 g/3½ oz can.

**Sausage and Apple Rice Salad** – grill 2 pork sausages until golden brown, then cool and cut into thin slices. Leaving the peel on, core and dice a firm, red-skinned apple and toss the pieces in a little lemon juice. Make the rice salad as above and stir in the sausage and apple pieces.

# Nasi Goreng

| METRIC/IMPERIAL | AMERICAN |
|---|---|
| 1 tablespoon oil | 1 tablespoon oil |
| 350 g/12 oz beef topside | ¾ lb top round steak |
| 2 rashers fatty bacon, chopped | 2 slices fatty bacon, chopped |
| 2 medium onions, sliced into rings | 2 medium onions, sliced into rings |
| 2 teaspoons curry powder | 2 teaspoons curry powder |
| ¼ teaspoon ground cloves | ¼ teaspoon ground cloves |
| ¼ teaspoon mixed spice | ¼ teaspoon apple spice |
| 1 teaspoon salt | 1 teaspoon salt |
| 1 ring canned pineapple chopped | 1 chopped canned pineapple ring |
| 150 g/5 oz cooked rice | ¾ cup cooked rice |

Heat the oil in a heavy-based frying pan (skillet). Cut the steak into fine slivers and stir-fry for 3 minutes; remove and reserve. Add the bacon and cook until crisp; remove and reserve. Add the onions and spices and fry until the onion is golden, then return the steak and bacon to pan with salt, pineapple and rice. Cook, stirring, over a medium heat for 5 minutes until rice is heated through.

Serve immediately with side dishes of salted peanuts and desiccated coconut.

# Spaghetti with Tomato and Bacon

| METRIC/IMPERIAL | AMERICAN |
|---|---|
| 1 tablespoon olive oil | 1 tablespoon olive oil |
| 100 g/4 oz lean bacon, diced | ½ cup diced lean bacon |
| 1 x 227 g/8 oz can tomatoes | 1 x 8 oz can tomatoes |
| 1 canned pimento, chopped | 1 canned pimiento, chopped |
| 175 g/6 oz spaghetti | 6 oz spaghetti |
| salt and freshly ground pepper | salt and freshly ground pepper |
| grated Pecorino or Parmesan cheese to serve | grated Pecorino or Parmesan cheese to serve |

Heat the oil in a heavy-based frying pan, add the bacon and fry gently for 5 minutes until the pieces start to become crisp. Add the tomatoes with their juice and the pimento and continue cooking over moderate heat for 10 minutes, stirring occasionally and pressing tomatoes to break them up.

Meanwhile cook the spaghetti in boiling salted water for 10 to 12 minutes. Drain well and place in warmed serving dish. Taste sauce and adjust seasoning, then pour over the spaghetti and toss gently.

Serve immediately with Pecorino or Parmesan cheese, with a green salad.

# Pasta with Bolognese Sauce

METRIC/IMPERIAL

2 tablespoons olive oil
2 rashers bacon, finely chopped
1 onion, chopped
1 stick celery, chopped
100 g/4 oz mushrooms, chopped
100 g/4 oz minced beef
50 g/2 oz chicken livers, chopped
2 tablespoons tomato purée
120 ml/4 fl oz red wine
250 ml/8 fl oz beef stock
1 tablespoon chopped fresh basil or
   ½ teaspoon dried
1 teaspoon sugar
freshly grated nutmeg
salt and freshly ground pepper
pasta, to serve, see below

AMERICAN

2 tablespoons olive oil
2 slices bacon, chopped
1 onion, chopped
1 stalk celery, chopped
1 cup chopped mushrooms
¼ lb ground beef
⅓ cup chopped chicken livers
2 tablespoons tomato paste
½ cup red wine
1 cup beef stock
1 tablespoon chopped fresh basil or
   ½ teaspoon dried
1 teaspoon sugar
freshly grated nutmeg
salt and freshly ground pepper
pasta, to serve, see below

Heat the oil in a large pan and gently fry the bacon, onion, celery and mushrooms until soft. Push vegetables to the side of the pan and add beef and chicken livers and continue cooking until the meat is brown. Stir in the tomato purée (paste), wine and stock, basil, sugar, and nutmeg and salt and pepper to taste. Bring to the boil, stirring, then cover the pan, reduce heat and simmer for 45 minutes.

**Tagliatelle alla Bolognese** – 15 minutes before the sauce is ready, cook 175 g/6 oz tagliatelle (ribbon noodles) in plenty of boiling salted water for about 12 minutes until tender but firm to the bite. Drain well, add a knob of butter and salt and pepper, then place in serving dish. Adjust the seasoning of the sauce then pour over the noodles. Pass a dish of grated Parmesan cheese and serve accompanied by a crisp green salad.

**Lasagne alla Bolognese** – make Bolognese Sauce. Cook 175 g/6 oz green lasagne in boiling salted water for 15 to 20 minutes until tender, drain and rinse then spread on a tea towel (cloth) to cool. Make a white sauce using 25 g/1 oz (¼ cup) flour, 25 g/1 oz (2 tablespoons) butter and 300 ml/½ pint (1¼ cups) milk and season with salt, pepper and nutmeg. Butter a small rectangular ovenproof dish and cover base with layers of lasagne. Spread half the Bolognese Sauce on top, then another layer of lasagne, the rest of the meat, then the remaining lasagne. Cover with the white sauce and sprinkle with 50 g/2 oz (½ cup) grated Parmesan cheese. Dot with butter and cook in preheated moderately hot oven (190°C/375°F, Gas Mark 5) for 20 to 25 minutes until bubbling. Serve immediately.

**Cannelloni** – make Bolognese Sauce, adding 2 tablespoons dry marsala and using a 227 g/8 oz can of peeled tomatoes instead of the stock; press the tomatoes during cooking to break them up. Make the white sauce as in Lasagne alla Bolognese above. Grease a shallow ovenproof dish (wide enough to take rolled lasagne). Use the Bolognese Sauce to fill 6 cannelloni tubes, arrange in the dish and surround with any remaining sauce. Cover completely with white sauce, then sprinkle with 50 g/2 oz (½ cup) grated Cheddar cheese. Dot with butter and cook in preheated moderate oven (180°C/350°F, Gas Mark 4) for 35 minutes. Serve immediately.

# Spaghetti with Gorgonzola

METRIC/IMPERIAL
*175 g/6 oz spaghetti*
*salt and freshly ground pepper*
*120 ml/4 fl oz single cream*
*100 g/4 oz Gorgonzola cheese,*
*.diced*
*25 g/1 oz butter*
*freshly grated nutmeg*
*2 spring onions, finely chopped*
*25 g/1 oz grated Parmesan cheese*
*chopped chives to garnish*

AMERICAN
*6 oz spaghetti*
*salt and freshly ground pepper*
*½ cup light cream*
*¼ lb Gorgonzola cheese, diced*
*2 tablespoons butter*
*freshly grated nutmeg*
*2 scallions, finely chopped*
*¼ cup grated Parmesan cheese*
*chopped chives for garnish*

Cook the spaghetti in plenty of boiling salted water for about 10 to 12 minutes until tender but not soft.

Meanwhile heat the cream in a pan, add the Gorgonzola and stir until melted. Add salt and freshly ground pepper to taste.

Drain the spaghetti, return to the pan and toss with the butter, nutmeg to taste, spring onions (scallions) and Parmesan cheese. Turn the spaghetti into a warmed serving dish, and pour over the sauce. Sprinkle with chives and serve immediately with a tomato and basil salad.

# Spaghettini with Herby Tomato Sauce

METRIC/IMPERIAL
*2 large ripe tomatoes*
*1 clove garlic, crushed*
*2 tablespoons chopped parsley*
*8 basil leaves, chopped*
*2 tablespoons olive oil*
*salt and freshly ground pepper*
*225 g/8 oz spaghettini or vermicelli*

AMERICAN
*2 large ripe tomatoes*
*1 clove garlic, crushed*
*2 tablespoons chopped parsley*
*8 basil leaves, chopped*
*2 tablespoons olive oil*
*salt and freshly ground pepper*
*½ lb spaghettini or vermicelli*

Peel and coarsely chop the tomatoes. Put the tomatoes, garlic, herbs and oil in a blender and blend to a purée. Heat the sauce gently in a pan to boiling point, then add salt and pepper to taste.

Meanwhile cook the pasta in plenty of boiling salted water until tender but still firm to the bite – 8 to 10 minutes. Drain well and toss immediately with the sauce.

# Creamy Noodles with Herbs

METRIC/IMPERIAL
225 g/8 oz tagliatelle or ribbon
  noodles
salt and freshly ground white
  pepper
1 clove garlic, crushed
25 g/1 oz butter
6 tablespoons single cream
1 tablespoon each chopped
  parsley, basil, chives and
  marjoram
grated Parmesan cheese, to serve

AMERICAN
½ lb tagliatelle or ribbon noodles
salt and freshly ground white
  pepper
1 clove garlic, crushed
2 tablespoons butter
6 tablespoons light cream
1 tablespoon each chopped
  parsley, basil, chives and
  marjoram
grated Parmesan cheese, to serve

Cook the noodles in plenty of boiling salted water until tender but still firm to bite – about 10 minutes. Drain thoroughly and toss in a large warmed serving bowl with the garlic and butter.

Heat the cream in a pan until nearly boiling, then stir in the herbs, salt to taste and plenty of freshly ground pepper. Pour the sauce over the buttered noodles and toss gently until the pasta strands are coated.

Serve with freshly grated Parmesan cheese and a mixed salad.

VARIATION:
**Creamy Noodles with Sorrel** – instead of the herbs, cook 100 g/4 oz (¼ lb) sorrel in 300 ml/½ pint (1¼ cups) chicken stock, then cool slightly and purée in a blender or food mill. Add the sorrel to the cream as in recipe above.

# Pasta with Garlic and Broccoli

METRIC/IMPERIAL
225 g/8 oz broccoli
4 tablespoons olive oil
3 cloves of garlic, chopped or
  crushed
salt and freshly ground pepper
about 300 ml/½ pint water
175 g/6 oz vermicelli or spaghetti

AMERICAN
½ lb broccoli
¼ cup olive oil
3 cloves of garlic, chopped or
  crushed
salt and freshly ground pepper
about 1¼ cups water
6 oz vermicelli or spaghetti

Trim any woody ends from the broccoli, then break into small florets. Put the olive oil and garlic in a heavy-based frying pan (skillet) and fry over medium heat. Season liberally with freshly ground pepper.

When the garlic is golden but not brown, add the broccoli, the water and the pasta broken into 5 cm/2 inch lengths. Mix well, then cover the pan and cook over moderate heat for 8 to 10 minutes. Stir occasionally so that the pasta does not stick to the pan. Add salt to taste at end of cooking time and serve immediately.

# Spinach Pesto

METRIC/IMPERIAL
40 g/1½ oz walnut pieces
2 cloves garlic, crushed
5 tablespoons water
225 g/8 oz spinach, chopped
120 ml/4 fl oz olive oil
25 g/1 oz grated Parmesan cheese
1 teaspoon salt
freshly ground pepper
225 g/8 oz freshly cooked pasta

AMERICAN
⅓ cup walnut pieces
2 cloves garlic, crushed
⅓ cup water
½ lb spinach, chopped
½ cup olive oil
¼ cup grated Parmesan cheese
1 teaspoon salt
freshly ground pepper
½ lb freshly cooked pasta

Place the walnuts, garlic and water in a blender or food processor fitted with the steel blade and process until the nuts are chopped. Add small amounts of spinach alternately with the oil and process until smooth. Add the cheese, salt and pepper to taste and blend. Toss the sauce with the hot pasta.

**Note:** any leftover sauce can be kept in a screw-top jar, covered with a little olive oil, in the refrigerator for up to 2 weeks.


# Noodles with Pesto

METRIC/IMPERIAL
1 large ripe tomato
40 g/1½ oz chopped fresh basil
2 cloves garlic, crushed
4 tablespoons pine kernels
50 g/2 oz grated Parmesan cheese
150 ml/¼ pint olive oil
175 g/6 oz freshly cooked ribbon
    noodles (tagliatelle)

AMERICAN
1 large ripe tomato
1 cup chopped fresh basil
2 cloves garlic, crushed
¼ cup pine nuts
½ cup grated Parmesan cheese
⅔ cup olive oil
6 oz freshly cooked ribbon noodles
    (tagliatelle)

Cut the tomato in half and grill (broil) skin-side-up until soft and quite blackened on the surface. Remove the skin and chop the flesh. Pound the basil in a mortar with a pestle, then add the garlic and nuts and pound again. Add the tomato and pound again, then the cheese. When all is smooth, add the oil drop by drop, as if making a mayonnaise, pounding constantly. Pour the sauce over the noodles, toss until the pasta strands are coated and serve at once.

**Note** – this quantity of sauce will be too much to serve two people but leftover sauce keeps well in a screw-top jar in the refrigerator if topped with a little extra olive oil. Try stirring a spoonful into fresh vegetable soup, or use as a dressing for freshly baked jacket potatoes, or with Tortellini (see page 176).

# Piquant Pasta

METRIC/IMPERIAL
*175 g/6 oz fettucine (narrow ribbon noodles)*
*salt*
*2 cloves garlic, crushed*
*1 small chilli, seeded and chopped*
*2 tablespoons olive oil*
*2 tablespoons chopped parsley*
*freshly ground pepper*

AMERICAN
*6 oz fettucine (narrow ribbon noodles)*
*salt*
*2 cloves garlic, crushed*
*1 small chili, seeded and chopped*
*2 tablespoons olive oil*
*2 tablespoons chopped parsley*
*freshly ground pepper*

Cook the noodles in boiling salted water for about 10 minutes until tender but still firm to the bite.

Meanwhile in a heavy-based frying pan (skillet), gently cook the garlic and chilli in the oil – they must not brown or they will be bitter. Drain the noodles and place in a warmed serving bowl. Pour over the hot oil with the garlic and chilli, add the parsley and pepper to taste and toss well.

# Salami Carbonara

METRIC/IMPERIAL
*100 g/4 oz salami in a piece*
*2 eggs, lightly beaten*
*2 tablespoons single cream*
*25 g/1 oz grated Parmesan cheese*
*1/4 teaspoon salt*
*freshly ground pepper*
*40 g/1½ oz butter*
*175 g/6 oz freshly cooked spaghetti*
*chopped chives or parsley to garnish*

AMERICAN
*1/4 lb salami in a piece*
*2 eggs, lightly beaten*
*2 tablespoons light cream*
*1/4 cup grated Parmesan cheese*
*1/4 teaspoon salt*
*freshly ground pepper*
*3 tablespoons butter*
*6 oz freshly cooked spaghetti*
*chopped chives or parsley for garnish*

Skin the salami and chop into small dice. Combine the eggs with the cream, cheese, salt and freshly ground pepper to taste.

Heat the butter in a large heavy-based frying pan (skillet) and lightly brown the salami. Add the hot freshly cooked and drained pasta, then pour in the egg mixture. Use two forks to toss the mixture over medium heat until the pasta is well coated. Serve immediately with fresh crusty bread, garnished with chives or parsley.

VARIATIONS:
**Ham Carbonara** – use cooked ham instead of the salami. Do not overcook this dish – the mixture should only be tossed in the pan for 1 to 2 minutes.
**Lamb or Beef Carbonara** – leftover cooked lamb or beef can be used, but heat thoroughly in the butter before adding the pasta.

# Buttered Noodles

METRIC/IMPERIAL
225 g/8 oz packet egg noodles
salt and freshly ground pepper
50 g/2 oz butter
2 spring onions, chopped
1 tablespoon poppy seeds

AMERICAN
½ lb egg noodles
salt and freshly ground pepper
¼ cup butter
2 scallions, chopped
1 tablespoon poppy seeds

Cook the noodles in plenty of boiling salted water until tender. Drain well and toss with the remaining ingredients. Serve at once.

# Spaghetti Provençale

METRIC/IMPERIAL
2 teaspoons olive oil
1 onion, chopped
1 clove garlic, crushed
½ green pepper, cored, seeded and chopped
1 small aubergine, chopped
1 x 227 g/8 oz can tomatoes
½ teaspoon dried basil
½ teaspoon dried oregano
salt and freshly ground pepper
100 g/4 oz spaghetti
50 g/2 oz Cheddar cheese, grated
25 g/1 oz grated Parmesan cheese

AMERICAN
2 teaspoons olive oil
1 onion, chopped
1 clove garlic, crushed
½ green pepper, seeded and chopped
1 small eggplant, chopped
1 x 8 oz can tomatoes
½ teaspoon dried basil
½ teaspoon dried oregano
salt and freshly ground pepper
¼ lb spaghetti
½ cup grated Cheddar cheese
¼ cup grated Parmesan cheese

Heat the oil in a heavy-based pan and cook the onion and garlic for 3 minutes. Add the green pepper, aubergine (eggplant), tomatoes with their juice, basil and oregano and plenty of salt and pepper. Bring to the boil, pressing gently on the tomatoes to break them up. Cover and simmer for 30 minutes.

Cook the spaghetti in boiling salted water for 15 minutes or until just tender. Drain and rinse with boiling water, then divide between two warmed serving plates and spoon the vegetables on top. Mix together the cheeses, then sprinkle over. Serve with a green salad.

# Chilli-Cheese Macaroni

METRIC/IMPERIAL
40 g/1 ½ oz butter
1 medium onion, finely chopped
2 sticks celery, finely chopped
½ red pepper, cored, seeded and
 chopped
1 teaspoon chilli powder
100 g/4 oz short-cut macaroni,
 cooked and drained
100 g/4 oz mature Cheddar
 cheese, diced
salt and freshly ground pepper
2 eggs
300 ml/½ pint milk

AMERICAN
3 tablespoons butter
1 medium-sized onion, finely
 chopped
2 stalks celery, finely chopped
½ red pepper, seeded and
 chopped
1 teaspoon chili powder
¼ lb elbow macaroni, cooked and
 drained
¼ lb sharp Cheddar cheese, diced
salt and freshly ground pepper
2 eggs
1 ¼ cups milk

Melt the butter in a heavy frying pan (skillet) and sauté the onion, celery
and red pepper until soft but not brown. Stir in the chilli powder, cook for 1
minute, then add the cooked macaroni, cheese and salt and pepper to
taste. Mix well, and spoon into a small greased baking dish.
 Beat the eggs and milk together and pour over the macaroni. Cook in a
preheated moderate oven (180°C/350°F, Gas Mark 4) for 35 minutes, or
until firm and golden brown on top.


# Tortellini in Cream Sauce

METRIC/IMPERIAL
175 g/6 oz tortellini
salt
150 ml/¼ pint single cream
1 tablespoon Pesto (see page 173)
freshly ground pepper
grated Parmesan cheese, to serve

AMERICAN
6 oz tortellini
salt
⅔ cup light cream
1 tablespoon Pesto (see page 173)
freshly ground pepper
grated Parmesan cheese, to serve

Cook tortellini in boiling salted water for 12 to 15 minutes. Drain well.
 Pour cream into a pan and heat gently to nearly boiling point. Remove
from heat and stir in pesto and pepper to taste. Add tortellini and toss well.
Divide between two warmed serving bowls and serve with Parmesan
cheese and a crisp green salad.

# Pasta and Tuna Salad

METRIC/IMPERIAL
*100 g/4 oz whole green beans*
*salt and freshly ground pepper*
*100 g/4 oz pasta shapes*
*3 tablespoons olive oil*
*4 fresh basil leaves, chopped*
*2 ripe tomatoes, cut in wedges*
*3 spring onions, chopped*
*1 x 200 g/7 oz can tuna in oil,*
*    drained*
*2 tablespoons chopped parsley*

AMERICAN
*¼ lb whole green beans*
*salt and freshly ground pepper*
*¼ lb pasta shapes*
*3 tablespoons olive oil*
*4 fresh basil leaves, chopped*
*2 ripe tomatoes, cut in wedges*
*3 scallions, chopped*
*1 x 7 oz can tuna in oil, drained*
*2 tablespoons chopped parsley*

Top and tail the beans if necessary. Cut into 2.5 cm/1 inch lengths. Bring a large pan of salted water to the boil and add the pasta shapes and beans. When the pasta is tender but still firm, drain immediately and refresh under cold water. Drain thoroughly.

Place the beans and pasta in a salad bowl and mix in olive oil, basil and salt and freshly ground pepper to taste. Toss gently with 2 forks to coat the beans and pasta with oil. Add the tomatoes, spring onions (scallions), tuna chunks and parsley. Toss lightly to combine.

Serve the salad at room temperature with chunks of wholemeal bread and butter.

VARIATION:
**Pasta Niçoise** – add black or green olives, some anchovy fillets and wedges of hard-boiled (hard-cooked) eggs to the above salad.

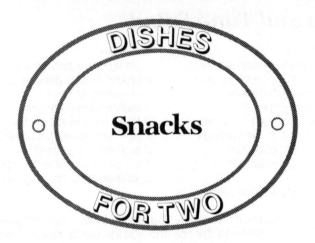

**DISHES**

**Snacks**

**FOR TWO**

# *Croque Monsieur*

METRIC/IMPERIAL
4 thin slices bread (not fresh)
butter
2 slices Emmental cheese
2 slices cooked ham
4 tablespoons milk
15 g/½ oz plain flour
salt and freshly ground pepper
1 egg
2 teaspoons olive oil
oil for shallow frying

AMERICAN
4 thin slices bread (not fresh)
butter
2 slices Swiss cheese
2 slices cooked ham
4 tablespoons milk
2 tablespoons all-purpose flour
salt and freshly ground pepper
1 egg
2 teaspoons olive oil
oil for shallow frying

Spread one side of each slice of bread with butter and use the cheese and ham to make two sandwiches. Trim off all the crusts.

Pour the milk on to a plate. Place the flour, seasoned with salt and pepper, on another plate. Beat together the egg and olive oil on a third plate. Dip each side of both sandwiches first in the milk, then the flour, then the egg, pressing the edges together securely.

Heat about 2.5 cm/1 inch of oil in a heavy-based frying pan (skillet). Fry the sandwiches, one at a time, pressing down with a fish slice for 1 minute, then cook for a further 2 minutes. Turn and cook other side in the same way.

Serve immediately with a mixed salad.

VARIATION:
**Croque Madame** – make sandwiches as above and top each one with a fried egg.

178

# Speedy Pizza Submarine

METRIC/IMPERIAL
1 x 227 g/8 oz can tomatoes,
    drained and chopped
1 clove garlic, crushed
4 black olives, stoned and chopped
1 tablespoon chopped fresh or
    1 teaspoon dried oregano
1 tablespoon olive oil
salt and freshly ground pepper
½ French loaf
6 thin slices Mozzarella cheese
6 slices salami
6 canned anchovy fillets
75 g/3 oz Parmesan cheese, grated

AMERICAN
1 x 8 oz can tomatoes, drained and
    chopped
1 clove garlic, crushed
4 black olives, pitted and chopped
1 tablespoon chopped fresh or
    1 teaspoon dried oregano
1 tablespoon olive oil
salt and freshly ground pepper
½ French loaf
6 thin slices Mozzarella cheese
6 slices salami
6 canned anchovy fillets
¾ cup grated Parmesan cheese

Put the tomatoes, garlic, olives, oregano, oil and salt and pepper to taste in a pan and simmer for 10 minutes.

Split the bread lengthwise and place on a baking sheet. Spoon the hot tomato mixture evenly on top and then add the cheese and salami slices alternately, slightly overlapping. Cut the anchovies into small pieces and scatter on top, then drizzle with the oil from the can. Sprinkle with the Parmesan cheese and place under a medium grill (broiler) for 4 to 6 minutes until the topping is golden and bubbly. Serve immediately.

# Curried Chicken Sandwich Snacks

METRIC/IMPERIAL
225 g/8 oz cooked chicken,
    chopped
1 stick celery, finely chopped
2 spring onions, finely chopped
1 tablespoon desiccated coconut
4 tablespoons mayonnaise
2 teaspoons curry powder
1 tablespoon lemon juice
½ green pepper, cored, seeded
    and finely chopped
salt and freshly ground pepper
8 slices buttered bread

AMERICAN
1 cup chopped cooked chicken
1 stalk celery, finely chopped
2 scallions, finely chopped
1 tablespoon shredded coconut
¼ cup mayonnaise
2 teaspoons curry powder
1 tablespoon lemon juice
½ green pepper, seeded and finely
    chopped
salt and freshly ground pepper
8 slices buttered bread

Mix all the ingredients together, except the bread. Place 4 slices of bread in a snackmaker (see Note) buttered side down, and divide the filling between them. Top with the remaining bread slices, buttered side up, and toast until crisp and brown.

**Note:** if you have not got a snackmaker, toast under a preheated moderate grill (broiler).

# Muffin Pizzas

METRIC/IMPERIAL
2 muffins or baps
1 x 227 g/8 oz can tomatoes
1 small clove garlic, crushed
½ teaspoon dried oregano
salt and freshly ground pepper
50 g/2 oz mature Cheddar cheese,
  grated
50 g/2 oz salami, diced
2 tablespoons grated Parmesan
  cheese

AMERICAN
2 English muffins or baps
1 x 8 oz can tomatoes
1 small clove garlic
½ teaspoon dried oregano
salt and freshly ground pepper
½ cup grated sharp Cheddar
  cheese
½ cup diced salami
2 tablespoons grated Parmesan
  cheese

Toast the muffins on both sides under the grill (broiler) then split open. Drain tomatoes and chop finely in a bowl. Mix in garlic, oregano and salt and pepper to taste. Spread evenly over the muffins, then top with the grated Cheddar cheese and salami. Sprinkle over the Parmesan cheese, then place under a medium hot grill (broiler) until the topping is bubbling. Serve immediately with a green salad.

VARIATIONS:
1. Mash together 198 g/7 oz can mackerel in tomato sauce and 50 g/2 oz grated Red Leicester cheese (brick cheese) with salt and pepper to taste.
2. Mash canned sardines or sild with gherkin relish and cream cheese.
3. Grill 4 streaky bacon rashers, crumble and mix with chopped canned tomatoes and chopped black olives. Sprinkle with Parmesan, grill till bubbling.

# Danish Surprise

METRIC/IMPERIAL
2 slices rye bread
butter, softened
grated horseradish
50 g/2 oz smoked salmon, cut into
  thin slices
1 Bismarck (pickled) herring fillet,
  cut into thin strips
15 g/½ oz lumpfish roe
2 tablespoons soured cream
2 sprigs dill weed or parsley

AMERICAN
2 slices rye bread
butter, softened
grated horseradish
½ cup smoked salmon strips
1 Danish pickled herring fillet, cut
  into thin strips
1 tablespoon lumpfish roe
2 tablespoons sour cream
2 sprigs dill weed or parsley

Lightly toast the bread and spread with butter blended with horseradish to taste. Cover with alternate strips of smoked salmon, herring and lumpfish roe.
Serve at once, topped with a spoonful of sour cream and a sprig of fresh dill or parsley.

# Fish in Pitta

METRIC/IMPERIAL
2 pitta breads
100 g/4 oz coleslaw
225 g/8 oz cod fillet, skinned
1 egg, beaten
40 g/1 ½ oz dry breadcrumbs
oil for shallow frying
mayonnaise to serve

AMERICAN
2 pitta breads
1 cup coleslaw
½ lb cod fillet, skinned
1 egg, beaten
½ cup dry bread crumbs
oil for shallow frying
mayonnaise to serve

Slit each pitta bread along one side with a sharp knife and spoon coleslaw inside.

Cut the fish into strips, then dip them first in the egg, then the breadcrumbs. Heat about 2.5 cm/1 inch oil in a heavy-based frying pan (skillet), add the fish and fry for 5 to 7 minutes, turning occasionally until crisp and golden all over. Drain on kitchen paper towels, then divide between the pitta breads. Top with a dollop of mayonnaise and serve immediately.

# Cheese Chowder

METRIC/IMPERIAL
50 g/2 oz butter
1 small onion, finely chopped
1 small carrot, finely chopped
2 sticks celery, finely chopped
¼ teaspoon each salt, paprika and
  dry mustard
1 tablespoon plain flour
1 x 425 g/15 oz can cream of
  chicken soup
300 ml/½ pint skimmed milk
50 g/2 oz mature Cheddar cheese,
  grated

AMERICAN
¼ cup butter
1 small onion, finely chopped
1 small carrot, finely chopped
2 stalks celery, finely chopped
¼ teaspoon each salt, paprika and
  dry mustard
1 tablespoon all-purpose flour
1 x 16 oz can cream of chicken
  soup
1 ¼ cups skimmed milk
½ cup grated sharp Cheddar
  cheese

Melt the butter in a pan, add the onion, carrot, celery, salt, paprika and dry mustard and fry, covered, for 5 minutes. Blend in the flour, cook for 1 minute, then stir in the chicken soup and milk.

Bring the chowder to the boil, stirring, then simmer, covered, for 10 minutes. Stir in the cheese, cook for 1 minute, then serve with warm French bread.

# Hot Corned Beef on Rye

METRIC/IMPERIAL
4 thick slices rye bread
4 tablespoons mayonnaise
2 teaspoons tomato ketchup
dash of Tabasco sauce
2 spring onions, chopped
salt and freshly ground pepper
100 g/4 oz sauerkraut, rinsed and
   well drained
4 slices corned beef
4 slices Gruyère or Jarlsberg
   cheese

AMERICAN
4 thick slices rye bread
1/4 cup mayonnaise
2 teaspoons tomato ketchup
dash of hot pepper sauce
2 scallions, chopped
salt and freshly ground pepper
1/4 lb sauerkraut, rinsed and well
   drained
4 slices corned beef
4 slices Swiss or Jarlsberg cheese

Toast the bread on one side only. Mix together the mayonnaise, ketchup, Tabasco (hot pepper) sauce, onions (scallions) and salt and pepper to taste. Spread on untoasted side of bread. Divide sauerkraut evenly between slices and top with corned beef and cheese.

   Grill (broil) for about 5 minutes until the cheese is melted. Serve immediately.


# Cheese and Date Dreams

METRIC/IMPERIAL
4 rashers streaky bacon
50 g/2 oz cream cheese, softened
50 g/2 oz stoned dates, chopped
4 slices white bread
1 egg
4 tablespoons milk
salt and freshly ground pepper
butter for frying

AMERICAN
4 slices bacon
1/2 cup cream cheese, softened
1/3 cup chopped pitted dates
4 slices white bread
1 egg
1/4 cup milk
salt and freshly ground pepper
butter for frying

Fry the bacon slowly in a pan until crisp. Remove and drain on kitchen paper towels. Cover and keep warm.

   Mix together the cream cheese and dates. Spread on two slices of bread and cover with the remaining bread. Beat the egg with the milk and salt and pepper to taste on a plate. Dip each sandwich into the mixture.

   Add a knob of butter to the bacon fat and fry the sandwiches on both sides until crisp and golden. Serve immediately topped with the bacon.

VARIATIONS:
**Fillings for Sandwiches** – instead of dates mix any of the following with the cream cheese: chopped walnuts; peeled prawns (shelled shrimp); drained canned tuna; mashed banana; diced green pepper; finely chopped onion; fresh herbs (parsley, chives, tarragon, thyme, basil).

# Cinnamon Nut Toast

METRIC/IMPERIAL
4 slices white bread
50 g/2 oz butter
1 ½ tablespoons honey
2 teaspoons ground cinnamon
2 tablespoons chopped mixed nuts

AMERICAN
4 slices white bread
¼ cup butter
1 ½ tablespoons honey
2 teaspoons ground cinnamon
2 tablespoons chopped mixed nuts

Toast the bread on one side only. Mix the remaining ingredients together and spread on the untoasted side. Place under a medium grill (broiler) and cook until the topping is bubbling. Cut into fingers to serve.

VARIATION:
**Oriental Toast** – use five-spice powder, available from Chinese food shops, instead of cinnamon.

# Chef's Club Sandwich

METRIC/IMPERIAL
6 thick slices white bread
butter for spreading
crisp lettuce leaves
4 slices Gruyère cheese
tomato slices
2 rashers back bacon, grilled
salt and freshly ground pepper
2 tablespoons mayonnaise
6 slices cooked chicken

AMERICAN
6 thick slices white bread
butter for spreading
crisp lettuce leaves
4 slices Swiss cheese
tomato slices
1 large slice Canadian bacon,
   broiled and cut in half
salt and freshly ground pepper
2 tablespoons mayonnaise
6 slices cooked chicken

Toast the bread on both sides, then butter one side of each slice.

On the first buttered side, place some lettuce, cheese, tomato and bacon and a little freshly ground pepper. Place second slice of toast on top, buttered side down, spread with mayonnaise and arrange more lettuce and chicken on top. Season with salt and pepper, then top with third slice of toast, buttered side down. Cut in two to serve. Repeat to make another sandwich. If like, garnish with stuffed olives.

# Soufflé Toasts

METRIC/IMPERIAL
4 eggs, separated
salt and freshly ground pepper
4 rashers bacon, cooked and
  chopped
4 tablespoons grated cheese
4 slices buttered toast
chopped parsley or chives to
  garnish

AMERICAN
4 eggs, separated
salt and freshly ground pepper
4 slices bacon, cooked and
  chopped
¼ cup grated cheese
4 slices buttered toast
chopped parsley or chives for
  garnish

Beat the egg yolks with salt and pepper to taste, then stir in the bacon and cheese. Whisk the egg whites until soft peaks form, then fold into the yolk mixture. Pile on to the toast, covering each slice completely. Grill (broil) under a low heat for 5 to 7 minutes, then serve garnished with parsley or chives.

# Quick Fry Supper

METRIC/IMPERIAL
2 tablespoons oil
175 g/6 oz ham, diced
2 tablespoons plain flour
2 tablespoons mild made mustard
1 tablespoon Worcestershire sauce
300 ml/½ pint milk
1 x 283 g/10 oz can green bean
  chunks, drained
225 g/8 oz cooked potatoes, sliced
50 g/2 oz Gruyère cheese, sliced
salt and pepper
green pepper rings to garnish

AMERICAN
2 tablespoons oil
¾ cup diced ham
2 tablespoons all-purpose flour
2 tablespoons mild prepared
  mustard
1 tablespoon Worcestershire sauce
1¼ cups milk
1 x 10 oz can green bean chunks,
  drained
½ lb cooked potatoes, sliced
2 oz Gruyère cheese, sliced
salt and pepper
green pepper rings for garnish

Heat the oil in a pan and fry the ham for 3 minutes. Remove with a slotted spoon and leave on one side. Stir in the flour and cook for 1 minute. Remove pan from heat and gradually add the mustard, Worcestershire sauce and milk. Heat, stirring, until the sauce thickens.

Add the ham, green beans, potatoes and cheese and heat through gently until the cheese melts. Add salt and pepper to taste. Transfer to two warmed serving plates and garnish with the green pepper rings. Serve with crusty fresh bread.

# Egg and Mushroom Cups

METRIC/IMPERIAL
2 large or 4 small round crusty rolls
olive oil
25 g/1 oz butter
2 eggs, beaten
1 x 213 g/7½ oz can creamed
   mushrooms
salt and freshly ground pepper

AMERICAN
2 large or 4 small round crusty rolls
olive oil
2 tablespoons butter
2 eggs, beaten
1 x 7½ oz can creamed
   mushrooms
salt and freshly ground pepper

Cut a thin slice from the top of the rolls and pull out the soft bread inside. Brush rolls inside and out with olive oil and place on a baking sheet.

Melt the butter in a small pan and stir in the eggs and creamed mushrooms. Cook gently until almost set, then remove from the heat and add salt and pepper to taste. Pile the mixture into the rolls, then bake in a preheated moderate oven (180°C/350°F, Gas Mark 4) for 10 minutes. Serve immediately.

# Scrambled Fish 'n' Egg

METRIC/IMPERIAL
4 eggs
salt and freshly ground pepper
25 g/1 oz butter
175 g/6 oz fillet smoked fish,
   cooked and flaked
2 tablespoons single cream
2 tablespoons mayonnaise
chopped chives to garnish

AMERICAN
4 eggs
salt and freshly ground pepper
2 tablespoons butter
1½ cups flaked smoked fish
2 tablespoons light cream
2 tablespoons mayonnaise
chopped chives for garnish

Beat the eggs and add salt and pepper to taste. Melt the butter in a non-stick pan and add the eggs. Cook, stirring, until nearly set. Fold in the fish, cream and mayonnaise.

Serve immediately, sprinkled with chives, with hot buttered toast and grilled tomato halves.

VARIATIONS:
**Mushroom Eggs** – lightly sauté 2 large flat mushrooms on both sides and use these as the base when serving the Scrambled Fish 'n' Egg.
**Special Egg Scramble** – instead of smoked fish and mayonnaise, flavour the eggs with: 100 g/4 oz (½ cup) chopped cooked ham; peeled prawns (shelled shrimp); diced garlic sausage or salami. Or mix in 2 finely chopped spring onions (scallions) and 50 g/2 oz whole kernel corn.

# Spanish Baked Eggs

METRIC/IMPERIAL
50 g/2 oz butter
1 clove garlic, crushed
100 g/4 oz sliced chorizo sausage
   or salami
1 green pepper, cored, seeded and
   finely chopped
4 eggs
salt and freshly ground pepper
4 tablespoons single cream

AMERICAN
¼ cup butter
1 clove garlic, crushed
¼ lb sliced chorizo sausage or
   salami
1 green pepper, seeded and finely
   chopped
4 eggs
salt and freshly ground pepper
4 tablespoons light cream

Heat the butter in a flameproof dish and gently fry the garlic, sausage and green pepper until the pepper is softened. Break the eggs over the top, add salt and pepper to taste, then spoon the cream over.

Cook in a preheated moderate oven (180°C/350°F, Gas Mark 4) for 8 to 10 minutes or until the whites are set but the yolks are still soft.


# Omelette Brayaude

METRIC/IMPERIAL
2 tablespoons dripping or oil
175 g/6 oz potatoes, peeled and
   diced
100 g/4 oz cooked ham, diced
6 eggs
15 g/½ oz butter, cut into slivers
salt
freshly ground pepper
3 tablespoons double cream
50 g/2 oz grated Gruyère cheese

AMERICAN
2 tablespoons pork drippings or oil
1 cup peeled and diced potatoes
½ cup diced ham
6 eggs
1 tablespoon butter, cut into slivers
salt
freshly ground pepper
3 tablespoons thick cream
½ cup grated Swiss cheese

Heat the dripping or oil in a large omelette pan, add the potatoes and fry briskly for 5 minutes, shaking the pan constantly. Lower the heat, cover and cook for 10 to 15 minutes until the potatoes are almost tender. Shake the pan occasionally to prevent sticking.

Add the ham, mixing very gently so as not to break the potatoes. Whisk the eggs together lightly, add the butter and salt and pepper to taste, then pour over the potatoes and ham. Increase the heat and cook until the underside is golden. Turn out on to a plate, then slide back into the pan, cooked side up. When the underside is cooked, cut the omelette in two and place each part on a warmed plate. Sprinkle with the cream and cheese and serve immediately with Broccoli in Wine (see page 123).

# Pipérade

METRIC/IMPERIAL

1 green or red pepper, cored,
    seeded and finely chopped
1 fresh chilli, seeded and chopped
1 onion, finely chopped
1 garlic clove, crushed
3 tablespoons oil
1 x 227 g/8 oz can tomatoes,
    drained and chopped
¼ teaspoon dried marjoram
4 eggs, beaten
salt and freshly ground pepper

AMERICAN

1 green or red pepper, seeded and
    finely chopped
1 fresh chili, seeded and chopped
1 onion, finely chopped
1 garlic clove, crushed
3 tablespoons oil
1 x 8 oz can tomatoes, drained and
    chopped
¼ teaspoon dried marjoram
4 eggs, beaten
salt and freshly ground pepper

Gently fry the pepper, chilli, onion and garlic in the oil until soft. Add the tomatoes and the marjoram. Cook over medium heat for 10 minutes, stirring occasionally, then pour the eggs over and add salt and pepper to taste. Increase the heat and cook, drawing the mixture from sides to middle with a palette knife until eggs are set.

Serve immediately with a crisp green salad.

# Baked Eggs en Cocotte

Butter individual shallow ovenproof dishes, pour 1 tablespoon cream into each and break in 2 eggs. Season with salt and pepper to taste and put another spoonful of cream, or a knob of butter on top.

Place dishes in a shallow pan, half-filled with hot water and cook in a preheated moderate oven (180°C/350°F, Gas Mark 4) for about 10 minutes or until the whites are just set and the yolks soft. Serve in the dishes, garnished with triangles of fried bread or Croûtons (see page 147).

VARIATION:

**Baked Eggs and Onions** – place a layer of golden fried onions in the dishes instead of the cream. Add the eggs and sprinkle with fresh breadcrumbs mixed with melted butter and a little grated Parmesan cheese. Cook in a preheated hot oven (220°C/425°F, Gas Mark 7) for 6 minutes.

# Chinese-Style Eggs

METRIC/IMPERIAL
4 eggs
oil for frying
1 tablespoon soy sauce
2 teaspoons vinegar
1 teaspoon brown sugar

AMERICAN
4 eggs
oil for frying
1 tablespoon soy sauce
2 teaspoons vinegar
1 teaspoon brown sugar

Fry each egg individually and, just before it is set, fold it over into a half moon shape, pressing the edges together with the egg slice. Remove from pan and keep warm.

When all eggs are cooked, add the soy sauce, vinegar and sugar to the pan and bring to the boil. Place eggs in the mixture and cook covered for 1 minute. Serve immediately with boiled rice.

VARIATIONS:
**Gingered Eggs** – finely chop 2 slices of fresh root ginger and add to the sauce.
**Sweet and Sour Eggs** – in a small pan heat together 1 tablespoon cornflour (cornstarch), 4 tablespoons (¼ cup) cold water, 1 tablespoon each soy sauce, tomato purée (paste) and vinegar, 2 tablespoons orange juice and 1 teaspoon brown sugar. Bring to the boil and simmer, stirring, until thick and translucent. Pour over the fried eggs to serve.

# Baked Eggs, Arnold Bennett

METRIC/IMPERIAL
225 g/8 oz cooked smoked
   haddock
3 eggs
120 ml/4 fl oz double cream
salt and white pepper
1 tablespoon each grated Cheddar
   and Parmesan cheese
butter

AMERICAN
½ lb cooked finnan haddie
   (smoked haddock)
3 eggs
½ cup heavy cream
salt and white pepper
1 tablespoon each grated Cheddar
   and Parmesan cheese
butter

Flake the haddock, discarding the skin and bones. Separate 1 egg, reserving the white. Add the yolk and one-third of the cream to the fish and mix in with salt and pepper to taste. Lightly whip the remaining cream, fold in the cheeses and salt and pepper to taste. Whisk the reserved egg white until stiff and fold in.

Butter 2 shallow ovenproof dishes and divide the fish mixture between them. Break an egg into each dish, then cover it with the cream and cheese mixture. Cook in a preheated moderately hot oven (200°C/400°F, Gas Mark 6) for 6 to 10 minutes. Serve immediately.

# Egg and Vegetable Fry

METRIC/IMPERIAL
1 medium aubergine, peeled and
  cut in thin slices
salt
4 tablespoons oil
2 large ripe tomatoes, quartered
1 clove garlic, peeled and crushed
1 bouquet garni
freshly ground pepper
4 eggs
100 g/4 oz ham, cut in thick strips
chopped parsley, to garnish

AMERICAN
1 medium eggplant, peeled and cut
  in thin slices
salt
4 tablespoons oil
2 large ripe tomatoes, quartered
1 clove garlic, peeled and crushed
1 bouquet garni
freshly ground pepper
4 eggs
¼ lb ham, cut in thick strips
chopped parsley, for garnish

Place the aubergine (eggplant) slices in a single layer on a plate, sprinkle with salt and leave for 20 minutes.

Meanwhile, heat 1 tablespoon oil in a heavy-based pan, add the tomatoes, garlic, bouquet garni and salt and pepper to taste. Cover the pan and cook gently for 10 minutes, crushing the tomatoes from time to time with a wooden spoon to break them up. Rub through a fine strainer (preferably not metal), return to the rinsed-out pan and keep hot.

Rinse the aubergines and dry on absorbent paper towels. Heat 2 tablespoons oil in a frying pan (skillet), add the aubergines and fry until golden on both sides. Remove with a slotted spoon and arrange on two warmed plates. Add remaining oil to the pan and fry the eggs to your liking. Add the strips of ham and heat through.

To serve, place the eggs on the aubergine slices, then top with the strips of ham and tomato sauce. Garnish with parsley and serve immediately.

# Chinese Egg Fried Rice with Ham

METRIC/IMPERIAL
3 tablespoons oil
2 large eggs, beaten
150 g/5 oz cooked long-grain rice
½ teaspoon salt
50 g/2 oz cooked ham, diced
1 tablespoon chopped spring onion
coriander leaves to garnish

AMERICAN
3 tablespoons oil
2 large eggs, beaten
¾ cup cooked long-grain rice
½ teaspoon salt
¼ cup diced cooked ham
1 tablespoon chopped scallion
Chinese parsley leaves for garnish

Heat the oil in a pan over a high heat. Pour in the beaten eggs and stir-fry for 1 second. Add the rice and salt and stir with the eggs until the rice grains are separated. Add the ham and spring onion (scallion) and stir-fry for 1 minute. Transfer to a serving dish and garnish with coriander (Chinese parsley) leaves. Serve hot.

# Eggs with Cucumber Sauce

METRIC/IMPERIAL
½ cucumber
40 g/1½ oz butter
1 tablespoon plain flour
150 ml/¼ pint hot chicken stock
½ tablespoon chopped dill weed
salt and freshly ground pepper
4 tablespoons double cream
2 hard-boiled eggs, halved

AMERICAN
½ cucumber
3 tablespoons butter
1 tablespoon all-purpose flour
⅔ cup hot chicken stock or broth
½ tablespoon chopped dill weed
salt and freshly ground pepper
¼ cup heavy cream
2 hard-cooked eggs, halved

Peel the cucumber and chop it roughly. Melt the butter in a saucepan and cook the cucumber, covered, for 5 minutes.

Sprinkle in the flour and cook for 1 minute, then add the stock. Simmer for 10 minutes, then add the dill, salt and pepper to taste, and stir in the cream.

Place two egg halves on each plate and spoon the cucumber sauce over. Serve with chunks of crusty bread.

# Eggs Sweet and Sour

METRIC/IMPERIAL
25 g/1 oz butter
½ green pepper, cored, seeded
  and chopped
1 onion, sliced
2 celery sticks, chopped
1 x 210 g/7½ oz can pineapple
  pieces
1 tablespoon tomato purée
1 teaspoon cornflour
1 tablespoon paprika pepper
2 teaspoons vinegar
1 teaspoon soy sauce
salt and freshly ground pepper
4 hard-boiled eggs, halved
chopped parsley to garnish

AMERICAN
2 tablespoons butter
½ green pepper, seeded and
  chopped
1 onion, sliced
2 stalks celery, chopped
1 x 7½ oz can pineapple pieces
1 tablespoon tomato paste
1 teaspoon cornstarch
1 tablespoon paprika
2 teaspoons vinegar
1 teaspoon soy sauce
salt and freshly ground pepper
4 hard-cooked eggs, halved
chopped parsley for garnish

Melt the butter in a pan and sauté the green pepper, onion and celery for 5 minutes.

Drain the juice from the pineapple and reserve. Add the fruit and tomato purée (paste) to the pan. Blend the cornflour (cornstarch) with the pineapple juice. Stir in the paprika, vinegar and soy sauce. Add to the pan and heat, stirring, until the sauce thickens.

Add salt and pepper to taste and stir in the eggs. Cover and simmer for 5 to 8 minutes. Transfer to a warmed serving dish and garnish with parsley. Serve with rice.

# Creamy Eggs and Onions

METRIC/IMPERIAL
225 g/8 oz onions
50 g/2 oz butter
1 tablespoon plain flour
400 ml/⅔ pint hot chicken stock
6 large sage leaves, chopped
6 tablespoons double cream
sea-salt and freshly ground pepper
2 hard-boiled eggs, halved

AMERICAN
½ lb onions
¼ cup butter
1 tablespoon all-purpose flour
2 cups hot chicken stock or broth
6 large sage leaves, chopped
6 tablespoons heavy cream
sea-salt and freshly ground pepper
2 hard-cooked eggs, halved

Peel the onions and chop them coarsely. Melt the butter in a pan and cook the onions, covered, for 10 minutes. Stir in the flour and cook for 1 minute, then add the stock.

Add the sage to the pan, cover and simmer slowly for 10 to 15 minutes until the onions are soft. Stir in the cream, and add salt and pepper to taste.

Put an egg in each bowl and spoon the sauce over. Serve with Garlic Croûtons (see page 147).

# Mediterranean Omelette

METRIC/IMPERIAL
15 g/½ oz butter
1 onion, chopped
50 g/2 oz mushrooms, sliced
1 small red pepper, cored, seeded
  and chopped
1 clove garlic, crushed
2 tomatoes, skinned and chopped
3 eggs
2 teaspoons water
1 teaspoon dried mixed herbs
salt and freshly ground pepper
2 teaspoons oil
25 g/1 oz grated Parmesan cheese

AMERICAN
1 tablespoon butter
1 onion, chopped
½ cup sliced mushrooms
1 small red pepper, seeded and
  chopped
1 clove garlic, crushed
2 tomatoes, peeled and chopped
3 eggs
2 teaspoons water
1 teaspoon dried mixed herbs
salt and freshly ground pepper
2 teaspoons oil
¼ cup grated Parmesan cheese

Melt the butter in a pan and sauté the onion, mushrooms, red pepper, garlic and tomatoes for 5 to 10 minutes or until soft. Remove with a slotted spoon and reserve.

Beat the eggs with the water, herbs and salt and pepper to taste. Heat the oil in an omelette pan and pour in the egg mixture. Cook over a medium heat for 1 minute or until the mixture is set on the bottom.

Spoon the vegetables over the omelette and continue to cook for 1 to 2 minutes, then sprinkle with Parmesan cheese and place under preheated grill (broiler) for 4 minutes. Cut into two and serve immediately.

# Spicy Egg Curry

METRIC/IMPERIAL
1 clove garlic, crushed
1 small onion, finely chopped
1 tablespoon oil
1 teaspoon each ground coriander
  and cumin
½ teaspoon chilli powder (or to
  taste)
freshly ground black pepper
2 tablespoons sesame seeds
½ teaspoon salt
150 ml/¼ pint plain yogurt
1 tablespoon lemon juice
4 hard-boiled eggs, shelled

AMERICAN
1 clove garlic, crushed
1 small onion, finely chopped
1 tablespoon oil
1 teaspoon each ground coriander
  and cumin
½ teaspoon chili powder (or to
  taste)
freshly ground black pepper
2 tablespoons sesame seeds
½ teaspoon salt
⅔ cup plain yogurt
1 tablespoon lemon juice
4 hard-cooked eggs, shelled

Cook the garlic and onion in the oil until soft. Add the spices, black pepper and sesame seeds and cook for 1 minute. Add the salt, yogurt and lemon juice and cook for 5 minutes but do not let it boil.

Halve the eggs and add them to the sauce. Cook until heated through, then serve with boiled rice or lentils and a green salad.

# Cheese and Bread Soufflé

METRIC/IMPERIAL
6 thin slices French bread
50 g/2 oz butter, softened
25 g/1 oz plain flour
150 ml/¼ pint milk
½ teaspoon made mustard
3 eggs, separated
75 g/3 oz mature Cheddar cheese,
  grated
salt and freshly ground pepper

AMERICAN
6 thin slices French bread
¼ cup softened butter
¼ cup all-purpose flour
⅔ cup milk
½ teaspoon prepared mustard
3 eggs, separated
¾ cup grated mature Cheddar
  cheese
salt and freshly ground pepper

Spread both sides of the bread with half the butter and use to line a greased 900 ml/1½ pint (3¾ cup) soufflé dish.

Melt the remaining 25 g/1 oz (2 tablespoons) butter in a pan, stir in the flour and cook for 1 minute. Remove from the heat and gradually blend in the milk. Cook the sauce, stirring, until it thickens. Cool slightly then beat in the mustard and egg yolks. Stir in the cheese and add salt and pepper to taste.

Whisk the egg whites until just stiff and carefully fold into the cheese mixture. Pour into the soufflé dish. Cook in a preheated moderately hot oven (200°C/400°F, Gas Mark 6) for 30 minutes or until well risen and golden brown. Serve immediately with a green salad.

# Crowns on Toast

METRIC/IMPERIAL
2 large eggs, separated
salt and freshly ground pepper
2 slices wholemeal toast, buttered
parsley sprigs to garnish

AMERICAN
2 large eggs, separated
salt and freshly ground pepper
2 slices wholewheat toast, buttered
parsley sprigs for garnish

Whisk the egg whites with salt and pepper to taste until soft peaks form. Pile half the egg white on to each slice of toast. Make a hollow in the centre and slip the yolk into the hollow.

Place on a baking sheet and cook in a preheated moderate oven (180°C/350°F, Gas Mark 4) for about 10 minutes until browned and the yolk is set. Serve immediately, garnished with parsley.

VARIATIONS:
**Ham Crowns** – to make this snack more substantial, place 2 slices of cooked ham on each piece of toast.
**Florentine Crowns** – place a layer of cooked leaf spinach (100 g/4 oz), then 50 g/2 oz (½ cup) diced Mozzarella cheese on the toast and continue as above.

# Hash Brown Omelettes

METRIC/IMPERIAL
2 medium potatoes, cooked and
    diced
1 tablespoon finely chopped onion
salt and freshly ground pepper
1 teaspoon lemon juice
2 tablespoons oil
2 tablespoons single cream
25 g/1 oz butter
4 eggs
chopped chives to garnish

AMERICAN
2 medium potatoes, cooked and
    diced
1 tablespoon finely chopped onion
salt and freshly ground pepper
1 teaspoon lemon juice
2 tablespoons oil
2 tablespoons light cream
2 tablespoons butter
4 eggs
chopped chives for garnish

Mix together the potatoes, onion, salt and pepper and lemon juice. Heat the oil in a heavy-based frying pan (skillet), then press the potato mixture in, shaping it into a flat cake. Cook very gently over a low heat until the underside is brown. Cut the potato cake in half and turn each half. Pour the cream over and continue cooking until second side is browned.

Heat half the butter in an omelette pan until sizzling but not browned. Beat 2 eggs and pour into the pan, then use a palette knife to draw the mixture from sides to middle so the uncooked egg runs underneath. When the underside is set but the top still runny, place half the potato cake on one side then fold the omelette over. Turn the omelette out on to a hot plate, sprinkle with chives. Keep warm while you make the second omelette.

# Basic Pancake (Crêpe) Batter

METRIC/IMPERIAL
*50 g/2 oz plain flour*
*½ teaspoon baking powder*
*¼ teaspoon salt*
*1 small egg*
*175 ml/6 fl oz milk*
*15 g/½ oz butter, melted*

AMERICAN
*½ cup all-purpose flour*
*½ teaspoon baking powder*
*¼ teaspoon salt*
*1 small egg*
*¾ cup milk*
*1 tablespoon melted butter*

Sift the flour, baking powder and salt into a mixing bowl. Make a well in the centre and add the egg, milk and butter, then gradually mix in the flour. Beat well, cover and leave to stand for 1 hour. (If preferred, all the ingredients can be put into a blender and mixed together.)

Heat a little extra butter in a crêpe pan. Use a small jug to pour in enough batter to coat the surface of the pan. Run the batter smoothly and evenly over the surface. Cook for about 1 minute until small bubbles appear, then use a spatula to turn the pancake over. Cook for 1 minute on the other side, or until set and golden brown. Lift out of the pan and fold in a clean towel. Repeat the process to make 6 pancakes in all.

SAVOURY FILLINGS:
**Spinach and Cheese** – fold 100 g/4 oz (½ cup) chopped, cooked and drained spinach with 4 tablespoons soured cream and 25 g/1 oz (¼ cup) grated Cheddar or Swiss cheese. Season with freshly ground black pepper and freshly grated nutmeg. Fill the pancakes (crêpes) with the mixture, roll up and arrange in an ovenproof serving dish. Make a cheese sauce: melt 25 g/1 oz (2 tablespoons) butter in a pan and stir in 1½ tablespoons flour and 1 teaspoon dry mustard. Cook for 1 minute, then gradually stir in 250 ml/8 fl oz (1 cup) milk and 50 g/2 oz (½ cup) grated cheese. Stir the sauce until it thickens, then pour over the rolled, stuffed pancakes (crêpes). Sprinkle with a little grated cheese and cook in a preheated moderately hot oven (200°C/400°F, Gas Mark 6) for 20 minutes.
**Spicy Crab or Chicken** – sauté 2 finely chopped spring onions (scallions) in 25 g/1 oz (2 tablespoons) butter. Stir in 2 teaspoons curry powder, fry for 1 minute, then add ½ teaspoon Worcestershire sauce, a dash of Tabasco, 4 tablespoons each soured cream and plain yogurt, and salt to taste. Fold in 100 g/4 oz (½ cup) crabmeat or chopped, cooked chicken and heat gently. Fill the pancakes with the crab or chicken mixture and arrange in a flameproof serving dish. Top with a little cream and place under a hot grill (broiler) to glaze.

SWEET FILLINGS:
**Jamaican Pineapple** – sauté 50 g/2 oz (½ cup) chopped fresh pineapple or chopped, well-drained canned pineapple in 25 g/1 oz (2 tablespoons) butter with 1 tablespoon brown sugar until lightly browned. Sprinkle over 1 tablespoon rum and cook for 1 minute more. Spread the pancakes (crêpes) with apricot jam, fill with the pineapple mixture, and arrange in a

flameproof serving dish. At the table, carefully set alight 1 tablespoon warm rum and pour over the pancakes (crêpes) while flaming. Serve with a bowl of chilled sour cream with a little brown sugar stirred through.
**Strawberry and Ice Cream** – drain a 312 g/11 oz can strawberries and place syrup in small pan. Boil until reduced by a half. Slice strawberries. Fold pancakes into quarters and arrange 3 on each plate. Cover with strawberries, a slice of vanilla ice cream and then pour the hot syrup over.

# *All-in-One Pancakes*

| METRIC/IMPERIAL | AMERICAN |
|---|---|
| *50 g/2 oz self-raising flour* | *½ cup self-rising flour* |
| *pinch of salt* | *pinch of salt* |
| *1 egg, lightly beaten* | *1 egg, lightly beaten* |
| *120 ml/4 fl oz milk* | *½ cup milk* |
| *flavouring ingredients (see below)* | *flavoring ingredients (see below)* |
| *oil for greasing pan* | *oil for greasing pan* |

Sift the flour and salt together. Mix the beaten egg and milk together and pour into the flour, folding through gently with a rubber spatula or a large metal spoon. Scatter flavouring ingredients over and fold in lightly.

Heat a large heavy frying pan (skillet) or griddle and grease the surface lightly. Place the mixture on in spoonfuls, dropping it from the tip of the spoon. When brown underneath and bubbles appear through the mixture, turn the pancakes with a metal spatula and cook the other side. Lift on to a cloth-covered wire rack. Regrease the pan before cooking each batch. Makes 12 small pancakes.

VARIATIONS:
**Ham and Herb** – mix together 2 tablespoons chopped fresh herbs (parsley, thyme, chives, oregano) with 2 slices chopped ham and add to the pancake mixture.
**Cheese and Asparagus** – mix together 25 g/1 oz (¼ cup) grated Cheddar cheese, 2 tablespoons drained and chopped, canned asparagus, ¼ teaspoon paprika and ¼ teaspoon cayenne and add to the pancake mixture. Sprinkle each pancake with a little extra grated cheese while hot.
**Apple and Sultana** – mix together 25 g/1 oz (¼ cup) chopped apple, 2 tablespoons sultanas (raisins), 1 tablespoon sugar and ¼ teaspoon ground cinnamon and add to the pancake mixture. Sprinkle the pancakes with a little extra sugar.
**Breakfast Pancakes** – make batter as above, adding 1 tablespoon sugar. Cook the pancakes and pile up in two stacks. Pour over golden or maple syrup to serve.

# Spinach and Cream Cheese Pancakes

METRIC/IMPERIAL
*100 g/4 oz spinach or sorrel*
*100 g/4 oz plain flour*
*pinch salt*
*1 egg*
*150 ml/¼ pint milk*
*lard for frying*
*15 g/½ oz butter, melted*
FILLING:
*225 g/8 oz cream cheese*
*salt and freshly ground pepper*
*2 tablespoons chopped chives*

AMERICAN
*¼ lb spinach or sorrel*
*1 cup all-purpose flour*
*pinch salt*
*1 egg*
*⅔ cup milk*
*lard for frying*
*1 tablespoon melted butter*
FILLING:
*1 cup cream cheese*
*salt and freshly ground pepper*
*2 tablespoons chopped chives*

Wash and drain the spinach or sorrel. Cook the leaves in a pan with a little water until soft, then rub through a sieve (strainer) to make a thin purée.

Sift the flour into a bowl with the salt. Beat in the egg and the milk then the spinach or sorrel purée. Allow the batter to stand for 10 minutes before using.

Season the cream cheese with salt and pepper and mix in the chopped chives.

Melt a little lard in a heavy-based pan and use the batter to make 8 small pancakes. Divide the filling between 4 of the pancakes and roll them up. Place on serving dish and pour over melted butter to serve.

**Note:** the remaining 4 pancakes can be stored in the refrigerator overnight. For a supper dish, layer the pancakes and a cheese sauce in a flameproof dish and sprinkle with cheese. Cook under a preheated grill (broiler) for about 10 to 15 minutes until heated through.

# Potted Cheese

METRIC/IMPERIAL
*225 g/8 oz cheese, grated*
*100 g/4 oz butter*
*6 tablespoons port, sherry, brandy*
*    or stout*
*pinch of pepper or cayenne*
*1 tablespoon chopped chives or*
*    fresh herbs*

AMERICAN
*2 cups grated cheese*
*½ cup butter*
*6 tablespoons port, sherry or*
*    brandy*
*pinch of pepper or cayenne*
*1 tablespoon chopped chives or*
*    fresh herbs*

Place all the ingredients in a blender or food processor fitted with the steel blade and process until smooth. Alternatively, cream the cheese and butter together with a wooden spoon, and gradually work in the flavourings. Spoon into a crockery bowl and store, tightly covered, in the refrigerator, where it will keep for weeks.

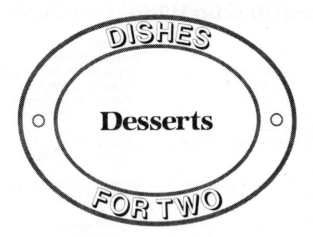

**DISHES**

**Desserts**

**FOR TWO**

# Canterbury Apples

METRIC/IMPERIAL
2 Granny Smith apples
50 g/2 oz butter
50 g/2 oz curd cheese
25 g/1 oz sultanas
25 g/1 oz brown sugar
½ teaspoon ground cinnamon

AMERICAN
2 large tart apples
¼ cup butter
¼ cup small curd cottage cheese
3 tablespoons raisins
2 tablespoons brown sugar
½ teaspoon ground cinnamon

Remove the cores from the apples and make a cut around the middle of each apple. Place in a shallow ovenproof dish greased with half the butter.

Blend together the curd cheese, sultanas (raisins), half the sugar and the cinnamon. Fill the centres of the apples with the cheese mixture. Press the rest on top and sprinkle with the remaining sugar.

Cook the apples in a preheated moderate oven (180°C/350°F, Gas Mark 4) for 1 hour. Serve warm with pouring cream or ice cream.

# Mango Dream Dessert

METRIC/IMPERIAL
1 ripe mango, peeled
1 tablespoon lemon or lime juice
1 tablespoon honey
250 ml/8 fl oz orange juice

AMERICAN
1 ripe mango, peeled
1 tablespoon lemon or lime juice
1 tablespoon honey
1 cup orange juice

Cut the mango flesh away from the seed and chop coarsely. Whirl with the remaining ingredients in a blender, pour into 2 stemmed glasses and serve with crisp sponge (lady) fingers.

# Yogurt Banana Whip

METRIC/IMPERIAL
2 small bananas
40 g/1½ oz brown sugar
2 teaspoons lemon juice
15 g/½ oz flaked almonds
2 teaspoons chopped stem ginger
150 ml/¼ pint plain yogurt
chocolate vermicelli to decorate

AMERICAN
2 small bananas
3 tablespoons brown sugar
2 teaspoons lemon juice
2 tablespoons sliced almonds
2 teaspoons chopped preserved
  ginger
⅔ cup plain yogurt
chocolate sprinkles to decorate

Mash the bananas and place in a pan with the sugar and lemon juice. Very slowly bring the mixture to the boil and continue to cook for 10 minutes. Remove the pan from the heat and leave to cool.

Stir in the nuts, ginger and yogurt. Blend well together, then spoon into two individual serving dishes. Just before serving, decorate with the chocolate vermicelli (sprinkles).

VARIATION:
To save cooking, make the dessert the night before. Stir the sugar, lemon juice, almonds and ginger into the yogurt and pile into glass dishes. Chill in the refrigerator overnight. Serve topped with fresh banana and Kiwifruit slices.

# Lemon Delight

METRIC/IMPERIAL
2 egg whites
25 g/1 oz ratafias, crushed
5 tablespoons double cream
grated rind and juice of 1 small
  lemon
3 tablespoons marsala
2 tablespoons caster sugar
chocolate curls to decorate

AMERICAN
2 egg whites
¼ cup crushed ratafias
6 tablespoons heavy cream
grated rind and juice of 1 small
  lemon
3 tablespoons marsala
2 tablespoons sugar
chocolate curls to decorate

Brush the inside of two glass dishes with some of the egg white and coat with the ratafias.

Whip the cream until thick, then stir in the lemon rind and juice, marsala and sugar. Whisk the remaining egg whites until stiff and fold into the lemon cream. Spoon into the dishes and chill well. Decorate with chocolate curls before serving.

# Apricot Cream

METRIC/IMPERIAL
6 ripe apricots, stoned and coarsely
  chopped
4 tablespoons milk
120 ml/4 fl oz double cream
1 tablespoon lemon juice
1 tablespoon sugar
4 ice cubes, crushed

AMERICAN
6 ripe apricots, pitted and coarsely
  chopped
¼ cup milk
½ cup heavy cream
1 tablespoon lemon juice
1 tablespoon sugar
4 ice cubes, crushed

Blend all the ingredients in a blender until smooth and creamy, then pour
into 2 tall stemmed glasses. Serve with crisp ginger biscuits.

# Summertime Apple Snow

METRIC/IMPERIAL
2 egg whites
25 g/1 oz caster sugar
1 x 100 g/4½ oz can apple purée
175 g/6 oz fresh or frozen and
  thawed raspberries
2 tablespoons icing sugar
sponge fingers to serve

AMERICAN
2 egg whites
2 tablespoons sugar
1 x 4½ oz can applesauce
1 cup fresh or frozen and thawed
  raspberries
2 tablespoons confectioners' sugar
lady fingers to serve

Whisk the egg whites until stiff, then lightly fold in the sugar. Place the
apple in a bowl and gently fold in the egg whites with a metal spoon.
  Divide the raspberries between two glass dishes, sprinkle with icing
(confectioners') sugar, then top with apple mixture. Serve immediately
with sponge (lady) fingers.

VARIATION:
Use any of the soft summer fruits as the base for this recipe.

# Sweet Fruit Cream

METRIC/IMPERIAL
100 g/4 oz strawberries, hulled
100 g/4 oz seedless black grapes
150 ml/¼ pint soured cream
5 tablespoons demerara sugar

AMERICAN
¼ lb strawberries, hulled
¼ lb seedless black grapes
⅔ cup sour cream
5 tablespoons light brown sugar

Arrange fruits in one layer in a shallow flameproof dish (about 18 cm/7 inch
by 13 cm/5 inch). Cover with the cream, then sprinkle over sugar to cover
cream completely. Place under a preheated hot grill (broiler) and cook until
sugar caramelizes – watch carefully to prevent the sugar from burning.
Cool, then refrigerate for 4 hours before serving.

# Cold Zabaglione

METRIC/IMPERIAL
50 g/2 oz granulated sugar
6 tablespoons water
2 egg yolks
1 tablespoon sweet sherry or
marsala
6 tablespoons double cream,
whipped

AMERICAN
1/4 cup sugar
6 tablespoons water
2 egg yolks
1 tablespoon sweet sherry or
marsala
6 tablespoons heavy cream,
whipped

Place the sugar and water in a pan and stir until the sugar dissolves, then boil until a thick syrup is formed.

Place the egg yolks in a bowl and gradually whisk in the syrup and sherry or marsala. Continue whisking until the mixture is thick and creamy. Fold in the whipped cream and spoon into serving dishes. When cool, cover and chill until serving time.

VARIATIONS:

**Pears with Zabaglione** – place a canned pear half in each dish and spoon zabaglione over. Serve chilled.

**Hot Zabaglione** – Place 2 egg yolks, 1 1/2 tablespoons of sugar and 6 tablespoons of sweet sherry or marsala in a heatproof, medium-sized bowl over, but not touching, a pan of gently simmering water. Whisk the mixture for about 8 to 10 minutes until thick and creamy. Pour into 2 serving glasses and serve with sponge (lady) fingers.

# Hot Compôte

METRIC/IMPERIAL
225 g/8 oz mixed dried fruits
(pineapple, pears, peaches, etc)
freshly made tea
150 ml/1/4 pint water
1 tablespoon clear honey
juice of 1/2 lemon
40 g/1 1/2 oz butter
25 g/1 oz demerara sugar
50 g/2 oz muesli cereal

AMERICAN
1/2 lb mixed dried fruits (pineapple,
pears, peaches, etc)
freshly made tea
2/3 cup water
1 tablespoon honey
juice of 1/2 lemon
3 tablespoons butter
1 1/2 tablespoons brown sugar
1/2 cup granola

Place the dried fruits in a bowl, cover with hot, strained tea and leave until cold. Drain the fruits well, then place in a pan with the water, honey and lemon juice. Bring to the boil, cover and cook gently for about 20 minutes until the fruit is tender. Turn into a shallow flameproof dish.

Melt the butter in a pan and add the sugar and muesli (granola). Mix well then sprinkle over the fruits. Place under a preheated moderate grill (broiler) until golden brown. Serve warm with pouring cream or yogurt.

# Crémets

| METRIC/IMPERIAL | AMERICAN |
|---|---|
| 120 ml/4 fl oz double cream chilled | ½ cup chilled heavy cream |
| 1 egg white | 1 egg white |
| fresh soft fruit, to serve | fresh soft fruit, to serve |
| sugar and cream, to serve | sugar and cream, to serve |

Whip the cream until stiff. Whisk the egg white in another bowl until stiff, then fold into the cream. Turn the mixture into two muslin (cheesecloth) lined crémet moulds (or use 2 small yogurt cartons with holes punched in the bottom). Cover and place in the refrigerator over a dish to catch the drips from the cream. Leave to drain for 3 to 6 hours.

Turn the crémets on to serving plates, surround with soft fruit, and serve with sugar and cream.

**Note:** chilled strawberries, raspberries or loganberries are the traditional accompaniments, but you could serve sliced banana or pineapple.


# Blackberry and Cream Crunch

| METRIC/IMPERIAL | AMERICAN |
|---|---|
| 225 g/8 oz fresh or frozen blackberries | 2 cups fresh or frozen blackberries |
| 1 tablespoon water | 1 tablespoon water |
| 1 tablespoon sugar | 1 tablespoon sugar |
| 120 ml/4 fl oz double or whipping cream | ½ cup heavy or whipping cream |
| 25 g/1 oz butter | 2 tablespoons butter |
| 100 g/4 oz digestive biscuits, crushed | 1½ cups graham cracker crumbs |

Place the blackberries in a pan with the water and sugar. Heat gently until the fruit is tender. Cool, then rub the fruit through a sieve (strainer) or purée in a blender or food processor.

Whisk the cream until very stiff. Melt the butter in a pan, then stir in the biscuit (cracker) crumbs and mix well.

Place alternate layers of crumb mixture, blackberry and cream in tall sundae glasses, finishing with the cream. Chill until ready to serve.

VARIATION:

**Finnish Trifles** – cook 225 g/8 oz (2 cups) cranberries in 2 tablespoons lemon juice for 10 minutes until they pop, then stir in 50 g/2 oz (⅓ cup) sugar and leave to cool. Whisk cream until stiff. Layer the cranberry sauce, cream and 25 g/1 oz (½ cup) fresh wholewheat breadcrumbs in tall glasses, finishing with a touch of sauce on the cream. Chill until ready to serve.

# Bananas Rio

METRIC/IMPERIAL
2 medium-ripe bananas
3 tablespoons orange juice
1 tablespoon lemon juice
2 tablespoons brown sugar
pinch of salt
15 g/½ oz butter
1 tablespoon freshly grated or
  desiccated coconut
whipped cream to serve

AMERICAN
2 medium-ripe bananas
3 tablespoons orange juice
1 tablespoon lemon juice
2 tablespoons brown sugar
pinch of salt
1 tablespoon butter
1 tablespoon freshly grated or
  shredded coconut
whipped cream to serve

Peel the bananas and arrange them in a buttered shallow casserole. Combine the orange and lemon juices, brown sugar and salt and pour over the bananas. Dot with butter and cook in a preheated moderately hot oven (200°C/400°F, Gas Mark 6) for 10 to 15 minutes.

Serve hot or warm, sprinkled with the coconut and topped with whipped cream.

# Crunchy Gooseberry Bake

METRIC/IMPERIAL
1 x 385 g/13½ oz can gooseberry
  pie filling
50 g/2 oz demerara sugar
juice of 1 orange
2 large slices bread, cut 1 cm/
  ½ inch thick
25 g/1 oz butter
½ teaspoon ground cinnamon

AMERICAN
1 x 14 oz can gooseberry pie filling
⅓ cup brown sugar
juice of 1 orange
2 large slices bread cut ½ inch
  thick
2 tablespoons butter
½ teaspoon ground cinnamon

Place the gooseberry filling in a 600 ml/1 pint (2½ cup) shallow ovenproof dish. Sprinkle with half the sugar, and the orange juice.

Remove the crusts, then cut the bread into 1 cm (½ inch) cubes. Melt the butter in a frying pan, add the cinnamon and bread cubes and toss until butter is absorbed. Arrange the bread on top of the fruit and then sprinkle with the remaining sugar.

Cook in a preheated moderate oven (180°C/350°F, Gas Mark 4) for 35 minutes until the topping is golden brown. Serve hot with whipped cream.

VARIATION:
**Plum Crunch** – use canned whole plums. Boil the syrup from the can with the orange juice until reduced and thick, then pour over the fruit. Mix 25 g/1 oz flaked (sliced) almonds with the fried bread cubes and bake as above.

# Apple and Walnut Dessert

| METRIC/IMPERIAL | AMERICAN |
|---|---|
| 50 g/2 oz self-raising flour | ½ cup self-rising flour |
| 25 g/1 oz butter, melted | 2 tablespoons melted butter |
| 1 small egg | 1 small egg |
| ½ teaspoon vanilla essence | ½ teaspoon vanilla |
| 1 teaspoon grated lemon rind | 1 teaspoon grated lemon rind |
| 75 g/3 oz brown sugar | ½ cup firmly packed brown sugar |
| 4 stoned dates, chopped | 4 chopped pitted dates |
| 1 tablespoon chopped walnuts | 1 tablespoon chopped walnuts |
| 2 apples, peeled, cored and diced | 2 apples, peeled, cored and diced |

Sift the flour into a bowl, make a well in the centre and add the melted butter, egg, vanilla and grated lemon rind. Mix well with a wooden spoon, then add the remaining ingredients and stir thoroughly.

Spoon the mixture into a well-greased shallow ovenproof dish and cook in a preheated moderately hot oven (200°C/400°F, Gas Mark 6) for 30 to 40 minutes until firm to the touch and well browned.

Serve hot with whipped cream, custard or ice-cream. Or serve cold, sliced and buttered.

# Surprise Pancakes

| METRIC/IMPERIAL | AMERICAN |
|---|---|
| 2 eggs, separated | 2 eggs, separated |
| 1 tablespoon caster sugar | 1 tablespoon sugar |
| ¼ teaspoon vanilla essence | ¼ teaspoon vanilla |
| good pinch of salt | large pinch of salt |
| 1 tablespoon plain flour · | 1 tablespoon all-purpose flour |
| 2 tablespoons milk | 2 tablespoons milk |
| butter | butter |
| maple or golden syrup to serve | maple syrup to serve |

Whisk the egg whites until frothy. Add the sugar, vanilla and salt and continue beating until stiff. Blend the egg yolks and flour together with a fork, then stir in the milk.

Grease a 20 cm/8 inch omelette pan with a little butter and heat. Pour in half the yolk mixture, spread evenly by rotating the pan and immediately spoon half the whites on one half. Cook for 1 minute, then use a spatula to lift up the half with the egg white filling and fold it over the other half. Cook for another minute to heat the whites through, then remove from pan. Place in a cool oven while you cook the second pancake. Serve hot with syrup poured over.

# Raspberry Fool

METRIC/IMPERIAL
*100 g/4 oz raspberries*
*1 tablespoon sugar*
*1 tablespoon lemon juice*
*120 ml/4 fl oz thick cold custard*
*150 ml/¼ pint double or whipping cream, whipped*
*2 fan wafers to decorate*

AMERICAN
*¼ lb raspberries*
*1 tablespoon sugar*
*1 tablespoon lemon juice*
*½ cup thick cold custard sauce*
*⅔ cup heavy or whipping cream, whipped*
*2 fan wafers to decorate*

Purée the raspberries in a blender until smooth, or rub through a sieve. Sweeten the fruit with sugar, and stir in the lemon juice. Combine with cold custard, mixing well, then fold in the whipped cream.

Spoon into individual stemmed glasses and decorate with fan wafers.

VARIATION:
**Strawberry Fool** – hull 100 g/4 oz washed strawberries, then purée. Add 1 tablespoon sugar and 1 tablespoon orange juice or orange liqueur (Grand Marnier or Curaçao). Fold through the cold custard with cream as above, allowing streaks of the fruit to be seen. Serve in stemmed glasses decorated with fan wafers or flaked (sliced) almonds.

# Sweet Dumplings with Syrup

METRIC/IMPERIAL
*100 g/4 oz self-raising flour*
*pinch of salt*
*2 tablespoons sugar*
*1½ teaspoons ground mixed spice*
*50 g/2 oz butter*
*75 g/3 oz sultanas*
*1 egg*
*120 ml/4 fl oz orange juice*
*golden or maple syrup, to serve*

AMERICAN
*1 cup self-rising flour*
*pinch of salt*
*2 tablespoons sugar*
*1½ teaspoons apple pie spice*
*¼ cup butter*
*½ cup raisins*
*1 egg*
*½ cup orange juice*
*corn or maple syrup to serve*

Sift the flour, salt, sugar and spice into a bowl. Rub (cut) in the butter and stir in the sultanas (raisins). Beat the egg with the orange juice, add to the flour and mix together.

Drop spoonfuls of the mixture into simmering water, then cover tightly and poach for 15 minutes. Remove dumplings with a slotted spoon.

To serve, split open, place a pat of butter inside each, then drizzle over golden (corn) or maple syrup.

# Iced Mincemeat Flambé

METRIC/IMPERIAL
vanilla ice cream
2 tablespoons mincemeat
2 tablespoons brandy

AMERICAN
vanilla ice cream
2 tablespoons mincemeat
2 tablespoons brandy

Place 2 scoops or slices of ice cream on each serving plate. Heat the mincemeat and spoon over, then warm the brandy, ignite, and pour flaming over the mincemeat. Serve at once.

VARIATION:
**Iced Sherried Mincemeat** – if you prefer not to flambé, add 2 tablespoons of sweet sherry to the mincemeat when heating through.

# Quick Rum Babas

METRIC/IMPERIAL
1 bought sponge cake layer
   (enough for 2 servings)
2 tablespoons honey
2 tablespoons water
1 tablespoon lemon juice
1 tablespoon dark rum
4 tablespoons double or whipping
   cream

AMERICAN
1 bought white cake layer (enough
   for 2 servings)
2 tablespoons honey
2 tablespoons water
1 tablespoon lemon juice
1 tablespoon dark rum
¼ cup heavy or whipping cream

Cut the cake into two rounds. Place in individual dishes. Bring the honey and water to a boil, then stir in the lemon juice and rum. Pour the hot syrup over the cake and, when cooled, chill until ready to serve. Whip the cream until stiff and spoon or pipe on top.

# Gingered Melon Balls

METRIC/IMPERIAL
1 honeydew melon
1 tablespoon honey
1 piece crystallized ginger, finely
   chopped
2 tablespoons gin (optional)
mint sprigs to decorate

AMERICAN
1 honeydew melon
1 tablespoon honey
1 piece candied ginger, finely
   chopped
2 tablespoons gin (optional)
mint sprigs to decorate

Scoop the flesh out of the melon in ball shapes and combine with the honey, ginger and gin, if using. Place in the freezer for 5 to 10 minutes, then spoon into melon shells and decorate with mint sprigs.

# Hot Brazil Sundaes

METRIC/IMPERIAL
*1 teaspoon butter*
*25 g/1 oz Brazil or cashew nuts,*
  *coarsely chopped*
*4 tablespoons single cream*
*25 g/1 oz brown sugar*
*1 banana, sliced*
*coffee ice cream to serve*

AMERICAN
*1 teaspoon butter*
*¼ cup coarsely chopped Brazil or*
  *cashew nuts*
*¼ cup light cream*
*2 tablespoons brown sugar*
*1 banana, sliced*
*coffee ice cream to serve*

Melt the butter in a small pan. Add the chopped nuts and stir until lightly toasted. Add the cream and brown sugar, bring to the boil, then simmer for 1 minute, stirring constantly.

Arrange the banana slices and scoops of coffee ice cream on serving plates and spoon over the hot sauce. Serve immediately.

# Apple Crisp

METRIC/IMPERIAL
*1 apple*
*2 slices well-buttered bread*
*40 g/1½ oz brown sugar*
*25 g/1 oz butter*
*caster sugar and ground cinnamon,*
  *mixed, to serve*

AMERICAN
*1 tart apple*
*2 slices well-buttered bread*
*3 tablespoons brown sugar*
*2 tablespoons butter*
*sugar and ground cinnamon,*
  *mixed, to serve*

Peel, core, and cut the apple into very thin slices. Remove crusts, then place bread, buttered side down, in a shallow casserole and sprinkle with half the brown sugar. Arrange apple slices on top and sprinkle with the rest of the brown sugar. Dot with the butter.

Cover the dish with buttered foil and cook in a preheated moderately hot oven (190°C/375°F, Gas Mark 5) for 25 to 30 minutes, until the bread is crisp and the apples soft. Sprinkle with sugar and cinnamon, and serve with pouring cream.

# Lemon Curd Custard

METRIC/IMPERIAL
1 tablespoon sugar
1½ tablespoons custard powder
pinch of salt
250 ml/8 fl oz milk
3 tablespoons lemon curd

AMERICAN
1 tablespoon sugar
1½ tablespoons Bird's English
  dessert mix
pinch of salt
1 cup milk
3 tablespoons lemon cheese

Blend the sugar, custard powder (dessert mix) and salt to a smooth paste with a little of the milk. Bring the remaining milk to near boiling, then stir in the custard powder mixture. Bring the sauce to the boil and simmer, stirring constantly, for 3 minutes. Stir in the lemon curd (cheese) until well blended. Cover, cool and chill.

Spoon the lemon custard into glasses and serve with sponge (lady) fingers or use to fill crisp meringue shells just before serving.

# Cottage Cheese Blintzes

METRIC/IMPERIAL
4 small pancakes, about 15 cm/
  6 inches in diameter (see basic
  pancake recipe page 194)
15 g/1 oz butter
½ tablespoon oil
FILLING:
175 g/6 oz cottage cheese, drained
1 egg yolk
½ teaspoon vanilla essence

AMERICAN
4 small pancakes, about 6 inches in
  diameter (see basic pancake
  recipe, page 194)
1 tablespoon butter
½ tablespoon oil
FILLING:
¾ cup cottage cheese, drained
1 egg yolk
½ teaspoon vanilla

Cook the pancakes as in recipe. Make the filling by blending the cheese, egg yolk and vanilla together. Fill the pancakes with the cheese mixture, tuck in the ends and roll up. Chill until required.

Heat the butter and oil in a heavy-based frying pan (skillet) and add the blintzes, seam-side down. Fry until golden brown, then turn carefully and fry the other side.

Serve at once, with a bowl of sugar and cinnamon mixed together and a jug of sour cream.

VARIATION:
**Lemon Curd Blintzes** – mix together 50 g/2 oz (½ cup) cream cheese and 3 tablespoons lemon curd until smooth. Use to fill pancakes as above, cook and serve with whipped cream.

# Quick Fruit Salad

METRIC/IMPERIAL
1 apple
1 tablespoon lemon juice
1 banana, sliced
1 x 385 g/13½ oz can pineapple
  chunks in own juice
whipped cream to serve

AMERICAN
1 tart apple
1 tablespoon lemon juice
1 banana, sliced
1 x 14 oz can pineapple chunks in
  own juice
whipped cream to serve

Finely chop the apple, discarding the core, and place in a bowl with the lemon juice, banana slices, pineapple chunks and juice. Mix well and chill for 1 hour. Serve with whipped cream.

VARIATIONS:
**Golden Fruit Salad** – mix together orange segments, halved apricots (fresh or canned) and melon chunks. Sprinkle with sugar and lemon or lime juice.
**Tropical Salad** – mix together pineapple pieces (fresh or canned), passion fruit and pawpaw, plus canned guavas with some of their juice, or fresh or canned mango slices.
**Red and White Fruit Salad** – mix together fresh strawberries, canned lychees and slices of red-skinned apple, with a little lychee juice and a squeeze of lemon juice.
**Red and Black Fruit Salad** – soak some dessert prunes in cold (strained) tea, then drain and add to chopped watermelon. Add 2 tablespoons orange juice and some flaked (sliced) almonds.
**Juicy Fruit Salad** – mix some canned mandarin oranges, white seedless grapes, sliced banana and 1 chopped mint leaf, together with some juice from can of mandarins.


# Crème Caribbean

METRIC/IMPERIAL
120 ml/4 fl oz soured cream
about 1 tablespoon soft brown
  sugar

AMERICAN
½ cup sour cream
about 1 tablespoon light brown
  sugar

Stir the cream to soften the texture, then add sugar to taste a little at a time, stirring well to dissolve it. Chill in the serving bowl.
    This cream is particularly good with fresh, poached or baked fruits.

# Hot Brandy Sauce

METRIC/IMPERIAL
*150 ml/¼ pint milk*
*1 tablespoon sugar*
*1 tablespoon cornflour*
*2 tablespoons brandy*

AMERICAN
*⅔ cup milk*
*1 tablespoon sugar*
*1 tablespoon cornstarch*
*2 tablespoons brandy*

Put the milk and sugar in a small pan and heat until nearly boiling. Blend the cornflour (cornstarch) with a little water, then stir into the pan. Cook the sauce over a low heat, stirring, for 4 minutes, then add brandy and pour into sauce boat.
    Serve the sauce hot, poured over ice cream or apple pie.

# Chocolate Mint Sauce

METRIC/IMPERIAL
*8 chocolate peppermint creams*
*2 tablespoons double cream*

AMERICAN
*8 chocolate peppermint creams*
*2 tablespoons heavy cream*

Place the chocolate creams in a heatproof glass bowl that will fit over a pan. Melt the chocolates over simmering water and stir in the cream.
    Serve the sauce warm over coffee ice cream or poached or canned pears.

# Hard Sauce

METRIC/IMPERIAL
*50 g/2 oz unsalted butter*
*50 g/2 oz caster or soft brown sugar*
*2 tablespoons brandy, rum, Grand Marnier or Cointreau, or ½ teaspoon vanilla essence*

AMERICAN
*¼ cup sweet butter*
*¼ cup sugar, or ⅔ cup light brown sugar*
*2 tablespoons brandy, rum, Grand Marnier or Cointreau, or ½ teaspoon vanilla*

Beat the butter until creamy and add the sugar and liqueur, a little at a time, beating until fluffy. Chill in the serving bowl. Serve with hot desserts.

# Tropical Meringue

METRIC/IMPERIAL
*15 g/½ oz brown sugar*
*25 g/1 oz butter*
*juice of 1 lemon*
*1 tablespoon rum*
*2 egg whites*
*25 g/1 oz caster sugar*
*25 g/1 oz desiccated coconut*
*2 firm ripe bananas*

AMERICAN
*1 tablespoon brown sugar*
*2 tablespoons butter*
*juice of 1 lemon*
*1 tablespoon rum*
*2 egg whites*
*2 tablespoons sugar*
*⅓ cup shredded coconut*
*2 firm ripe bananas*

Place the brown sugar and butter in a pan and heat gently until melted, then stir in the lemon juice and rum. Whisk the egg whites until stiff, then fold in the sugar and coconut.

Peel the bananas and slice lengthwise, then arrange in a shallow buttered ovenproof dish. Pour over the rum sauce and top with the meringue. Cook in a preheated moderate oven (180°C/350°F, Gas Mark 4) for 10 to 15 minutes. Serve immediately.

VARIATIONS:
**Peach Macaroon Meringue** – arrange 4 canned peach halves in the ovenproof dish and fill them with 6 crushed macaroons mixed with 2 tablespoons raspberry jam. Whisk the egg whites until stiff, fold in the sugar and coconut and pile on the top. Bake as above.
**Apple Meringue** – place 2 slices of madeira or sponge cake in the dish and spread with 2 tablespoons apricot jam. Top with 4 tablespoons canned pie filling and sprinkle with cinnamon. Top with stiffly beaten egg whites (fold in sugar and coconut if liked) and bake as above.
**Gooseberry Meringue** – place 100 g/4 oz (1 cup) canned gooseberry pie filling in the dish and cover with 6 crushed ginger biscuits. Pile stiffly beaten egg whites (fold in sugar and ½ teaspoon ground ginger) and bake as above.

# Minted Melon Appetizer

METRIC/IMPERIAL
1 Ogen melon
50 g/2 oz strawberries, hulled and
    sliced
5 cm/2 inch piece cucumber, sliced
    and quartered
freshly ground sea-salt
finely grated rind and juice of
    1 small orange
1 tablespoon chopped mint
a few lettuce leaves
2 mint sprigs to garnish

AMERICAN
1 Ogen melon
½ cup hulled and sliced
    strawberries
2 inch piece cucumber, sliced and
    quartered
freshly ground sea-salt
finely grated rind and juice of
    1 small orange
1 tablespoon chopped mint
a few lettuce leaves
2 mint sprigs for garnish

Cut the melon in half and discard the seeds. Cut the flesh into 1 cm/½ inch cubes or scoop into balls; reserve the melon halves. Place the melon in a bowl with the strawberries and cucumber and a sprinkling of sea-salt. Mix the orange rind and juice with the chopped mint, then pour on to the salad and mix gently together.

Shred the lettuce and use to line the melon shells. Spoon the salad on top, pouring in any orange juice from the bowl. Serve chilled as an appetizer, garnished with sprigs of mint.

VARIATION:
**Minted Melon Dessert** – combine the melon, strawberries, orange rind and juice in a bowl as above, then top with a scoop of vanilla ice cream and 1 teaspoon crème de menthe liqueur. Serve with crisp biscuits.

211

# Lettuce and Walnut Salad

METRIC/IMPERIAL
6 leaves iceberg lettuce
25 g/1 oz walnut halves
1 teaspoon French mustard
½ teaspoon sugar
1 tablespoon wine vinegar
3 tablespoons olive oil
salt and freshly ground pepper

AMERICAN
6 leaves iceberg lettuce
½ cup walnut halves
1 teaspoon Dijon-style mustard
½ teaspoon sugar
1 tablespoon wine vinegar
3 tablespoons olive oil
salt and freshly ground pepper

Rinse and dry the lettuce well. Place the lettuce on serving plates and top with the walnuts.

Mix together the mustard, sugar, vinegar, oil, and salt and pepper to taste and pour over the salad. Toss the lettuce lightly until glistening, then serve as a starter, or as a side salad.


# Ham Mousse Avocados

METRIC/IMPERIAL
225 g/8 oz cooked ham
2 tablespoons mayonnaise
salt
cayenne pepper
25 g/1 oz butter, softened
1 tablespoon port or brandy
1 large ripe avocado
1 tablespoon lemon juice
fresh mint leaves to garnish

AMERICAN
½ lb cooked ham
2 tablespoons mayonnaise
salt
cayenne
2 tablespoons softened butter
1 tablespoon port or brandy
1 large ripe avocado
1 tablespoon lemon juice
fresh mint leaves for garnish

Cut the ham into small pieces, place in a blender or food processor fitted with the steel blade and process until smooth. Place the ham in a bowl and stir in the mayonnaise, salt and cayenne to taste, softened butter and port or brandy. Beat until smooth and chill for 1 hour.

Halve the avocado, remove the stone (seed) and sprinkle with lemon juice. Spoon the ham mousse into the cavities, mounding it up. Garnish with mint and serve with buttered brown bread.

# Quick Liver Pâté

METRIC/IMPERIAL
75 g/3 oz coarse liver sausage
50 g/2 oz softened butter
25 g/1 oz cream cheese
1 tablespoon cream
1 teaspoon lemon juice or dry
  sherry
onion salt
freshly ground pepper

AMERICAN
⅓ cup country-style liver sausage
¼ cup softened butter
2 tablespoons cream cheese
1 tablespoon cream
1 teaspoon lemon juice or dry
  sherry
onion salt
freshly ground pepper

Place the liver sausage in a bowl and blend in half the butter and the cream cheese. Stir in the cream, lemon juice or sherry, onion salt and pepper to taste and mix well.

Spoon into two individual small dishes and smooth over the tops. Cover each dish with a layer of melted butter and chill for 30 minutes before serving with midget gherkins (dill pickles) and hot toast.

# Prawn and Melon Cocktails

METRIC/IMPERIAL
1 small ripe melon
50 g/2 oz peeled prawns
1 teaspoon capers
1 stick celery, finely chopped
2 tablespoons mayonnaise
2 teaspoons tomato purée
½ teaspoon Worcestershire sauce
salt and freshly ground pepper
chopped parsley to garnish

AMERICAN
1 small ripe melon
½ cup shelled shrimp
1 teaspoon capers
1 stalk celery, minced
2 tablespoons mayonnaise
2 teaspoons tomato paste
½ teaspoon Worcestershire sauce
salt and freshly ground pepper
chopped parsley for garnish

Cut the melon in half, scoop out the seeds, and chill.

Mix together the prawns (shrimp), capers and celery. Combine the mayonnaise, tomato purée (paste), Worcestershire sauce and salt and pepper to taste. Stir the prawn (shrimp) mixture into the dressing and just before serving, spoon into the melon halves.

Garnish with chopped parsley and serve with thinly sliced brown bread and butter.

# Avocado and Apple Starter

METRIC/IMPERIAL
1 red dessert apple
1 tablespoon raisins
1 tablespoon chopped nuts
2 celery sticks, chopped
2 tablespoons mayonnaise
1 tablespoon lemon juice
1 ripe avocado
salt and freshly ground pepper

AMERICAN
1 red-skinned dessert apple
1 tablespoon raisins
1 tablespoon chopped nuts
2 stalks celery, chopped
2 tablespoons mayonnaise
1 tablespoon lemon juice
1 ripe avocado
salt and freshly ground pepper

Core and dice the apple. Mix the apple with the raisins, chopped nuts and celery. Add the mayonnaise and lemon juice and toss lightly.

Just before serving, halve the avocado and remove the stone (seed).

Remove the flesh, cut into dice and mix gently into the salad. Add salt and pepper to taste. Spoon the mixture in the avocado shells and serve.

# Champignons en Cocotte

METRIC/IMPERIAL
100 g/4 oz button mushrooms
15 g/½ oz butter
salt and freshly ground pepper
150 ml/¼ pint double cream
25 g/1 oz Parmesan cheese, grated
parsley sprigs to garnish

AMERICAN
1 cup button mushrooms
1 tablespoon butter
salt and freshly ground pepper
⅔ cup heavy cream
¼ cup grated Parmesan cheese
parsley sprigs for garnish

Divide the mushrooms between two buttered ramekin dishes and dot with butter. Sprinkle with salt and pepper to taste, then pour over the cream.

Top with Parmesan cheese and place under a preheated moderate grill (broiler) for 10 minutes. Garnish with parsley sprigs and serve with Melba toast.

214

# Mussels in Sauce Vin Blanc

METRIC/IMPERIAL
*1 kg/2 lb fresh mussels*
*4 spring onions*
*4 stalks parsley*
*1 sprig thyme*
*freshly ground pepper*
*50 g/2 oz butter*
*250 ml/8 fl oz dry white wine*
*1 tablespoon plain flour*
*4 tablespoons single cream*
*1 egg yolk*
*chopped parsley to garnish*

AMERICAN
*2 lb fresh mussels*
*4 scallions*
*4 stalks parsley*
*1 sprig thyme*
*freshly ground pepper*
*¼ cup butter*
*1 cup dry white wine*
*1 tablespoon all-purpose flour*
*¼ cup light cream*
*1 egg yolk*
*chopped parsley for garnish*

Thoroughly scrub each mussel with a good stiff brush and plenty of water to remove any mud or seaweed. Pull off the beard that clings around the edges. Soak the mussels in water – they should disgorge any sand. Discard any mussels which do not shut tightly or don't shut when tapped.

Put the mussels in a large wide pan with the spring onions (scallions), herbs, pepper, half the butter and the wine. Cover the pan and cook over a high heat for 5 minutes, shaking the pan now and then. Remove the mussels as they open, discarding empty half of each shell, and arrange in a large bowl (or individual warmed soup plates). Keep warm.

Strain the cooking liquid and bring to the boil in a clean pan. Mix the remaining butter with the flour and stir into the liquid, a little at a time, until slightly thickened. Beat the cream with the egg yolk and add to the sauce. Heat the sauce, stirring constantly, until it thickens slightly – do not let the sauce boil. Pour the sauce over the mussels and sprinkle with chopped parsley. Serve at once with crusty bread.

# Mouclade

METRIC/IMPERIAL
1.5 litres/2½ pints fresh mussels
200 ml/⅓ pint dry white wine
1 bay leaf
1 thyme sprig
3 parsley stalks, bruised
25 g/1 oz butter
2 shallots, peeled and finely
    chopped
120 ml/4 fl oz double cream
pinch of cayenne pepper
2 egg yolks
1 teaspoon curry powder
salt
freshly ground pepper
TO SERVE:
Croûtes (see page 147)
chopped parsley

AMERICAN
3 pints/6 cups fresh mussels
about 1 cup dry white wine
1 bay leaf
1 thyme sprig
3 parsley stalks, bruised
2 tablespoons butter
2 shallots, peeled and finely
    chopped
½ cup heavy cream
pinch cayenne pepper
2 egg yolks
1 teaspoon curry powder
salt
freshly ground pepper
FOR SERVING:
Croûtes (see page 147)
chopped parsley

Scrub the mussels and discard any that are open and will not close when tapped. Bring the wine to the boil in a large pan with the bay leaf, thyme and parsley stalks. Add the mussels and shake the pan constantly over high heat until the shells open, about 5 minutes. Remove mussels from pan with slotted spoon, discarding any that have not opened, and set aside.

Continue boiling the liquid in the pan. Meanwhile, melt the butter in a separate pan, add the shallots and fry gently for 3 minutes. Strain the mussel liquid and stir slowly into shallots. Stir in two-thirds of the cream and the cayenne, bring to the boil and boil for 1 minute.

Put the egg yolks in a bowl with the remaining cream and curry powder and mix well with a fork. Gradually stir in 2 tablespoons of the hot sauce, then stir the mixture slowly into the sauce over the lowest possible heat. Do not let the sauce boil or it will separate. Taste and adjust seasoning.

Remove mussels from shells and add to the sauce. Heat through for 1 minute, stirring constantly. Pile on to freshly made Croûtes, sprinkle with parsley and serve immediately.

# Seafood Poulette

METRIC/IMPERIAL
350 g/12 oz white fish fillets
225 g/8 oz scallops
25 g/1 oz butter
2 spring onions, chopped
6 sprigs parsley
50 g/2 oz mushrooms, sliced
175 ml/6 fl oz hot water
4 tablespoons dry white wine
120 ml/4 fl oz single cream
1 egg yolk
1 tablespoon chopped chives

AMERICAN
¾ lb white fish fillets
½ lb scallops
2 tablespoons butter
2 scallions, chopped
6 sprigs parsley
½ cup sliced mushrooms
¾ cup hot water
¼ cup dry white wine
½ cup light cream
1 egg yolk
1 tablespoon chopped chives

Cut the fish fillets into smallish pieces. Remove any brown beards from the scallops. Butter a flameproof dish and layer in the spring onions (scallions) and parsley, then the fish, scallops and mushrooms. Add the water and drizzle the wine over. Cover with buttered paper with a tiny hole in the centre. Bring just to simmering point, cover and cook slowly for 8 to 10 minutes.

Lift the fish, scallops and mushrooms on to a hot serving dish and keep warm. Discard the parsley and boil the liquid in the pan until reduced by one-third. Add the cream and cook for a few minutes more. Beat 3 tablespoons of this liquid with the egg yolk, then pour back into the pan and reheat gently, stirring until thickened. Do not let the sauce boil. Spoon the sauce over the fish and sprinkle with chives.

# Smoked Trout with Horseradish Sauce

METRIC/IMPERIAL
2 smoked trout, about 350 g/12 oz
  each
120 ml/4 fl oz double cream
1 tablespoon grated horseradish
salt and freshly ground pepper
TO SERVE:
4 crisp lettuce leaves
8 black olives
4 lemon wedges
chopped parsley

AMERICAN
2 smoked trout, about ¾ lb each
½ cup heavy cream
1 tablespoon grated horseradish
salt and freshly ground pepper
TO SERVE:
4 crisp lettuce leaves
8 ripe olives
4 lemon wedges
chopped parsley

First skin the trout: run a knife down the centre of each side and lift the two halves off the bone, turn over and repeat on the other side. Skin the other fish. You will have 8 small fillets.

Whip the cream until stiff, then fold in the horseradish. Add salt and pepper to taste, taking into account the smokey flavour of the trout. Arrange the fillets on the lettuce and garnish with olives and lemon. Sprinkle with parsley and serve with the horseradish sauce and hot toast.

# Trout with Riesling

METRIC/IMPERIAL
*75 g/3 oz butter*
*75 g/3 oz mushrooms, chopped*
*salt*
*freshly ground pepper*
*2 trout, gutted and cleaned through*
*the gills*
*2 shallots, peeled and finely*
*chopped*
*250 ml/8 fl oz Riesling*
*4 tablespoons double cream*

AMERICAN
*⅓ cup butter*
*¾ cup chopped mushrooms*
*salt*
*freshly ground pepper*
*2 trout, gutted and cleaned through*
*the gills*
*2 shallots, peeled and finely*
*chopped*
*1 cup Riesling*
*4 tablespoons heavy cream*

Melt 25 g/1 oz (2 tablespoons) butter in a pan and add two-thirds of the mushrooms and salt and pepper to taste. Stuff the trout with this mixture. Cover the base of a well-buttered baking dish with the shallots, place the trout on top and pour over the wine. Sprinkle with salt and pepper. Cover the dish and bake in a preheated moderately hot oven (200°C/400°F, Gas Mark 6) for 20 minutes.

Lift the trout out and carefully peel away the skin. Arrange trout on warmed plates and keep hot. Strain the cooking juices into a heavy-based pan and boil rapidly until reduced by two-thirds. Stir in the cream and heat gently for 2 to 3 minutes, stirring constantly. Remove from heat and whisk in remaining butter a little at a time. Taste and adjust seasoning, then pour over the fish and serve immediately with boiled new potatoes and a mixed salad or green vegetable.

# Mussels Marinière

METRIC/IMPERIAL
1.5 litres/2½ pints fresh mussels
50 g/2 oz butter
2 shallots, peeled and finely
 chopped
1 clove garlic, peeled and crushed
300 ml/½ pint dry white wine
1 bouquet garni
freshly ground pepper
2 tablespoons chopped parsley

AMERICAN
3 pints/6 cups fresh mussels
¼ cup butter
2 shallots, peeled and finely
 chopped
1 clove garlic, peeled and crushed
1¼ cups dry white wine
1 bouquet garni
freshly ground pepper
2 tablespoons chopped parsley

Scrub the mussels and discard any that are open and will not close when tapped. Melt the butter in a large pan, add the shallots and garlic and fry gently until tender but not coloured. Stir in the wine, add the bouquet garni and bring to the boil. Boil for 2 minutes, then add pepper to taste and the mussels.

Over high heat shake the pan constantly or stir the mussels until the shells open. Remove from pan with slotted spoon and discard any that have not opened. Boil the liquid rapidly until reduced by half. Discard the bouquet garni, then return mussels to pan with the parsley. Heat through for 1 minute, shaking the pan constantly. Divide mussels and sauce between two deep serving bowls and serve immediately with crusty bread.

# Scallops with Cider and Cream

METRIC/IMPERIAL
6 scallops on shells
4 tablespoons butter
2 shallots, peeled and finely
 chopped
120 ml/4 fl oz dry cider
salt and pepper
2 tablespoons double cream

AMERICAN
6 scallops on shells
4 tablespoons butter
2 shallots, peeled and finely
 chopped
½ cup hard cider
salt and pepper
2 tablespoons heavy cream

Detach the white scallop meat from the shells and separate the red coral. Cut away the muscular skin on the outside of the white meat. Wash and drain well. Scrub 2 shells and dry thoroughly.

Melt 25 g/1 oz/2 tablespoons butter in a pan, add the shallots (scallions) and fry gently for 2 to 3 minutes. Pour in the cider and bring to the boil, then add the scallops and coral with salt and pepper. Cover and simmer gently for 12 to 15 minutes. Remove scallops and corals with a slotted spoon and divide between cleaned shells. Keep hot.

Boil the cooking liquid rapidly until reduced by half, then stir in the cream and bring to near boiling. Remove pan from heat and add the remaining butter a little at a time, whisking vigorously until dissolved. Taste and adjust seasoning, then pour over the scallops and serve immediately.

# Grilled (Broiled) Fish

METRIC/IMPERIAL

2 fish steaks, fillets or small whole
   fish, cleaned
40 g/1½ oz butter
1 tablespoon plain flour, seasoned
   with salt and freshly ground
   pepper

AMERICAN

2 fish steaks, fillets or small whole
   fish, cleaned
3 tablespoons butter
1 tablespoon all-purpose flour,
   seasoned with salt and freshly
   ground pepper

If cooking whole fish, slash one side diagonally two or three times so that the heat can penetrate. Line the grill (broiler) pan or a shallow metal tray with foil and place under high heat for 3 minutes. Add the butter and heat until the foam subsides. Meanwhile, coat the fish lightly with seasoned flour.

Place the fish in the pan and turn until coated in the butter, then cook without turning until the flesh turns white and flakes easily when tested with a fork – this will take 8 minutes for 2.5 cm/1 inch thick fish, 5 minutes if thinner.

VARIATIONS:

**German-Style Fish** – while the fish is cooking as above, melt 25 g/1 oz (3 tablespoons) butter in a frying pan (skillet), add 25 g/1 oz flaked (sliced) almonds and cook, stirring, until browned. Stir in 4 tablespoons single cream, 1 tablespoon lemon juice and 1 tablespoon chopped olives or spring onions (scallions). Add salt and pepper to taste, stir gently until hot but not boiling, then pour this sauce over the fish and serve with potato croquettes and a green salad.

**Fish with Tarragon** – before grilling whole fish, place them in a marinade of 1 crushed clove garlic, 6 to 8 chopped tarragon leaves and 2 tablespoons lemon juice, and leave for 30 minutes. Mix 50 g/2 oz (¼ cup) butter with 1 teaspoon oil, 1 tablespoon chopped tarragon leaves and sea-salt, then form into a roll and chill. Grill (broil) the fish and serve topped with the tarragon butter.

**Fish Maître d'Hôtel** – grill the fish as above and serve topped with Parsley Butter (see page 146) mixed with 1 tablespoon lemon juice.

**Fish and Cucumber Kebabs** – cut the fish fillets into chunks and coat in seasoned flour. Thread on to 2 skewers, alternating with a thick chunk of cucumber and a cube of buttered bread. Brush with butter and grill, turning frequently for 5 to 7 minutes. Serve with Sour Cream Dressing (see page 148) and a green salad.

# Normandy Stuffed Crab

| METRIC/IMPERIAL | AMERICAN |
|---|---|
| 1 dressed crab (about 500 g/1 lb) | 1 dressed crab (about 1 lb) |
| 65 g/2½ oz butter | 5 tablespoons butter |
| 2 shallots, peeled and finely chopped | 2 shallots, peeled and finely chopped |
| 1 small onion, peeled and finely chopped | 1 small onion, peeled and finely chopped |
| 1 clove garlic, peeled and crushed | 1 clove garlic, peeled and crushed |
| 1 tablespoon chopped parsley | 1 tablespoon chopped parsley |
| 50 g/2 oz fresh white breadcrumbs | 1 cup soft white bread crumbs |
| salt | salt |
| freshly ground pepper | freshly ground pepper |
| 4 tablespoons dry cider | 4 tablespoons hard cider |

Twist off the crab legs and claws, crack them open and remove the meat with pincers or a skewer. Pull the body of the crab away from its shell and take out all the meat. Discard the stomach sac, the pale grey fronds ('dead men's fingers') and any greenish matter. Scoop out the dark meat with a teaspoon. Flake all the extracted crabmeat and remove any cartilage. Thoroughly scrub inside of shell and reserve.

Melt 40 g/1½ oz (3 tablespoons) butter in a pan, add the shallots and onion and fry gently until translucent. Add the crabmeat, garlic, parsley, 40 g/1½ oz (¾ cup) breadcrumbs and salt and pepper to taste. Add the cider and cook gently for 10 minutes, then stuff the mixture inside the cleaned crab shell. Sprinkle with remaining breadcrumbs and dot with remaining butter.

Bake in a preheated hot oven (220°C/425°F, Gas Mark 7) for 10 minutes. Serve hot, straight from the shell, with Beans with Poulette Sauce (see page 104).

# Chicken Auvergne

METRIC/IMPERIAL

1 tablespoon chopped dried
  mushrooms
4 tablespoons dry white wine
2 half chicken breasts
1 tablespoon plain flour
25 g/1 oz butter
4 tablespoons olive oil
2 tablespoons sherry
1 small aubergine
salt and freshly ground pepper
2 medium tomatoes
knob of butter

AMERICAN

1 tablespoon chopped dried
  mushrooms
¼ cup dry white wine
2 half chicken breasts
1 tablespoon all-purpose flour
2 tablespoons butter
¼ cup olive oil
2 tablespoons sherry
1 small eggplant
salt and freshly ground pepper
2 medium-sized tomatoes
pat of butter

Soak the mushrooms in the wine. Dust the chicken breasts with the flour. In a large frying pan (skillet), heat the butter and 1 tablespoon of the oil and brown the chicken on each side. Heat the sherry and pour over the chicken. Cover the pan, reduce the heat and cook very slowly for about 25 minutes, or until the chicken is tender.

Meanwhile cut the aubergine (eggplant) in slices, sprinkle with salt and leave for 30 minutes. Rinse the slices, dry well and fry until golden in the remaining oil. Season the chicken with salt and pepper to taste, remove and keep warm. Do not rinse out the pan – keep it for the gravy.

Arrange the aubergine (eggplant) slices on a heated serving dish and keep warm. Thickly slice the tomatoes and sauté in the same pan, slip off and discard the skins. Arrange the tomatoes over the aubergine (eggplant). Place the chicken on top. Keep warm.

Place the soaked mushrooms and the wine in the reserved pan and bring to the boil, stirring the brown bits from the bottom. Swirl in a little butter, taste for seasoning, and spoon over the chicken. Serve with Herby New Potatoes (page 108).

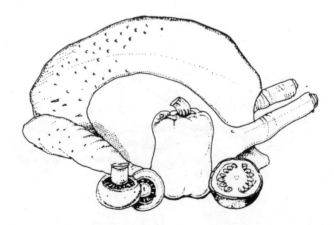

# Spicy Drumsticks

METRIC/IMPERIAL
1 teaspoon curry paste
1 small onion, chopped
120 ml/4 fl oz plain yogurt
2 chicken drumsticks

AMERICAN
1 teaspoon curry paste
1 small onion, chopped
½ cup plain yogurt
2 chicken drumsticks

Mix together the curry paste, onion and yogurt. Arrange the drumsticks in a glass dish and pour the mixture over, turning the drumsticks so that they are well coated. Cover and chill for 2 hours or more.

Place the drumsticks in an oiled baking dish and pour the yogurt mixture over. Cook in a preheated moderately hot oven (200°C/400°F, Gas Mark 6) for 15 minutes. Turn the chicken, cook for a further 15 to 20 minutes or until the juices run clear and the flesh is very tender. Serve hot with Rösti (see page 112) and Mixed Beans with Garlic Butter (see page 103).

# Indian Chicken

METRIC/IMPERIAL
2 tablespoons peanut oil
2 onions, finely chopped
1 tablespoon canned green
  peppercorns, drained and
  chopped
1 cm/½ inch piece fresh root ginger,
  grated
½ teaspoon ground turmeric
½ teaspoon ground mace
¼ teaspoon ground coriander
¼ teaspoon ground cinnamon
2 small chicken thighs, halved
1 teaspoon cornflour
250 ml/8 fl oz chicken stock
1 apple, peeled, cored and diced
1 tablespoon desiccated coconut,
  toasted, to serve

AMERICAN
2 tablespoons peanut oil
2 onions, finely chopped
1 tablespoon canned green
  peppercorns, drained and
  chopped
½ inch piece fresh ginger root,
  grated
½ teaspoon ground turmeric
½ teaspoon ground mace
¼ teaspoon ground coriander
¼ teaspoon ground cinnamon
2 small chicken thighs, halved
1 teaspoon cornstarch
1 cup chicken stock or broth
1 apple, peeled, cored and diced
1 tablespoon shredded coconut,
  toasted, to serve

Heat the oil in a large frying pan (skillet), add the onions and cook gently until golden. Add the green peppercorns, cook for 1 minute, then stir in the ginger and spices. Add the chicken pieces and cook for about 10 minutes until brown all over.

Blend the cornflour (cornstarch) with the chicken stock, pour into the pan and cook, stirring, until it boils and thickens. Simmer for 5 minutes. Add the apple, cover and simmer for another 10 minutes. Serve the Indian Chicken, sprinkled with toasted coconut, with plain boiled rice.

# Poussins Maintenon

METRIC/IMPERIAL
*2 x 350 g/12 oz poussins*
*olive oil*
*salt and freshly ground pepper*
*4 chicken livers*
*4 flat mushrooms, sliced*
*4 slices cooked tongue or ham*
*½ teaspoon chopped fresh or a*
  *pinch of dried thyme*
*2 slices white bread*
*2 tablespoons dry white wine*
*1 tablespoon water*
*2 tablespoons single cream*

AMERICAN
*2 x ¾ lb poussins*
*olive oil*
*salt and freshly ground pepper*
*4 chicken livers*
*4 flat mushrooms, sliced*
*4 slices cooked tongue or ham*
*½ teaspoon chopped fresh or a*
  *pinch of dried thyme*
*2 slices white bread*
*2 tablespoons dry white wine*
*1 tablespoon water*
*2 tablespoons light cream*

Use poultry shears to cut along both sides of the backbones of poussins, then remove. Turn poussins breast side up and press with rolling pin to flatten. Push 2 skewers through each poussin to keep in shape. Rub the poussins all over with oil and salt and pepper. Place on a foil-lined grill (broiler) pan and cook under a preheated medium grill (broiler) for 10 minutes on each side – the chickens should be 7.5 cm/3 inches from the heat.

Meanwhile prepare the garnish: sauté the chicken livers very quickly in 1 tablespoon olive oil, remove and add the mushrooms to the pan. Shred the cooked tongue or ham and add salt and pepper to taste and the thyme. Stir until heated through, then remove from the heat and keep warm.

Cut the slices of bread into 2 large rounds, fry in oil until golden, then drain on kitchen paper towels.

To assemble the dish, place the fried bread on individual plates, top each with the mushroom and tongue mixture, then a poussin. Garnish with slices of chicken liver.

Add the white wine, water and cream to the grill (broiler) pan. Bring to the boil, stirring in the brown bits until smooth. Season to taste and spoon over the chicken. Serve with Mange-Tout (see page 103).

VARIATION:
**Grilled Poussins with Barbecue Sauce** – mix together 2 tablespoons tomato purée, 1 teaspoon Worcestershire sauce, 1 teaspoon brown sugar, 1 tablespoon vinegar, 1 tablespoon oil, salt and pepper and a crushed garlic clove. Prepare and grill the poussins as above, basting them frequently with the sauce. Serve with the juices from the pan.

# Yakitori

METRIC/IMPERIAL
*350 g/12 oz boneless chicken*
*2 chicken livers*
*2 spring onions, cut into short lengths*
MARINADE:
*1 tablespoon sake or dry sherry*
*2 teaspoons soy sauce*
*1 clove garlic, crushed*
*½ teaspoon sugar*
*2 slices fresh root ginger, finely chopped*
TERIYAKI SAUCE:
*4 tablespoons bottled teriyaki sauce*
*1 tablespoon sake or dry sherry*
*4 tablespoons chicken stock*

AMERICAN
*¾ lb boneless chicken*
*2 chicken livers*
*2 scallions, cut into short lengths*
MARINADE:
*1 tablespoon sake or dry sherry*
*2 teaspoons soy sauce*
*1 clove garlic, crushed*
*½ teaspoon sugar*
*2 slices fresh ginger root, finely chopped*
TERIYAKI SAUCE:
*¼ cup bottled teriyaki sauce*
*1 tablespoon sake or dry sherry*
*¼ cup chicken stock or broth*

Combine the marinade ingredients in a small bowl. Mix the teriyaki ingredients in a separate flat dish. Cut the chicken into bite-size pieces. Trim the livers, and cut each one in half. Add the livers to the marinade and leave, covered, in the refrigerator for at least 1 hour. Soak 4 bamboo (satay) skewers.

Thread chicken pieces, spring onion (scallions) and livers on to skewers. Turn the filled skewers around in the teriyaki mixture, coating all sides. Leave for 2 hours in the teriyaki sauce, turning twice.

Preheat the grill (broiler) and line the rack with foil. Grill (broil) the yakitori for 3 minutes on one side, brushing with teriyaki sauce. Turn and cook the other side, brushing again with sauce. Serve at once with plain boiled rice and Oriental Spinach (see page 121).

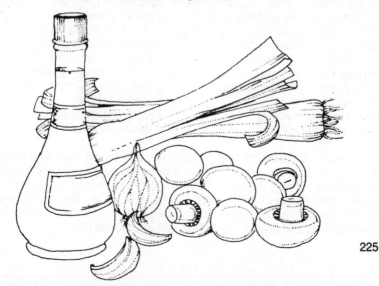

# Pot-Roast Tarragon Chicken

METRIC/IMPERIAL
*2 sprigs fresh tarragon*
*1 x 1.25 kg/2½ lb oven-ready*
  *chicken*
*4 rashers fatty bacon, chopped*
*salt and freshly ground pepper*
*120 ml/4 fl oz wine*
*250 ml/8 fl oz chicken stock*
*1 carrot, chopped*
*1 onion, chopped*
*a little cornflour mixed to a paste*
  *with water*

AMERICAN
*2 sprigs fresh tarragon*
*1 x 2½ lb roasting chicken*
*4 slices bacon, chopped*
*salt and freshly ground pepper*
*½ cup wine*
*1 cup chicken stock or broth*
*1 carrot, chopped*
*1 onion, chopped*
*a little cornstarch mixed to a paste*
  *with water*

Place one sprig of tarragon inside the chicken. Heat the bacon in a flameproof dish and cook until the fat runs. Add the chicken and brown all over, turning carefully so as not to pierce the skin. Add salt and pepper to taste, remaining tarragon, wine, stock and vegetables and cover the dish tightly with a lid or foil.

Cook the chicken over a low heat or in a preheated moderate oven (160°C/325°F, Gas Mark 3) for 2 hours. Skim fat from cooking liquid, reduce by boiling, then thicken with cornflour (cornstarch) to make gravy.

Serve with Courgette (Zucchini), Scallop (see page 156) and Sweet Potato Fries (see page 115).

**Note:** there will be enough chicken left over for a second meal.

# Creole Roast Chicken

METRIC/IMPERIAL
*2 x 350 g/12 oz poussins*
*25 g/1 oz fresh white breadcrumbs*
*1 banana, peeled and mashed*
*1 clove garlic, crushed*
*15 g/½ oz chopped nuts*
*1 teaspoon desiccated coconut*
*juice of 1 lime or ½ lemon*
*good pinch cayenne pepper*
*salt and pepper*
*freshly grated nutmeg*
*2 tablespoons oil*

AMERICAN
*2 x ¾ lb poussins*
*½ cup soft white bread crumbs*
*1 banana, peeled and mashed*
*1 clove garlic, crushed*
*2 tablespoons chopped nuts*
*1 teaspoon desiccated coconut*
*juice of 1 lime or ½ lemon*
*good pinch cayenne pepper*
*salt and pepper*
*freshly grated nutmeg*
*2 tablespoons oil*

Stuff the poussins with a mixture made by combining breadcrumbs, banana, garlic, nuts, coconut, lime or lemon juice, cayenne and salt, pepper and nutmeg to taste. Place in a roasting tin with the oil and cook in a preheated moderately hot oven (200°C/400°F, Gas Mark 6) for 40 to 50 minutes until juices run clear when legs are pierced with a fine skewer. Serve with baked onions, fried bananas and boiled rice.

# Chicken in Red Wine

METRIC/IMPERIAL
1 ½ tablespoons oil
40 g/1 ½ oz butter
750 g/1 ½ lb chicken, cut into
    4 serving pieces
8 small pickling onions, peeled
50 g/2 oz smoked bacon, derinded
    and diced
1 tablespoon plain flour
½ to ⅔ bottle good red wine
1 bouquet garni
2 cloves garlic, peeled and bruised
½ teaspoon sugar
freshly grated nutmeg
salt
freshly ground pepper
100 g/4 oz button mushrooms
4 Croûtes (see page 147)
1 tablespoon brandy

AMERICAN
1 ½ tablespoons oil
3 tablespoons butter
1 ½ lb chicken, cut into 4 serving
    pieces
8 pearl onions, peeled
¼ cup diced smoked bacon
1 tablespoon all-purpose flour
½ to ⅔ bottle good red wine
1 bouquet garni
2 cloves garlic, peeled and bruised
½ teaspoon sugar
freshly grated nutmeg
salt
freshly ground pepper
¼ lb button mushrooms
4 Croûtes (see page 147)
1 tablespoon brandy

Heat the oil and butter in a large flameproof casserole, add the chicken pieces and fry gently, turning frequently until golden on all sides. Remove with slotted spoon and set aside. Pour off half the fat from the casserole, then add the onions and bacon. Fry over moderate heat until lightly coloured, then sprinkle in the flour and cook for 1 minute. Gradually blend in the wine and bring to the boil. Add the bouquet garni, garlic, sugar, nutmeg, salt and pepper to taste. Replace the chicken, cover and simmer for 15 minutes. Add the mushrooms and continue cooking gently for a further 30 minutes or until the chicken is tender.

Remove chicken with slotted spoon and place on Croûtes on warmed plates. Keep hot. Pour the brandy into the sauce and cook, uncovered, for 5 minutes. Remove bouquet garni and garlic, then taste and adjust seasoning. Pour the sauce over the chicken and serve immediately with rice or boiled potatoes and a mixed salad.

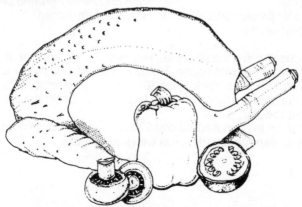

227

# Cold Chicken with Walnut Sauce

METRIC/IMPERIAL
1 x 1.25 kg/2½ lb chicken
1 onion, sliced
1 carrot, sliced
1 stick celery, sliced
2 sprigs parsley
½ bay leaf
salt
8 peppercorns
25 g/1 oz white bread, diced
50 g/2 oz walnut pieces
freshly ground pepper

AMERICAN
1 x 2½ lb chicken
1 onion, sliced
1 carrot, sliced
1 stalk celery, sliced
2 sprigs parsley
½ bay leaf
salt
8 peppercorns
½ cup diced white bread
½ cup walnut pieces
freshly ground pepper

Place the chicken in a large pan and almost cover with cold water. Remove the chicken and add the onion, carrot, celery, parsley, bay leaf, salt and peppercorns. Bring to the boil, replace the chicken, bring to the boil again and cover. Reduce the heat and simmer for about 1 hour until tender, then turn off the heat and leave to cool in the liquor. Do this the night before.

When cold, remove the chicken from the pan, skin and cut into joints. Arrange on a serving plate. Put the bread and 250 ml/8 fl oz (1 cup) of strained cooking liquid into a blender or food processor fitted with the steel blade and blend at high speed, gradually adding the walnut pieces, until smooth. Add salt and pepper to taste. Spoon the sauce over the chicken and serve with jacket-baked potatoes and a crisp green salad.
**Note:** there will be enough chicken left over for a second meal.


# Poussins in Baskets

METRIC/IMPERIAL
2 x 350 g/12 oz oven-ready
   poussins
25 g/1 oz butter
salt and freshly ground pepper
2 rashers fatty bacon

AMERICAN
2 x ¾ lb dressed poussins
2 tablespoons butter
salt and freshly ground pepper
2 slices fatty bacon

Place the poussins in a roasting pan. Rub with butter, sprinkle with salt and pepper and cover with bacon. Roast in a preheated moderately hot oven (200°C/400°F, Gas Mark 6) for 30 to 40 minutes until the juices run clear when the legs are pierced with a fine skewer. Drain the poussins on kitchen paper towels.

Place a napkin in an individual small basket, add a poussin and surround with crisp French fries. Eat with your fingers.

# Peking Fried Duckling

| METRIC/IMPERIAL | AMERICAN |
|---|---|
| 2 tablespoons coarsely ground black peppercorns | 2 tablespoons coarsely ground black peppercorns |
| 1 x 1.5 kg/3 lb duckling | 1 x 3 lb duckling |
| 2 tablespoons salt | 2 tablespoons salt |
| 2 spring onions, minced | 2 scallions, minced |
| 2 tablespoons chopped root ginger | 2 tablespoons chopped ginger root |
| 250 ml/8 fl oz stock | 1 cup stock |
| 50 g/2 oz plain flour, sifted | ½ cup all-purpose flour, sifted |
| 5 tablespoons water | 5 tablespoons water |
| 1 tablespoon soy sauce | 1 tablespoon soy sauce |
| 1 egg white | 1 egg white |
| oil for deep frying | oil for deep frying |
| sprigs of coriander to garnish | sprigs of Chinese parsley for garnish |

Toast the peppercorns in a pan over a low heat for 2 minutes, then crush. Rub the duck inside and out with the salt, pepper, spring onions (scallions) and ginger. Cover the duck and leave for 5 hours.

Place the duck on a rack in a roasting pan, add the stock, then cover whole pan tightly with foil. Steam-roast in a preheated moderate oven (190°C/375°F, Gas Mark 5) for 1¾ to 2 hours until tender. Use poultry shears to divide the duck into four pieces. (Reserve two pieces of duckling for another meal.) Mix together the flour, water, soy sauce and egg white in a bowl and beat until smooth. Rub over the two duck pieces.

Heat the oil in a large deep-fryer to 180°C/350°F. Deep fry the duckling until golden brown; drain. Serve garnished with coriander (Chinese parsley) and accompanied by plain boiled rice.

# Braised Duckling and Turnips

METRIC/IMPERIAL
1 x 1.5 kg/3 lb duckling
2 sprigs fresh thyme
1 tablespoon oil
salt and freshly ground pepper
120 ml/4 fl oz wine or marsala
250 ml/8 fl oz chicken stock
350 g/12 oz white turnips,
 quartered
6 button onions, peeled
1 teaspoon sugar
2 tablespoons single cream

AMERICAN
1 x 3 lb duckling
2 sprigs fresh thyme
1 tablespoon oil
salt and freshly ground pepper
½ cup wine or marsala
1 cup chicken stock or broth
¾ lb white turnips, quartered
6 button onions, peeled
1 teaspoon sugar
2 tablespoons light cream

Prick the duckling skin with a fork. Place the thyme sprigs inside the bird. Heat the oil in a frying pan (skillet) and brown the duckling all over. Sprinkle with salt and pepper. Place the duckling on a rack in a roasting pan, pour in the wine or marsala and half the stock, cover with foil and cook in preheated moderate oven (160°C/325°F, Gas Mark 3) for 1 hour.

Add the turnips, button onions and sugar to the frying pan and cook, stirring, until brown all over. Remove the duckling and pour off excess fat from pan. Add turnips and button onions to the pan, replace the rack with duck, add remaining stock, cover and cook for a further hour.

Place the duckling and vegetables on a serving plate and keep warm. Pour off the excess fat from roasting tin, then boil the pan juices rapidly to reduce. Add cream and salt and pepper to taste, and pour into a sauceboat. Serve immediately.
**Note:** there will be enough duckling left over for a second meal.

# Pheasant Casserole

METRIC/IMPERIAL
*75 g/3 oz butter*
*2 carrots, scraped and thinly sliced*
*2 onions, peeled and chopped*
*1 pheasant (about 1 kg/2 lb weight),*
   *cleaned and cut into 4 pieces*
*1 tablespoon plain flour*
*1½ tablespoons brandy*
*170 ml/6 fl oz good red wine*
*150 ml/¼ pint chicken stock*
*salt*
*freshly ground pepper*
*50 g/2 oz button mushrooms, sliced*
*4 rashers streaky bacon, derinded*
   *and chopped*
*8 pickling onions, peeled*

AMERICAN
*6 tablespoons butter*
*2 carrots scraped and thinly sliced*
*2 onions, peeled and chopped*
*1 pheasant (about 2 lb weight),*
   *cleaned and cut into 4 pieces*
*1 tablespoon all-purpose flour*
*1½ tablespoons brandy*
*¾ cup good red wine*
*⅔ cup chicken stock*
*salt*
*freshly ground pepper*
*½ cup sliced button mushrooms*
*4 slices fatty bacon, chopped*
*8 pearl onions, peeled*

Melt half the butter in a flameproof casserole, add carrots and onions, cover and fry gently for 5 minutes. Add the pheasant pieces and fry until lightly coloured on all sides. Sprinkle in the flour and cook, stirring, until all the fat has been absorbed. Add the brandy, set alight and when flames have died down, add the wine, stock, salt and pepper. Bring to the boil, cover and simmer gently for 20 minutes.

Meanwhile, melt remaining butter in another flameproof casserole. Add the mushrooms, bacon and onions and fry briskly until lightly coloured. Remove pheasant pieces from other casserole and place on top of mushrooms, bacon and onions. Strain over the pheasant cooking liquid, reserving vegetables (see Note), then cover and simmer gently for 30 to 45 minutes until pheasant is tender.

Taste sauce and adjust seasoning, then serve with Buttered Noodles (see page 175) and green vegetable of choice.

**Note:** if you reserve the vegetables you can use these to make an accompaniment for the casserole instead of noodles. Mash the vegetables with salt and pepper and a few drops of Worcestershire sauce. Remove crusts and cut two slices of bread into triangles, then spread with mashed vegetables. Fry until crisp and golden in a little hot oil and serve with the pheasant.

# Casseroled Quails

METRIC/IMPERIAL
12 brined vine leaves
4 oven-ready quail
4 streaky bacon rashers, derinded
65 g/2½ oz butter
salt
freshly ground pepper
about 5 fl oz/¼ pint dry white wine
    or half wine and half chicken
    stock
4 slices bread, crusts removed

AMERICAN
12 brined vine leaves
4 dressed quail
4 fatty bacon slices, rinds removed
5 tablespoons butter
salt
freshly ground pepper
about ⅔ cup dry white wine, or half
    wine and half chicken stock
4 slices bread, crusts removed

Soak vine leaves in hot water for 30 minutes, drain, then dry thoroughly. Wrap each quail in 3 vine leaves, leaving the birds' heads protruding. Tie a rasher (slice) of bacon on top of each bird with trussing thread or string. Melt one third of the butter in a small flameproof casserole and fry the quail gently on all sides for a few minutes, turning them carefully with tongs.

Sprinkle with salt and pepper and pour in enough wine, or wine and stock, to come halfway up the sides of the quail. Bring to the boil, then reduce heat, cover and simmer for 25 to 30 minutes until the quail are tender when pierced with a skewer. Remove the quail from the casserole. Untie, reserve bacon and discard vine leaves. Boil the cooking liquid vigorously until reduced by half, then return quail and bacon to casserole and heat through. Meanwhile, fry the bread in the remaining butter until golden brown on both sides. Place two on each warmed plate and arrange one quail and one piece of bacon on each slice. Adjust seasoning of cooking juices, then sprinkle over the quail. Serve immediately.

# Rabbit in Cream

METRIC/IMPERIAL
500 g/1 lb oven-ready rabbit, cut
    into pieces
2 tablespoons plain flour, seasoned
    with salt, pepper and paprika
50 g/2 oz butter
2 onions, thinly sliced
120 ml/4 fl oz soured cream

AMERICAN
1 lb rabbit, cut into pieces
2 tablespoons all-purpose flour,
    seasoned with salt, pepper and
    paprika
¼ cup butter
2 onions, thinly sliced
½ cup sour cream

Coat the rabbit with seasoned flour. Heat the butter in a heavy flameproof casserole and brown the pieces well on all sides. Add the onions and cream to the casserole, stir to mix in the brown bits and cover tightly.

Cook in a preheated cool oven (160°C/325°F, Gas Mark 3) for about 1 hour, or until very tender.

# Melt-in-the-Mouth Steaks

METRIC/IMPERIAL
2 rump steaks (about 225 g/8 oz
  each and 2 cm/¾ inch thick)
1 bay leaf, crushed
2 cloves, lightly crushed
4 cloves garlic, peeled
5 tablespoons oil
2 onions, peeled and sliced into
  rings
salt
freshly ground black pepper
4 tablespoons red wine vinegar
2 tablespoons capers, drained and
  finely chopped
1 tablespoon plain flour
250 ml/8 fl oz hot beef stock

AMERICAN
2 top round steaks (about ½ lb
  each and ¾ inch thick)
1 bay leaf, crushed
2 whole cloves, lightly crushed
4 cloves garlic, peeled
5 tablespoons oil
2 onions, peeled and sliced into
  rings
salt
freshly ground black pepper
4 tablespoons red wine vinegar
2 tablespoons capers, drained and
  chopped
1 tablespoon all-purpose flour
1 cup hot beef stock

Put the steaks in a bowl with bay leaf and cloves, 2 cloves garlic cut into slivers, and the oil. Leave to marinate for 8 hours or overnight.

The next day, remove the steaks, strain and reserve the marinade. Place half the onions in the bottom of a flameproof casserole with 1 clove garlic, chopped. Put steaks on top, sprinkle with salt, pepper, vinegar, then cover with remaining onions and the final garlic clove, chopped.

Cover the casserole with a concave lid or a deep ovenproof plate and fill this with water. The casserole should be simmered over very gentle heat for 1½ hours and should not be uncovered during this time. Keep the lid or plate topped up with water as it evaporates during cooking.

Remove steaks and place on warmed plates. Keep hot. Add the capers to the casserole with the flour. Cook for 1 minute, stirring, then gradually stir in the stock. Taste and adjust seasoning and cook, stirring, until thick. Pour over the steaks, sprinkle with reserved marinade and serve immediately with Glazed Carrots (see page 124) and New Potatoes Maître d'Hotel (see page 109).

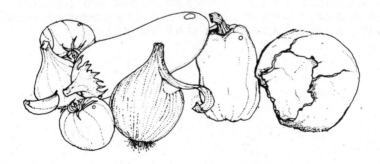

# Steaks with Bercy Butter

METRIC/IMPERIAL
*Bercy Butter (see page 146)*
*2 entrecote (sirloin/porterhouse)*
  *steaks, about 1 cm/½ inch thick*
*15 g/½ oz butter*
*1 tablespoon oil*
*salt*
*freshly ground pepper*

AMERICAN
*Bercy Butter (see page 146)*
*2 entrecote (sirloin) steaks, about*
  *½ inch thick*
*1 tablespoon butter*
*1 tablespoon oil*
*salt*
*freshly ground pepper*

Make the Bercy Butter according to the method on page 146, then chill. To cook the steaks, heat the butter and oil in a heavy-based frying pan (skillet) and fry the steaks for 3 to 5 minutes each side according to taste. Sprinkle the steaks with salt and pepper, then place on warmed plates. Top with the prepared butter and serve immediately with Spiced Green Beans (see page 106) and grilled tomatoes.

# Carpetbag Steak

METRIC/IMPERIAL
*2 x 225 g/8 oz rump steaks, 3.5 cm/*
  *1½ inches thick*
*freshly ground salt and black*
  *pepper*
*8 fresh oysters*
*1 tablespoon lemon juice*
*75 g/3 oz butter*

AMERICAN
*2 x ½ lb top round or Swiss steaks,*
  *1½ inches thick*
*freshly ground salt and black*
  *pepper*
*8 fresh shucked oysters*
*1 tablespoon lemon juice*
*6 tablespoons butter*

Make a deep cut in the side of each steak to form pockets. Grind pepper over the steaks and in the pockets. Mix the oysters with the lemon juice, then put 4 in each steak with the juice. Close up openings with skewers.

Heat 50 g/2 oz (¼ cup) butter in a heavy-based frying pan, add the steaks and cook quickly for 1 minute on both sides. Reduce the heat and cook gently for 15 to 20 minutes, turning twice. (Cook longer for well-done steak.)

Place the steaks on serving plates and top each with 15 g/½ oz (1 tablespoon) of butter and salt and freshly ground pepper. Serve with sauté potatoes and a mixed salad with French dressing.

# Boeuf Bourguignon

METRIC/IMPERIAL

1 medium onion, peeled and sliced
1 parsley sprig
1 thyme sprig
1 bay leaf, crushed
600 g/1 ¼ lb chuck steak or top
  rump, cut into 6 pieces
1 tablespoon brandy
250 ml/8 fl oz full-bodied red wine
2 tablespoons oil
25 g/1 oz butter
50 g/2 oz lean bacon, derinded and
  cut into thin strips
8 pickling onions, peeled
100 g/4 oz mushrooms, sliced
2 tablespoons flour
250 ml/8 fl oz beef stock
1 clove garlic, peeled and crushed
1 bouquet garni
salt
freshly ground pepper

AMERICAN

1 medium onion, peeled and sliced
1 parsley sprig
1 thyme sprig
1 bay leaf, crushed
1 ¼ lb stewing beef or top rump, cut
  into 6 pieces
1 tablespoon brandy
1 cup full-bodied red wine
2 tablespoons oil
2 tablespoons butter
⅓ cup lean bacon, cut into thin
  strips
8 pearl onions, peeled
1 cup sliced mushrooms
2 tablespoons flour
1 cup beef stock
1 clove garlic, peeled and crushed
1 bouquet garni
salt
freshly ground pepper

Layer onion slices, herbs and meat in bowl, then mix together brandy, wine and oil and pour over. Cover and leave to marinate for at least 4 hours.

Melt the butter in flameproof casserole, add bacon and fry over moderate heat until starting to crisp. Remove bacon with slotted spoon and set aside. Add small onions and fry until lightly coloured, then remove with slotted spoon and set aside. Add mushrooms and fry for 1 minute, then remove and drain on absorbent paper towels.

Remove beef pieces from marinade, then strain the marinade and reserve the liquid. Dry beef thoroughly, add to casserole and fry over brisk heat until browned all over. Sprinkle in the flour and cook for 1 minute, then gradually stir in the strained marinade and the stock. Bring to the boil, add garlic, bouquet garni, salt and pepper to taste, cover tightly and simmer gently for 1 ½ hours. Skim surface of any fat, then add the bacon, onions and mushrooms. Simmer for further 30 minutes or until beef is tender.

Discard bouquet garni, taste and adjust seasoning. Transfer to warmed serving dish and serve immediately with Buttered Noodles (see page 175) and a green salad.

# Beef Rolls in Wine

METRIC/IMPERIAL
2 large slices topside of beef,
  pounded until thin
1 clove garlic, crushed
salt and freshly ground pepper
100 g/4 oz sausagemeat
1 onion, finely chopped
½ teaspoon dried thyme
1 carrot, quartered
50 g/2 oz butter
120 ml/4 fl oz red wine
1 tablespoon tomato purée
1 teaspoon Worcestershire sauce
1 teaspoon vinegar
1 teaspoon brown sugar

AMERICAN
2 large slices top round of beef,
  pounded until thin
1 clove garlic, crushed
salt and freshly ground pepper
¼ lb sausagemeat
1 onion, finely chopped
½ teaspoon dried thyme
1 carrot, quartered
¼ cup butter
½ cup red wine
1 tablespoon tomato paste
1 teaspoon Worcestershire sauce
1 teaspoon vinegar
1 teaspoon brown sugar

Cut each piece of beef in half, spread a little garlic on each and season with salt and pepper to taste. Mix the sausagemeat with the onion and thyme and spread a layer over each steak. Place a piece of carrot in the middle, and roll up the steaks. Tie with string.

Melt the butter in a flameproof casserole and gently brown the rolls on all sides. Combine the wine, tomato purée (paste), Worcestershire sauce, vinegar and sugar and pour over the meat. Cover the casserole tightly and cook in a preheated moderate oven (180°C/350°F, Gas Mark 4) for 1 hour, or until the rolls are very tender. Serve with Courgette (Zucchini) Scallop (see page 156) and Oven-Cooked New Potatoes (see page 108).

# Indonesian Meatballs and Rice

METRIC/IMPERIAL
25 g/1 oz desiccated coconut
225 g/8 oz finely minced beef
¼ teaspoon coriander seeds,
   ground
¼ teaspoon cumin seeds, ground
salt and freshly ground pepper
1 egg
2 tablespoons oil
100 g/4 oz long-grain rice
½ teaspoon turmeric
¼ teaspoon chilli powder
300 ml/½ pint water

AMERICAN
⅓ cup shredded coconut
½ lb finely ground beef
¼ teaspoon coriander seeds,
   ground
¼ teaspoon cumin seeds, ground
salt and freshly ground pepper
1 egg
2 tablespoons oil
⅔ cup long-grain rice
½ teaspoon turmeric
¼ teaspoon chili powder
1¼ cups water

Place the coconut in a bowl with the meat, coriander, cumin and a
generous amount of salt and pepper. Add the egg and mix well. With
flour-covered hands, shape the mixture into 1 cm/½ inch balls.
   Heat 1 tablespoon oil in a frying pan (skillet) and stir-fry the rice, turmeric
and chilli powder for 3 minutes. Add the water and some salt and bring to
the boil. Stir, cover and simmer for 15 minutes or until the rice is tender.
   Heat remaining oil in a frying pan and fry the meatballs for about
5 minutes, turning frequently. Pile on to the rice to serve.

# Wiener Schnitzel

METRIC/IMPERIAL
2 x 100 g/4 oz thin veal escalopes
2 tablespoons plain flour, seasoned
   with salt and pepper
1 egg, beaten
25 g/1 oz dry breadcrumbs
2 tablespoons vegetable oil
50 g/2 oz butter
1 hard-boiled egg
2 anchovy fillets

AMERICAN
2 x 4 oz thin veal cutlets
2 tablespoons all-purpose flour,
   seasoned with salt and pepper
1 egg, beaten
¼ cup dry bread crumbs
2 tablespoons vegetable oil
¼ cup butter
1 hard-cooked egg
2 anchovy fillets

Place the veal between sheets of greaseproof (waxed) paper and beat
with a rolling pin until very thin. If the escalopes (cutlets) are large, cut in
two. Coat with seasoned flour, dip in beaten egg and then in crumbs,
firming them on with the flat of hand. Chill the veal for 10 minutes.
   Heat the oil in a frying pan, then add the butter and heat until the foam
subsides. Fry the veal briskly in the pan for 3 or 4 minutes until the
undersides are golden, then turn and cook the other sides. Remove the
veal from the pan and drain. Arrange veal in a hot serving dish and garnish
with the chopped white and sieved yolk of a hard-boiled (hard-cooked) egg
and a rolled anchovy fillet.

# Beef Stroganoff

| METRIC/IMPERIAL | AMERICAN |
| --- | --- |
| 350 g/12 oz rump or topside | ¾ lb fillet steak |
| 2 tablespoons plain flour | 2 tablespoons all-purpose flour |
| salt and freshly ground pepper | salt and freshly ground pepper |
| ½ teaspoon ground mace | ½ teaspoon ground mace |
| 150 g/5 oz long grain rice | ¾ cup long grain rice |
| 1 tablespoon oil | 1 tablespoon oil |
| 25 g/1 oz butter | 2 tablespoons butter |
| ½ teaspoon ground cumin | ½ teaspoon ground cumin |
| 1 onion, finely chopped | 1 onion, finely chopped |
| 50 g/2 oz mushrooms, finely sliced | ½ cup finely sliced mushrooms |
| 3 tablespoons water | 3 tablespoons water |
| 1 tablespoon vinegar | 1 tablespoon vinegar |
| 120 ml/4 fl oz soured cream | ½ cup sour cream |
| chopped parsley to garnish | chopped parsley for garnish |

Finely slice the beef across the grain to make 5 cm/2 inch lengths. Mix together the flour, salt, pepper and mace on a plate and toss the beef until coated. Cook the rice in plenty of boiling salted water.

Meanwhile heat the oil and butter in a large heavy-based frying pan (skillet). Add the cumin and onion and fry gently for 3 minutes. Raise the heat slightly, add the beef and stir-fry until brown all over. Add the mushrooms and cook for 1 minute then add the water and vinegar. Cover the pan and cook gently for 5 minutes.

Drain the rice and fluff it with a fork, then place on a warmed serving dish. Stir the sour cream into the meat and cook until just heated through. Spoon the meat mixture over the rice. Garnish with parsley and serve immediately with a crisp mixed salad.

VARIATION:
**Beef Stroganoff and Noodles** – serve white or green tagliatelle (broad noodles) instead of rice, and use freshly grated nutmeg instead of cumin.

# Veal Chops Rosé

METRIC/IMPERIAL
2 large veal chops
1 tablespoon plain flour, seasoned
  with salt and pepper
50 g/2 oz butter
120 ml/4 fl oz rosé wine
120 ml/4 fl oz soured cream

AMERICAN
2 large veal chops
1 tablespoon all-purpose flour,
  seasoned with salt and pepper
¼ cup butter
½ cup rosé wine
½ cup sour cream

Lightly dust the veal chops on both sides with seasoned flour. Heat the butter in a heavy-based sauté or frying pan (skillet) and brown the chops on both sides. Season with salt and pepper to taste. Add the wine to the pan, cover, and simmer gently for 20 minutes or until the chops are tender.

Remove the chops and keep warm. Scrape up the brown bits from the bottom of the pan and add the sour cream. Heat the sauce without boiling, taste for seasoning, and pour over the chops. Serve on a bed of Buttered Noodles (see page 175).

# Cordon Bleu Escalopes (Cutlets)

METRIC/IMPERIAL
2 x 100 g/4 oz thin veal escalopes
2 slices smoked ham
2 slices Gruyère cheese
seasoned flour
1 egg, beaten
dried breadcrumbs for coating
2 tablespoons vegetable oil
50 g/2 oz butter
lemon wedges

AMERICAN
2 x ¼ lb thin veal cutlets
2 slices smoked ham
2 slices Swiss cheese
seasoned flour
1 egg, beaten
dry bread crumbs for coating
2 tablespoons vegetable oil
¼ cup butter
lemon wedges

Put the veal between sheets of greaseproof (wax) paper and beat with a rolling pin until they are very thin. Cut each one in two and on one half of each escalope place a slice of ham and slice of cheese. Top with remaining half escalopes and secure on each side with wooden cocktail sticks (toothpicks).

Coat each veal "sandwich" with seasoned flour, dip in beaten egg and then in crumbs, firming them on with the flat of the hand. Wrap in waxed paper or plastic film and chill for 30 minutes.

Heat the oil and butter in a large frying pan (skillet) and when the foam subsides, add the veal and fry for 5 to 7 minutes on each side until crisp and golden. Remove the cocktail sticks (toothpicks) and serve immediately with lemon wedges, croquette potatoes and a crisp green salad.

# Noisettes of Lamb and Lettuce

METRIC/IMPERIAL
2 lamb loin chops, cut double
  thickness and boned
salt and freshly ground pepper
2 rashers bacon
25 g/1 oz butter
4 large lettuce leaves
120 ml/4 fl oz chicken stock
4 tablespoons single cream

AMERICAN
2 lamb loin chops, cut double
  thickness and boned
salt and freshly ground pepper
2 slices bacon
2 tablespoons butter
4 large lettuce leaves
½ cup chicken stock or broth
¼ cup light cream

Curl each chop into a round shape. Season well with salt and pepper.
Wrap a strip of bacon around each and secure with a wood cocktail stick.
   Heat the butter in a flameproof casserole and gently brown the chops for
about 4 minutes on each side. Blanch the lettuce leaves, one at a time, by
dipping into boiling water for 3 seconds, then into cold water. Dry gently
with kitchen paper towels. Remove the cocktail sticks (toothpicks) and
wrap each chop in two lettuce leaves. Replace in the casserole seam-side
down, pour the chicken stock over, cover tightly, and cook in a preheated
moderately hot oven (200°C/400°F, Gas Mark 6) for 20 minutes.
   Place the chops on a warmed serving plate and stir the cream into the
liquid left in the casserole. Bring to boiling point, taste for seasoning, and
spoon over the chops. Serve with Lentils with Parsley Butter (see page 100).

# Peruvian Lamb

METRIC/IMPERIAL
1.5 kg/3 lb shoulder of lamb
salt and freshly ground pepper
2 onions, sliced
1 carrot, sliced
120 ml/4 fl oz hot beef stock
250 ml/8 fl oz hot strong black
  coffee
1 tablespoon sugar
120 ml/4 fl oz single cream

AMERICAN
3 lb shoulder of lamb
salt and freshly ground pepper
2 onions, sliced
1 carrot, sliced
½ cup hot beef stock
1 cup hot strong black coffee
1 tablespoon sugar
½ cup light cream

Season the lamb well with salt and pepper. Place the vegetables in a
greased ovenproof dish, put the lamb on top, and cook in a preheated
moderately hot oven (200°C/400°F, Gas Mark 6) for 30 minutes. Mix
together the stock, coffee and sugar and pour over the lamb. Reduce the
heat to moderate (180°C/350°F, Gas Mark 4) and continue roasting,
basting frequently for 1 hour.
   Transfer the lamb to a warm plate. Skim off any fat, then rub the
contents of the roasting pan through a sieve or purée in a blender. Reheat
the sauce to boiling point, stir in the cream, and serve in a sauce boat with
the lamb, roast potatoes and Spiced Green Beans (see page 106).

# Moussaka

| METRIC/IMPERIAL | AMERICAN |
|---|---|
| 1 medium aubergine, sliced | 1 medium eggplant, sliced |
| salt and freshly ground pepper | salt and freshly ground pepper |
| 225 g/8 oz minced beef | ½ lb ground beef |
| 3 tablespoons oil | 3 tablespoons oil |
| 1 large onion, sliced | 1 large onion, sliced |
| 1 clove garlic, crushed | 1 clove garlic, crushed |
| 2 tablespoons tomato purée | 2 tablespoons tomato paste |
| 15 g/½ oz butter | 1 tablespoon butter |
| 1 tablespoon plain flour | 1 tablespoon all-purpose flour |
| ½ teaspoon dry mustard | ½ teaspoon dry English mustard |
| 175 g/6 fl oz milk | ¾ cup milk |
| 50 g/2 oz mature Cheddar, grated | ½ cup grated sharp cheese |
| 1 egg yolk | 1 egg yolk |

Place the sliced aubergine (eggplant) in a glass dish, sprinkle with salt and leave to drain for 15 minutes.

Meanwhile fry the beef in a hot, heavy-based frying pan (skillet) without added fat until well browned. Remove from pan and reserve. Add 1 tablespoon oil to pan and fry onion slices until golden on both sides. While they are cooking, drain the aubergine (eggplant), rinse and drain again.

Remove onions and reserve. Add remaining 2 tablespoons oil to the pan, add garlic and aubergine (eggplant) slices and fry until golden on both sides.

In 2 individual ovenproof dishes, layer the aubergine (eggplant), onions and mince, seasoning each layer well. Divide the tomato purée (paste) between each dish, spreading it over the top layer. Leave to cool.

Melt the butter in a small pan, add the flour and mustard and cook for 1 minute without browning. Stir in the milk and stir until the sauce thickens. Remove from the heat and stir in half the cheese, then the egg yolk. Pour the sauce over the two dishes and sprinkle with remaining cheese. Cook in a preheated moderate oven (180°C/350°F, Gas Mark 4) for 45 minutes. Serve with a green salad.

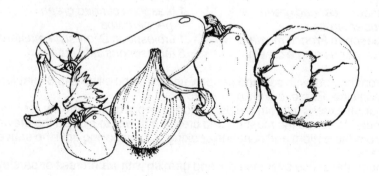

# Persian Lamb Steaks

METRIC/IMPERIAL
2 lamb steaks
2 tablespoons lemon juice
¼ teaspoon ground cardamom
½ teaspoon coriander seeds,
    ground
120 ml/4 fl oz plain yogurt
25 g/1 oz butter
1 small onion, chopped
¼ teaspoon ground ginger or
    2 slices fresh root ginger,
    chopped
salt and freshly ground pepper

AMERICAN
2 lamb steaks
2 tablespoons lemon juice
¼ teaspoon ground cardamom
½ teaspoon coriander seeds,
    ground
½ cup plain yogurt
2 tablespoons butter
1 small onion, chopped
¼ teaspoon ground ginger or
    2 slices fresh ginger root,
    chopped
salt and freshly ground pepper

Place the lamb steaks in a glass dish. Mix together the lemon juice, cardamom, coriander and yogurt and pour over the lamb. Turn the steaks and leave, covered, for 1 hour.

Melt the butter in frying pan (skillet), add the onion and ginger and cook for 2 to 3 minutes, stirring. Add lamb steaks and fry for 6 to 8 minutes on each side until tender. Remove and keep warm. Skim or pour away any fat in the pan, then add any remaining marinade, and a little milk if necessary, and make a gravy by scraping up the brown bits from the bottom of the pan. Add salt and pepper to taste, pour the gravy over the steaks and serve with Persian Crusty Rice (see page 108).

# Pork with Green Peppercorns

METRIC/IMPERIAL
2 pork steaks or chops
salt and freshly ground pepper
1 tablespoon oil
watercress or parsley to garnish
SAUCE:
1 teaspoon canned green
    peppercorns
1 tablespoon French mustard
6 tablespoons single cream

AMERICAN
2 pork chops
salt and freshly ground pepper
1 tablespoon oil
watercress or parsley for garnish
SAUCE:
1 teaspoon canned green
    peppercorns
1 tablespoon Dijon-style mustard
6 tablespoons light cream

Season the pork with salt and pepper, and fry in the oil for 6 to 8 minutes on each side. Remove and keep warm.

Pour off excess fat from the pan, add the peppercorns and stir for 1 minute, then add the mustard and cream. Stir well to pick up the brown bits from the bottom and continue cooking without boiling until the sauce thickens.

Spoon the sauce over the pork and garnish with watercress or parsley.

# Pork Chops in Wine Sauce

METRIC/IMPERIAL
2 pork chops, trimmed of fat
salt
freshly ground pepper
1 teaspoon dried oregano
2 tablespoons pork dripping or oil
2 large ripe tomatoes, skinned and
  chopped, or 1 x 227 g/8 oz can
  tomatoes
200 ml/⅓ pint red wine
1 tablespoon snipped chives
1 tablespoon butter
1 tablespoon flour

AMERICAN
2 pork chops, trimmed of fat
salt
freshly ground pepper
1 teaspoon dried oregano
2 tablespoons pork drippings or oil
2 large ripe tomatoes, peeled and
  chopped, or 1 x ½ lb can
  tomatoes
about 1 cup red wine
1 tablespoon snipped chives
1 tablespoon butter
1 tablespoon flour

Sprinkle the chops with mixture of salt, pepper and oregano. Heat the fat in a heavy-based frying pan (skillet), add the chops and fry over brisk heat for 2 to 3 minutes each side until browned. Lower the heat, cover and cook gently for 30 minutes or until tender.

Meanwhile, purée the fresh or canned tomatoes and juice in an electric blender or vegetable mill.

Transfer the chops to warmed plates and keep hot. Pour the wine into the pan and stir, scraping up any sediment on the bottom. Add the tomatoes and chives and salt and pepper to taste. Cook over high heat for 5 minutes, then whisk in small balls of the butter and flour mixed together. Cook until sauce thickens, then pour over chops and serve with creamed potatoes and Minted Peas (see page 102).

# Soufflé Romantica

METRIC/IMPERIAL
25 g/1 oz butter
1 x 310 g/10½ oz can condensed
  mushroom soup
4 eggs separated
salt and freshly ground pepper

AMERICAN
2 tablespoons butter
1 x 10½ oz can condensed
  mushroom soup
4 eggs, separated
salt and freshly ground pepper

Grease a 900 ml/1½ pint (3¾ cup) soufflé dish, then tie a band of foil around the outside to stand 5 cm/2 inches above the rim.

Place the soup in a pan and heat through gently. Beat the egg yolks until thick and creamy, add to the soup and cook for 2 minutes, stirring. Do not allow to boil. Whisk the egg whites until stiff. Fold a little of the soup mixture into them, then add the remainder. Add salt and pepper to taste, then pour into the prepared dish.

Cook the soufflé in a preheated moderately hot oven (190°C/375°F, Gas Mark 5) for 35 minutes until well risen and golden brown. Remove the foil collar and serve immediately with a green salad.

# Pork with Mushrooms and Cream

METRIC/IMPERIAL
*350 g/12 oz pork fillet*
*50 g/2 oz button mushrooms*
*2 tablespoons plain flour*
*50 g/2 oz clarified butter*
*2 tablespoons sherry or vermouth*
*4 tablespoons soured cream*
*2 teaspoons chopped mixed fresh*
   *herbs*
*salt and freshly ground pepper*
*175 ml/6 fl oz stock*
*fried mushroom caps to garnish*

AMERICAN
*¾ lb pork tenderloin*
*½ cup button mushrooms*
*2 tablespoons all-purpose flour*
*¼ cup clarified butter*
*2 tablespoons sherry or vermouth*
*¼ cup sour cream*
*2 teaspoons chopped mixed fresh*
   *herbs*
*salt and freshly ground pepper*
*¾ cup stock or broth*
*fried mushroom caps for garnish*

Cut the pork into 2.5 cm/1 inch thick slices. Place the pork between sheets of cling film (plastic wrap) and flatten slightly with a rolling pin. Trim mushroom stalks and wipe caps with a damp cloth. This can all be done ahead of time.

Coat the pork with the flour, shaking off any surplus. Heat the butter in a sauté pan (skillet) and, when foam subsides, add the pork in a single layer. Fry briskly until crisp underneath; turn and fry other side. Add the mushrooms and cook for 5 minutes, shaking the pan frequently. Pour in the sherry or vermouth and bring to the boil, scraping up brown bits from bottom of pan. Cook gently for a minute or two.

Lower the heat and stir in the sour cream. Add the herbs, salt and pepper to taste and mix well. Stir in sufficient stock just to cover the pork. Cook gently for 7 to 10 minutes or until the pork is tender. Add salt and pepper to taste.

Make a border of creamed potatoes on a serving plate and spoon in the pork and sauce. Garnish with fried mushroom caps and serve immediately.

# Pot-Roasted Pork with Madeira

METRIC/IMPERIAL
*50 g/2 oz butter*
*1 onion, finely chopped*
*2 carrots, finely chopped*
*2 sticks celery, finely chopped*
*50 g/2 oz mushrooms, thinly sliced*
*1 hand of pork, boned*
*1 teaspoon fresh or ¼ teaspoon*
  *dried thyme*
*1 bay leaf*
*salt and freshly ground pepper*
*250 ml/8 fl oz Madeira*

AMERICAN
*¼ cup butter*
*1 onion, finely chopped*
*2 carrots, finely chopped*
*2 stalks celery, finely chopped*
*½ cup thinly sliced mushrooms*
*1 pork arm roast, boned*
*1 teaspoon fresh or ¼ teaspoon*
  *dried thyme*
*1 bay leaf*
*salt and freshly ground pepper*
*1 cup Madeira*

Heat the butter in a flameproof casserole and add the onion, carrots, celery and mushrooms. Cover and cook for 5 minutes. Place the pork on the vegetables, add the thyme and bay leaf to the pan, and add salt and pepper to taste. Pour in the Madeira, cover tightly, and cook over a low heat for 2 hours or until the meat is very tender. Remove the pork and keep warm.

Discard the bay leaf and purée the sauce and vegetables in a blender, or push through a sieve (strainer). Reheat the sauce until boiling and adjust the seasoning. Serve the meat sliced with sauce, boiled new potatoes and Spiced Green Beans (see page 106).
**Note:** there will be enough pork left over for a second meal.

# Baked Ham and Pineapple Parcels

METRIC/IMPERIAL
*butter*
*2 gammon steaks*
*made mustard*
*1 tablespoon chopped chives or*
  *spring onions*
*2 slices fresh or canned pineapple*
*1 tablespoon brown sugar, mixed*
  *with 1 teaspoon vinegar*

AMERICAN
*butter*
*2 ham steaks*
*prepared mustard*
*1 tablespoon chopped chives or*
  *scallions*
*2 slices fresh or canned pineapple*
*1 tablespoon brown sugar, mixed*
  *with 1 teaspoon vinegar*

Cut 2 large heart shapes from non-stick parchment or greaseproof (waxed) paper. Fold and then open out. Butter one half of the shapes and place the steaks on this side. Spread each steak with mustard to taste, sprinkle with chives or spring onion (scallions). Top with the pineapple and the brown sugar mixture.

Fold second side over and roll edges to seal well. Place the parcels on baking tray and cook in preheated hot oven (200°C/400°F, Gas Mark 6) for 30 minutes. Serve with jacket-baked potatoes and a Curly Endive and Apple Salad (see page 132).

# Pork in Pastry

METRIC/IMPERIAL
*225 g/8 oz pork fillet*
*1 tablespoon oil*
*25 g/1 oz liver sausage*
*few drops of anchovy essence*
*salt and freshly ground pepper*
*2 teaspoons chopped fresh mixed*
  *herbs (chives, parsley, thyme)*
*225 g/8 oz frozen puff pastry,*
  *thawed*
*1 egg, beaten*

AMERICAN
*½ lb port tenderloin*
*1 tablespoon oil*
*¼ cup liverwurst*
*few drops of anchovy essence*
*salt and freshly ground pepper*
*2 teaspoons chopped fresh mixed*
  *herbs (chives, parsley, thyme)*
*½ lb frozen puff pastry, thawed*
*1 egg, beaten*

Cut the pork into 4 slices and fry on both sides for 1 minute in the hot oil. Mix together the liver sausage, anchovy essence and salt and pepper to taste, then spread on each slice of pork and sprinkle with herbs.

Roll out the pastry thinly and cut into 4 portions. Wrap each pork slice neatly in dough, sealing the joins with a little beaten egg. Use the trimmings to make decorative shapes and arrange on the parcels with egg. Chill for at least 1 hour.

Glaze the tops with the remaining egg and cook in a preheated moderately hot oven (200°C/400°F, Gas Mark 6) for 20 minutes. Reduce the heat to moderate (160°C/325°F, Gas Mark 3) and cook for a further 15 minutes.

Serve with Oven-Cooked New Potatoes (see page 108) and Beans with Poulette Sauce (see page 104).

## *Sweet Soufflé Omelette*

| METRIC/IMPERIAL | AMERICAN |
|---|---|
| *3 eggs, separated* | *3 eggs, separated* |
| *1 tablespoon sugar* | *1 tablespoon sugar* |
| *2 teaspoons plain flour* | *2 teaspoons all-purpose flour* |
| *1 tablespoons single cream* | *1 tablespoon light cream* |
| *grated rind of ½ lemon* | *grated rind of ½ lemon* |
| *pinch of salt* | *pinch of salt* |
| *15 g/½ oz butter* | *1 tablespoon butter* |
| *2 tablespoons jam, warmed* | *2 tablespoons jam, warmed* |
| *caster sugar for dusting* | *sugar for dusting* |

Preheat the oven to moderately hot (190°C/375°F, Gas Mark 5). Lightly beat the egg yolks with the sugar, flour, cream and lemon rind. Whisk the egg whites with the salt until firm peaks form. Pour the yolk mixture into the whites and fold in gently.

Heat the butter in a large omelette pan or other heavy pan that can go in the oven. When the butter is sizzling, but not brown, pour in the omelette mixture. Gently level the top. Place the pan in the oven for 12 to 15 minutes or until golden and risen (do not open the door before 10 minutes).

Spoon the warm jam down the centre, fold the omelette over, dust with caster sugar and slide on to a heated dish. Serve immediately.

VARIATIONS:
**Flamed Soufflé Omelette** – warm 1 tablespoon rum, set light to it and pour flaming over the omelette.
**Alaska Soufflé Omelette** – fill the centre of the omelette with slices of vanilla ice cream, and drizzle caramel sauce over after folding. Serve at once.

# Fruit Fondue

| METRIC/IMPERIAL | AMERICAN |
|---|---|
| a selection of fresh fruits, to serve | a selection of fresh fruits, to serve |
| SAUCE: | SAUCE: |
| 120 ml/4 fl oz soured cream | ½ cup sour cream |
| 1 teaspoon desiccated coconut | 1 teaspoon shredded coconut |
| 1 tablespoon chopped walnuts | 1 tablespoon chopped walnuts |
| 1 tablespoon sieved apricot jam | 1 tablespoon strained apricot jam |
| 1 teaspoon finely chopped preserved ginger | 1 teaspoon finely chopped candied ginger |

Combine all the ingredients for the sauce and divide between 2 small bowls. Chill until ready to serve.

On a plate arrange a selection of fruits to choose from for dipping: pineapple chunks, apple slices, banana slices, melon cubes, grapes, cherries, strawberries or raspberries.

# Mandarin Layer Dessert

| METRIC/IMPERIAL | AMERICAN |
|---|---|
| 1 x 312 g/11 oz can mandarin oranges | 1 x 11 oz can mandarin oranges |
| 120 ml/4 fl oz whipping or double cream | ½ cup heavy cream |
| 100 g/4 oz Nice biscuits | ¼ lb plain sweet cookies |
| 2 tablespoons dry sherry | 2 tablespoons pale dry sherry |

Purée half the drained mandarins in a blender or by rubbing through a sieve. Whip the cream until stiff, then fold in the fruit purée.

In a small glass dish, arrange a layer of biscuits (cookies), each one dipped quickly into sherry, topped by a layer of the mandarin cream. Repeat until both are used, then decorate the top of each dessert with reserved mandarins. Chill for at least 2 hours to allow flavours to develop.

VARIATIONS:
**Mocha Delight** – use chocolate chip cookies and flavour the cream with 1 teaspoon instant coffee powder dissolved in 1 tablespoon coffee liqueur.
**Ginger Cream** – use ginger biscuits (cookies) and fold 25 g/1 oz finely chopped preserved stem ginger into the cream.
**Chocolate Finger Layer** – use packaged chocolate fingers but do not dip into the sherry – simply crush and fold into the whipped cream. Or, if preferred, fold in crème de menthe liqueur to give a minty chocolate flavoured dessert.

# Stir-Fried Fruit Salad

METRIC/IMPERIAL
40 g/1 ½ oz brown sugar
2 tablespoons lemon juice
4 tablespoons reserved syrup from
  the fruit
2 canned peach halves, drained
  and halved
1 banana, quartered
2 canned pineapple rings, drained
  and quartered
2 tablespoons rum or brandy

AMERICAN
¼ cup brown sugar
2 tablespoons lemon juice
¼ cup reserved syrup from the fruit
2 canned peach halves, drained
  and halved
1 banana, quartered
2 canned pineapple rings, drained
  and quartered
2 tablespoons rum or brandy

Place the sugar and lemon juice in heavy-based frying pan (skillet) or wok and cook, stirring, until the sugar dissolves. Add the syrup from the canned fruit and cook for 2 minutes, then add all the fruit and stir-fry for 2 to 3 minutes until heated through. Add the rum or brandy, wait 15 seconds, then light it. Serve the fruit salad when the flames subside.

# Grand Marnier Cream

METRIC/IMPERIAL
1 egg
25 g/1 oz caster sugar
2 tablespoons Grand Marnier
120 ml/4 fl oz double cream

AMERICAN
1 egg
2 tablespoons sugar
2 tablespoons Grand Marnier
½ cup heavy cream

Using a wire whisk or hand-held electric beater, whisk the egg and the sugar in a heatproof bowl over a pan of simmering water, until the mixture is pale and fluffy. Remove from the heat and stir in half the Grand Marnier. Cover the bowl with cling film (plastic wrap) and chill.

An hour before serving time, whip the cream until it just holds its shape. Add the egg mixture, drizzle the remaining Grand Marnier round the sides and fold all together until well blended. Pile into 2 tall glasses and chill until ready to serve.

VARIATIONS:
**Passionfruit (Granadilla) Cream** – fold in 2 tablespoons creamed passionfruit (granadilla) pulp and omit the Grand Marnier.
**Orange-Mango Cream** – fold in 2 tablespoons canned mango pulp and 1 tablespoon Cointreau instead of the Grand Marnier.

# Strawberry Fluff

METRIC/IMPERIAL
*100 g/4 oz strawberries*
*2 tablespoons Grand Marnier or*
  *Cointreau*
*2 tablespoons icing sugar*
*1 teaspoon grated orange rind*
*1 egg white, stiffly beaten*
*120 ml/4 fl oz double or whipping*
  *cream, whipped*

AMERICAN
*¼ lb strawberries*
*2 tablespoons Grand Marnier or*
  *Cointreau*
*2 tablespoons confectioners' sugar*
*1 teaspoon grated orange rind*
*1 egg white, stiffly beaten*
*½ cup heavy or whipping cream,*
  *whipped*

Hull the strawberries and cut into slices. Mix the strawberries with the Grand Marnier or Cointreau, sugar and orange rind. Chill in the refrigerator for 30 minutes.

Just before serving, fold the egg white into the cream, then add the strawberries and combine lightly. Spoon into tall chilled glasses.

VARIATION:
Raspberries, loganberries or blackberries can be used instead of strawberries, and use sweet sherry, marsala or port instead of Grand Marnier or Cointreau.

# Honeyed Apricots with Brandy

METRIC/IMPERIAL
*10 ripe apricots*
*175 g/6 oz honey*
*2 tablespoons lemon juice*
*2 tablespoons water*
*2 tablespoons brandy*

AMERICAN
*10 ripe apricots*
*1 cup honey*
*2 tablespoons lemon juice*
*2 tablespoons water*
*2 tablespoons brandy*

Plunge the apricots into boiling water, leave them for a minute, then rinse in cold water. The skins should slip off easily. Cut the peeled apricots in half and remove the stones (pits).

Place the honey, lemon juice and water in a pan and bring to the boil. Add the apricots, reduce the heat and simmer very gently for 8 to 10 minutes, or until the fruit is tender when pierced with a fine skewer. Leave the apricots to cool in the syrup, then stir in the brandy. Chill and serve over vanilla ice cream.

# Glazed Butterscotch Apples

METRIC/IMPERIAL
2 large tart apples
25 g/1 oz butter
pinch of salt
2 tablespoons brown sugar
1 teaspoon ground cinnamon
whipped cream or ice cream, to
  serve

AMERICAN
2 large tart apples
2 tablespoons butter
pinch of salt
2 tablespoons brown sugar
1 teaspoon ground cinnamon
whipped cream or ice cream, to
  serve

Peel and core the apples and cut each one into 8 wedges. Heat the butter in a frying pan (skillet) and add the apples. Cover the pan and cook over a very low heat, turning now and again, for about 10 minutes until the apples begin to soften.

Sprinkle with salt, sugar and cinnamon and continue cooking and turning for 10 to 15 minutes until the apples are quite soft.

Serve warm with cream or ice cream. If wished, a little dark rum may be heated, poured over the apples, and set alight.

# Tipsy Melon Cups

METRIC/IMPERIAL
1 medium Ogen melon
2 tablespoons orange liqueur
120 ml/4 fl oz double cream,
  whipped
4 maraschino cherries

AMERICAN
1 medium Ogen melon
2 tablespoons orange liqueur
½ cup heavy cream, whipped
4 maraschino cherries

Cut the melon in half and remove the seeds. Scoop out the flesh with a melon baller or teaspoon and place in a bowl, reserve shells. Add the orange liqueur to the melon and mix well. Leave to soak in the refrigerator.

Just before serving, spoon the melon mixture back into the melon halves and decorate with cream and cherries.

# Creamy Peaches

METRIC/IMPERIAL
2 large ripe peaches
2 tablespoons brown sugar
120 ml/4 fl oz soured cream

AMERICAN
2 large ripe peaches
2 tablespoons brown sugar
½ cup sour cream

Pour boiling water over the peaches, leave for 2 minutes, then slip off the skins. Cut into halves, remove stone (pits) and slice thinly.

Arrange the peaches in two shallow glass dishes. Mix together the brown sugar and the cream, then pile on top of peaches. Chill until serving time.

# Strawberry Peaches

METRIC/IMPERIAL
1 large ripe peach, peeled
1 tablespoon lemon juice
100 g/4 oz ripe strawberries, hulled
1 tablespoon kirsch
1 tablespoon caster sugar
3 tablespoons orange juice
whipped cream, to serve

AMERICAN
1 large ripe peach, peeled
1 tablespoon lemon juice
¼ lb ripe strawberries, hulled
1 tablespoon kirsch
1 tablespoon sugar
3 tablespoons orange juice
whipped cream, to serve

Halve the peach, remove the stone (pit) and sprinkle with lemon juice.
Purée the strawberries and mix with the kirsch, sugar and orange juice. Divide the strawberry mixture between two glass dishes. Top each with a peach half, cut side up, and fill with whipped cream.

# Tropical Cream

METRIC/IMPERIAL
1 ripe banana
1 passionfruit
50 g/1 tablespoon sugar
pinch of salt
2 tablespoons pineapple juice
1 teaspoon lemon juice
120 ml/4 fl oz double or whipping
   cream, whipped

AMERICAN
1 ripe banana
1 granadilla
1 tablespoon sugar
pinch of salt
2 tablespoons pineapple juice
1 teaspoon lemon juice
½ cup heavy or whipping cream,
   whipped

Mash the banana. Peel and mash the passionfruit (granadilla). Mix both fruits with sugar, salt and juices. Fold in the cream.
Spoon into tall stemmed glasses and chill overnight. Serve with crisp biscuits.

# Grapefruit Brûlée

METRIC/IMPERIAL
1 grapefruit
½ teaspoon ground cinnamon
2 tablespoons demerara sugar

AMERICAN
1 grapefruit
½ teaspoon ground cinnamon
2 tablespoons light brown sugar

Halve the grapefruit. Use a grapefruit knife to remove the flesh by cutting between the membranes. Place the flesh in bowl with cinnamon and half the sugar. Remove the membranes from grapefruit halves and fill the halves with flesh mixture.
Sprinkle over remaining sugar then cook under preheated grill (broiler) until top is golden brown. Serve hot with pouring (light) cream or yogurt.

# Toffee Meringue Glacé

METRIC/IMPERIAL
2 tablespoons brown sugar
2 teaspoons golden syrup
1 tablespoon milk
15 g/½ oz butter
½ teaspoon vanilla essence
2 meringue nests
2 scoops vanilla ice cream

AMERICAN
2 tablespoons brown sugar
2 teaspoons light corn syrup
1 tablespoon milk
1 tablespoon butter
½ teaspoon vanilla
2 meringue nests
2 scoops vanilla ice cream

Place the sugar, syrup, milk, butter and vanilla in a pan. Heat gently, stirring until the sugar dissolves, then bring to the boil. Continue to boil for 3 to 4 minutes, stirring continuously.

Place the meringues on two serving dishes, add the ice cream and spoon a little of the sauce over the top. Serve the remaining sauce separately.

# Figs Paradiso

METRIC/IMPERIAL
225 g/8 oz ripe figs
1 slice fresh root ginger, shredded
dry white wine to cover
4 tablespoons honey
TO SERVE:
double or whipping cream, lightly
   whipped
1 tablespoon flaked almonds

AMERICAN
½ lb ripe figs
1 slice fresh ginger root, shredded
dry white wine to cover
4 tablespoons honey
TO SERVE:
heavy whipping cream, lightly
   whipped
1 tablespoon sliced almonds

Wash the figs and place in a pan with the ginger. Add enough wine to come to the top of the figs and bring to the boil. Stir in the honey, and cook gently for about 20 minutes until the figs are tender. Leave to cool then chill.

Serve the figs topped with cream and a sprinkling of almonds.

# Index

PDO 83-428